The World as Teacher

The World as Teacher

•

Harold Taylor

1969
Doubleday & Company, Inc.
Garden City, New York

Research sponsored by the American Association of Colleges for Teacher Education under United States Office of Education Contract No. OE–6–10–116.

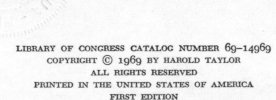

LIBRARY OF CONGRESS CATALOG NUMBER 69–14969

TITLE IN BCL 2nd ED

Contents

Introduction

I came to write this book because I had been troubled for a long time by some questions in education and social change which I found I did not know enough about to answer intelligently.

Start with the question of human survival, go on a little further to ask where are the forces among us in support of life and against destruction, and then ask how these forces can be organized to create magnanimous societies and a just and peaceable world order.

You are then at the center of most of what matters in the world—the dampening down and resolution of racial and nationalist hatreds, the creation of new and deep-going forms of art and experience, the heightening of a sense of life and its possibilities, the discovery of new and generous relations between and among persons, the abolition of war as an instrument of politics, the creation of a world belief that life on earth is all we have to work with and that at all costs it must be preserved and nourished. That and a great deal more.

The philosophers, the poets, the artists, scientists, technologists, and statesmen move among these questions in various ways, in speculative thought, lyrical statement, scientific inquiry, political theory, social invention. But sooner or later it is necessary, if the questions are to be answered, to talk and think about education, in the largest possible sense of that word.

When you begin to do that, if you are going to be helpful, you must then become practical. What education? For whom? What kind? What is in it? How is it done? Who does it? Where? With whose money? Under whose control?

And then, finally, necessarily, who teaches the teachers to do whatever it is that must be done, and who decides what must be done? Unless you can say something useful about that, it seems to me that you simply remain suspended in a state of speculation and rhetoric. You are not answering the main questions, but either fighting them or decorating them. Education is only as good or as bad as the teachers who plan it and carry it on.

Although I have held strong views about many of these issues for some time and have talked and written about them, I had never gone through a sustained examination of what might be done to connect the forces of education to the solution of world problems, or of what others had said, thought, and done about that connection.

I now have—in the case of the American educational system, the one nearest at hand—and after three years of study, research, writing, talking, and traveling to schools, colleges, and universities here and abroad, have turned in a report of practical findings[1] to the American Association of Colleges for Teacher Education and the United States Office of Education, where in each instance a group of congenial colleagues had extended an invitation and sponsored the enterprise. This book is based on that report, and contains the main ideas developed in it about the education of teachers in an understanding of the world and its problems, and about some possibilities that exist for changing the world through what teachers do in it. What teachers or anyone else can learn about world affairs depends on how sensitive they are to the political, social, and cultural life around them in their own society and in the world at large. Or, to put it differently, to understand the world's affairs and the nature of world society, it is necessary to be interested in and conscious of the issues which are alive in one's own culture. In this, teachers are no different from the rest of mankind. It is everyone's educational problem to learn how to think perceptively and act intelligently in the context of modern society, with society now defined on a global and not on a local scale.

The education of teachers to understand the world must therefore deal not merely with formal courses in foreign cultures, international relations, world history, and so on, but with the quality of intellectual, social, and personal experience available to those who are going to teach in the colleges, schools, or anywhere else.

---

[1] Published for its membership by the American Association of Colleges for Teacher Education, 1201 Sixteenth Street NW, Washington, D.C., May 2, 1968, under the title *The World and the American Teacher*. A brief account of the method and scope of the study is included in Appendix A, pp. 280–85.

This is true whether the field is the arts, the humanities, the sciences, or the field of world affairs itself. Whatever they teach, teachers should be educated in a way calculated to raise the level of their awareness of what is happening to mankind in the world's contemporary circumstance.

This means that those who are becoming teachers should have a chance to cross over, through their studies and their personal experience, to a culture different from the one in which they have been born and raised. Through entering other lives they begin to enter the world, and to provide themselves with something to compare themselves with, and by comparison to learn to look at mankind from a broader perspective. Since most American teachers are unquestioning members of the white middle class who have seldom had a chance to move outside that milieu into a wider world, their educational need is for a broader range of experience with cultures and people unlike themselves. Without that, academic studies designed to prepare them to teach about the world will have little effect on the growth of their understanding of social issues and human values, since the issues will either go unobserved or be seen from too narrow a view.

Throughout the book I have resisted as well as I can the temptation to denounce weaknesses in the system of education I have been examining, since that kind of denunciation is already in unusual supply and, in any case, is about at the same level of significance as shooting fish in a barrel. I have tried to report fairly what I have found, and where I have found weaknesses, I have looked for their cause, with a view to laying a foundation for overcoming the weaknesses. The recommendations I have made stem from the idea that education is the means by which societies and persons become conscious of themselves and of the changes going on within societies and persons, the better to discover what changes are desirable and how best to bring them about. The emphasis is upon the quality of the teacher's experience.

No sharp distinction can be made between what is involved in learning to be a teacher, and what is involved in becoming a person of intellectual and cultural substance, able to act in and on the world. For those who are teaching teachers, it is a matter of how, through arranging a series of appropriate experiences in intellectual, social, and cultural affairs, the student can learn to understand himself and others, to think clearly, to gain a body of knowledge about man, nature, and the world, and to teach what he has learned to others, by the example of his own life and the knowledge he has gained in it. The sooner he begins practicing the art of getting his own knowledge, thinking for himself, working, studying, and acting with other people, and teaching what he knows whenever he has a chance, the better will be his education and the use to which it will be put in the practice of his art.

What then is at stake is a radical reform of the whole style of instruction in the colleges and universities, with drastic revision in the academic system, from lectures to credits to grades, in order to free the student to do his own learning. But that is a long story, part of which this book is devoted to telling. The story begins with the fact that the best way to learn how to teach is to learn how to live, fully, generously, and sensitively, and that you learn to teach in the same way you learn to live—by involving yourself deeply in the thing itself.

Holderness, New Hampshire
July 1968

The World as Teacher

1

The Dimension of the Problem

. . . the unity of knowledge, the nature of human communities, the order of society, the order of ideas, the very notions of society have changed, and will not return to what they have been in the past. What is new is not new because it has never been before, but because it has changed in quality . . . so that the world alters as we walk in it, so that the years of a man's life measure not some small growth or rearrangement or moderation of what he learned in childhood, but a great upheaval . . . The global quality of the world is new; our knowledge of and sympathy with remote and diverse people, our involvement with them in practical terms and our commitment to them in terms of brotherhood . . .

ROBERT OPPENHEIMER
speaking at Columbia University,
December 27, 1954

The child enters the world without knowledge of it and without having taken an attitude toward it. In the long run, what he can know and believe about the world depends on the attitude he learns to take toward it and toward himself. His early years are spent in exploring what the world contains, how he feels about what he discovers, how to cope with the small private sector which he occupies. Although this exploration is not usually called education, that is what it is. It is a set of personal experiences in which the child's senses and emotions are so completely fused with his intellect that he does not separate the knowledge he possesses from the way he feels about it, and, in a sense, he can only learn what he wants to learn.

His capacity to go on learning more about the world depends on his openness to it and the opportunities for extending his range. The child who has never been more than three blocks from home, or a mile from his father's rice paddy, who can't read and who knows no one who is not like himself, is condemned to a narrow orbit of self-awareness, a meager knowledge of the world at large, and a very slim chance that he will ever know more than he does.

In one way or another, in more or less degree, everyone suffers from a similar limitation. That is the problem in teaching about world affairs, or, to put it more accurately, in teaching and learning about the world. The size of the sector in which each learns to move depends for its broadening on the arousal of interest in knowing what exists in the broader dimension of an environment which extends beyond one's own. It is not enough to be told about Africa, Asia, Europe, or Kansas in the classrooms of the world. Everything that is told or presented is told to persons in various states of capacity to respond. It is not so much what is said, but what is heard. There is such a thing as total capacity to respond, which in the most fortunate of cases means that geniuses among the children are interested in everything that is interesting, including the Africans, Asians, Europeans, Kansans, or mathematics. But that is a situation seldom to be found in the American public school system, or the American universities, or anywhere else in the schools and colleges of the world.

Through the normal course of growing up in his own culture, each child is taught what he is intended to know, and his sense of identity, his attitudes, depend on the cultural milieu in which they are developed and what he has been taught to believe about himself. In order to know anything, it is necessary to be able to relate it to something already known, to look at the world from one's own point of view. But to do that means narrowing the world to a single perspective, thus distorting the reality of what can only be seen clearly and truthfully from a larger view and from many perspectives.

". . . for men," as Erik Erikson says, "not being a natural species any more, and not a mankind as yet—need to feel that they are of some special kind (tribe or nation, class or caste, family, occupation, or type), whose insignia they will wear with vanity and conviction, and defend (along with the economic claims they have staked out for their kind) against the foreign, the inimical, the not-so-human kinds. Thus it comes about that they can use all their proud skills and methods most systematically against other men, even in the most advanced states of rationality and civilization, with the conviction that they could not morally afford not to do so."[1]

We can read the history of world education as the way in which, in successive generations since civilization began, the size of the group to which one was attached gradually increased in the spread of its loyalties, from the family to the tribe, from the tribe to a village, from one village to other villages until the shared loyalty and sense of identity could extend to a city-state. The sense of personal and group identity was sharpened and defined by conflict and war, reinforced by cultural and religious unity, and the rallying points for the assertion of that identity were around ideas of physical courage, faithfulness to one's own, and pride of conquest.

In the most optimistic reading of contemporary history, we could now say that we have reached a stage at which it has become necessary for the educated man to extend the dimension of his loyalty to the entire human race. The conception of education itself must now be one which locates man intellectually in a universe described by scientists, artists, and writers, and in a cultural setting as big as the globe. To enjoy any longer the luxury of defining one's nation, one's society, or oneself in terms of pride of ancestry, social superiority, or power of destruction is not only supremely dangerous to the survival of the race, but intellectually and socially obsolete.

In order to be truly educated, each must have a full sense of the nature of modern man and of the world he lives in, and I do not see how that sense can be achieved by the kind of education now being provided by most of the schools, colleges, universities, and educational systems of the world. They have fallen behind the reality of world society and are presenting conceptions of man and his world comparable to the pre-Copernican system of ideas in the post-Copernican period.

To create a new beginning, it is necessary to understand modern man as a single member of the human race with infinite individual variations, and not as the representative of a single culture, nation, society, or continent. There is no East and West, North and South. There are different people living in different places, under different conditions, and, through the happy circumstance of the spread of modern knowledge, we now have access to the full variety of their lives and natures, with more to be learned the longer we live.

[1] "Youth: Fidelity and Diversity," in *Conflict Resolution and World Education*; ed. by Stuart Mudd; Dr. W. Junk Publishers, The Hague, 1966, p. 40.

It is now the task of education, on a world scale, to put together the scattered fragments of the world's knowledge of itself in a form which can become the basis for a new kind of education in human affairs. I urge the effort to achieve this kind of education not for any other reason than that it lifts the conception of human nature to the level at which it belongs. There is new and global knowledge of man to be gained by those who care to seek it out, from poetry, theater, sociology, philosophy, anthropology, religion, the arts, on every continent, and the fascination of the art of education in the modern world lies in the number of different ways one can learn to understand how human beings have created themselves out of the accidents of their own environment and their own history.

The principal fact of the modern world is not its massive unrest, although that is its most visible characteristic, but its growing and necessary unity—the interpenetration of all lives by every other, the coming together of peoples, cultures, and societies to accomplish common and contradictory purposes. The teacher is at the center of his own culture and of this process of interpenetration. By what he teaches and by what he learns, he has it within his power to join with other teachers and their students in every part of the world to create the elements of unity in a world culture. That is what he must now do.

For a world transformation is under way, partly through the blind and unavoidable impulses in contemporary history which are driving societies into revolutionary situations, where the need for political and social reform has not kept pace with the legitimate expectations and demands of the dispossessed and the unprivileged, partly through conscious changes in the thinking and policies of countries who hold the major sources of political, military, and economic power. The social and political systems of the world are now affecting each other in fundamental ways, creating a fluid state of rapid change in international alignments and interrelationships.

Never having known each other at first hand, the world's people have never before had the opportunity for such massive conflict or for such massive cooperation. Confronting each other across the world, men can now see the face of actual hate, the intensities of national pride, the discrepancies of wealth and poverty, the threats of political coercion. Armed with the ultimate weapons, men can now see the path to mass destruction, without knowing what other paths can lead away from it, while millions more have joined together to fight for their claim to be heard in the places decisions are made about their future.

The decisions were made in the past by white Western élites in control of the world. In a new perspective, the present turmoil in the United States and abroad is a consequence of the disintegration of the old order and a transitional stage into the new, where the poor, the ignorant, the uneducated and the deprived are demanding that the élites give up the power of control and share it with those whose lives are affected. In the modern world, there are no foreign problems, only human problems shared by all societies—racial conflict, poverty, unemployment, educational shortages, political antagonisms, individual freedom, threats to personal security.

In another dimension, ideological, secular, and religious beliefs are finding new accommodations with each other, of a kind few would have predicted at the middle of this century. The great religions, Hinduism, Buddhism, Christianity, Islam, are in the process of discovering, through a world-wide ecumenical movement, a set of shared values which have to do, not with theological dogma, but with what Pope John in *Pacem in Terris* has called, "the common good of the entire human family."

At the moment the balance of forces which put war, violence, hatred, and ignorance on one side, and peace, security, human well-being, social progress, and education on the other, seem tipped toward violence as the norm in world affairs. It is clear that the present stage of world history demands the intense commitment of those who have intellectual, educational, and social resources at their disposal to do everything in their power to tip the balance in the opposite direction.

The necessity to do so becomes even more urgent when we face the fact that a new generation, larger than ever before in a world-wide population expansion, is growing up in an unstable environment in which the older modes of authority have lost their grip. The new expectations of the young are challenging, everywhere in the world, the authority of the older generation and its patterns of control. In this country, where by 1970 more than half the population will be below the age of twenty-five, a new generation of students has created a national community among themselves, a subculture within the larger society, with its own interests, attitudes, ideas, and ambitions. The educated American young have become involved in the issues of international affairs, and the problems of human rights, war and peace, the politics of change, and the reform of education have become matters of central concern. They see the problems of world society in the same light as those of their own.

The solutions they propose and act upon, the unifying beliefs, are based on the conviction that the older generation and the established order in any society cannot assume the right of control over the younger generation, either before or after it reaches its majority. The young, they are saying, have equal rights as citizens, regardless of their age group and, as certified citizens, black or white, have their own ideas about how to run the society and its educational system. Since they are the ones education is done to, they claim special qualifications for knowing what it is, how it is working, and how it should work. Maximum participation by the poor, says the Poverty legislation. Yes, say the students, and maximum participation by the young, poor or otherwise.

Elsewhere around the world there is a comparable constituency, alive to the fact that they can exercise political and social power, conscious of discrepancies between the privileges of the rich and the position of the poor. The young Indonesians who united against Sukarno, the Korean youth who opposed the dictatorship of Rhee, the Spanish students who reject the educational control of Franco, the Soviet young who question, through poetry and the arts, the social policy and politics of their elders, have their counterparts in other societies around the world, in Poland, France, Italy, Czechoslovakia, Africa, Asia, Latin America, and Europe. They are forming their own leadership from their own ranks, and where there is no accommodation between them and their elders, they can and will form the basis for revolutionary action, responsible or irresponsible, as the circumstances provide.

It is in this sense that the education and accommodation of the new generation becomes a primary matter of concern for the societies of the world as they enter the second half of what has been announced as the Development Decade, a time when the resources of the United Nations and allied organizations and governments were pledged to narrow the gap between the have and the have-not countries. The unhappy fact is that during the first half of the ten years, the have-not countries are finding that even with foreign help and their own development programs, food, supplies, production of goods, housing, and jobs have either barely kept up to their rising populations or have fallen behind. The gap has widened, not narrowed, and the basic problem grinds its way back to the absence of educated manpower to give leadership in planning and trained capacity in action.

THE CONTEXT OF EDUCATION

It is in the context of these considerations that I wish to deal with the education of teachers in an understanding of the world, and to define the terms in which the idea of world education acquires its meaning. By education I mean the way in which each person becomes aware of himself and his place in the world at large, and learns how best to conduct himself in it and to contribute to it. To achieve that awareness, he needs the opportunity to explore the world's geography, its people, including those of his own society, to learn through science the physical characteristics and foundations of nature, through language, the arts, and philosophy to learn the ideas, experiences, and expressions of mankind. These are the world's affairs, and although they include such matters as the history of governments, their international relationships, their wars, victories, defeats, and the rise and fall of empires and civilizations, the culminating point in education comes when one has learned to understand the nature and character of the world itself in its contemporary manifestation, and one has learned how to do something useful in it.

This is not to say that all education must deal with the contemporary, but that all education *is* ultimately contemporary, and that it has links with the entire world. The mind of primitive man is, in history or in the present, linked directly to our own. The primitive, the pre-industrial and the post-industrial cultures and educational systems of the world are linked together by their common efforts to deal with the problems of human existence, no matter how different they may be in the ways they set about doing it. Says Margaret Mead:

> While anthropologists seek for ways of describing man that will apply to all cultures at all times in history, anthropology remains closely bound to the living detail of the way special men have lived at given times and place . . . The precious concrete reference is never lost. Real Indians hunt

real buffalo, or stare at the sun until they fall unconscious, or fast in the lonely wilderness seeking a guardian spirit for life . . .[2]

The educator, like the anthropologist, the philosopher, the poet, or the psychologist must take for his province the infinite variety of human nature and human cultures, blending together the general characteristics one can find among the details with the concrete reality of specific men, women, and children who have lived under specific circumstances at certain times. The generalization without the detail is banal and essentially meaningless; the detail without the pattern in history and culture becomes meaningless by fragmentation.

Or, to put it in different terms, in the words of Joseph Campbell:

> In his life-form the individual is necessarily only a fraction and distortion of the total image of man. He is limited either as a male or as female; at any given period of his life he is again limited as child, youth, mature adult, or ancient; furthermore, in his life-role he is necessarily specialized as craftsman, tradesman, servant or thief, priest, leader, wife, nun or harlot; he cannot be all. Hence, the totality—the fullness of man—is not in the separate member, but in the body of the society as a whole; the individual can be only an organ. From his group he has derived his techniques of life, the language in which he thinks, the ideas on which he thrives; through the past of that society descended the genes that built his body. If he presumes to cut himself off, either in deed or in thought and feeling, he only breaks connection with the sources of his existence.[3]

To make connection with the sources of one's existence is the ultimate purpose of education, and no one can become a full-bodied teacher without learning to make that connection. This means a shift in educational perspective to a world point of view, one now made necessary by the shift in the circumstances of world society.

The education of teachers is the focal point around which the shift must be made. Without teachers whose own knowledge and attitudes are in tune with the demands which world society now makes for the application of new knowledge, there is little chance that new perspectives can be introduced into the structure and content of modern education, in the United States or anywhere else.

Immediately then, the question is raised, Who will teach the

[2] *The Golden Age of American Anthropology*, ed. by Margaret Mead and Ruth L. Bunzel; George Braziller, New York, p. 1.
[3] *The Hero With a Thousand Faces*, Joseph Campbell; Pantheon Books, New York, 1949, pp. 382–83.

teachers, how will they be taught, how can they teach themselves?

That is the central question and the one which America is now forced to answer. At this point, we in the United States *are* the world's most powerful economic, social, military, and political force. We possess a vast and latent power for taking initiatives in cultural and educational change on a world scale. Whether we like it or not, or whether anyone else likes it, with our mass media, our science, our technology, our cultural and educational institutions, our mass transport and urban problems, we are the forerunners of what mass societies will some day be. Despite our location here on a local continent, we live in the middle of the world and serve as a point of linkage between the thousands of elements which make up the cultural and social fabric of world society.

Having been handed the leadership of the world as a gift from history, a gift seldom given and quickly taken away, we now have a chance to show what we can do with it. We have a special chance to use our cultural and educational resources to make the entire country into a general friendly meeting-ground and laboratory in social change, to which students and teachers from everywhere in the world may come to try to find solutions to the world's educational problems while working with us on ours and their own.

We have within our fifty states a fascinating assortment of underdeveloped countries, pre-industrial societies, post-industrial urban centers, bad housing, ghettos, rural slums, wealthy suburbs, beautiful farms, bad schools, good schools, mediocre universities, great ones, anti-intellectuals, poets, philistines, dancers, surf-riders, television programs, research centers, think tanks, anti-think tanks, rebels, conformists, mass culture and high art, all of which has to be seen to be believed and which is, in a curious way, the wonder of the world. There is no reason why we cannot make of this assortment a campus for the world, while the world can, under the right circumstances, become a campus for everyone, including the Americans.

In saying this I am not proposing a new kind of American cultural imperialism, or a program of making friends and allies through education, or a new display of the arrogance of power, but something quite simple and appropriate—the use of our money, our institutions, and our cultural resources to improve the quality of education throughout the world, considering America to be one part of the world where this kind of work can actually be done. We have already come part way to this point of view, with the 100,000 students and 10,000 scholars here from abroad each year, with the new International Education Act of 1966, with the international work of our foundations, universities, and voluntary organizations. The new initiatives on our part will have to come from the joint efforts of intellectuals here and abroad, from the American campuses where teachers are now being educated, and from the schools where American teachers are already teaching.

THE ARGUMENT FOR INTERNATIONALISM

If we need other reasons for immediate American initiatives in developing a world-wide sense of community with an educational system to match, the primary and most practical one lies in the fact that unless action is taken in those quarters where there is genuine power to act, the civilization we now have may very well blow itself up. There is little point in reviewing again the brute facts of the present and future power of nuclear weapons and the danger to world civilization which their presence imposes on everyone. The nuclear confrontation is already here, and there are too few counterforces to the destructive tendencies in international politics to assure the continuity of humanitarian principles. Unless we throw the weight of our energies behind those principles, what momentum there now exists in the direction of a world community may cease altogether.

Another and equally compelling reason is the moral, and practical, imperative that the West must share with the rest of the world the huge accumulation of knowledge it has gained in its own climb to social and economic security. By knowing more about other cultures and their situation we can help to adapt and reshape our knowledge to their needs, so that others may adapt what they need to their own social and personal use. The injection of new knowledge and ideas from other cultures into our own gives heightened vitality to both. It gives each culture something to assimilate, something with which to compare itself, and to judge.

Until recently, the major argument for American international involvement in cultural and educational affairs has had to do with our national and international security. It has been argued that our educational system should make provision for teaching world affairs and non-Western cultures in order that American citizens can understand the nature of world society and the problems of American foreign policy. It is obvious that without a broad educational base in foreign languages and foreign cultures, the American educational system as a whole will be unable to develop enough citizens, scholars, and experts in foreign cultures and international affairs to supply the manpower needed to cope with the formation and application of our foreign policy, both inside and outside of government. Nor could it deal with the need for a broader professional education for lawyers, businessmen, public administrators, and engineers who conduct American affairs overseas. The rationale behind the National Defense Education Act is of this kind. Education in this instance becomes an instrument of national security. Foundation and Government grants for area studies, international affairs centers, and research institutes have been based on similar reasoning.

Although these areas of research and scholarship are an essential ingredient in the store of American knowledge, for whatever use it may be put, the knowledge itself has not permeated the educational system as a whole, largely because there is no direct connection between the developments within the knowledge industry and the education of teachers within the schools and colleges. It is time now to put these elements together, and the place to do it is in the universities and schools where teachers are prepared, in the schools and among the teachers where the young are now being educated.

The irony in the present situation is that just at the point in time when we should be using a major part of our intellectual resources in advancing the cause of international education in our schools and colleges, the major foundations and the United States Congress are pulling back from the support of international studies. After passing the International Education Act in 1966, and establishing the central proposition that American education is part of a system of world education and world culture, the United States Congress has refused to appropriate the money to carry out its own provisions. This is resulting, as Karl Deutsch points out, in a kind of unilateral intellectual disarmament by the United States. "Our intellectual competence in finding adequate solutions or policies for our current problems is not as good as our present commitments and interests require; but some of the coming problems will make these inadequacies in our knowledge far more serious, and potentially fatal.

"For the United States as a national society," says Deutsch, "the coming decades will be a period of increasing vulnerability and lessening control of world affairs, together with increasing potential occasions for violent foreign conflict. We know that population growth will continue to be rapid in many developing countries for much of the next ten or twenty years. Indeed, all the world's desperate and rebellious adults of the 1970s and mid-1980s already have been born. Unless someone kills them, they are likely to grow up; and unless someone helps them soon to help themselves, they will grow up radically discontented. Food supplies are hardly likely to keep pace with population growth in many of these countries. Their people will become worse fed, better armed, more discontented, and more numerous . . . It will take more—not less—knowledge, skill, and competence for the next generation of American leaders to cope with these international problems for the 1970s and 1980s. To reduce the intellectual sources of this knowledge now, by cutting back on international research, might prove to be a truly fateful decision—a national decision that should not be taken lightly or as a result of absentmindedness."[4]

THE COMMUNITY AND ITS CULTURE

It will be clear at the outset that the achievement by Americans of a broad and enlightened outlook toward the world is the result not merely of what is done by teachers in the classrooms or of scholars in the universities, no matter how well they have been prepared for their mission. The American child in early and in later life is immersed in a total context, and the context shifts from big cities in the north to rural areas in the south, from poverty to affluence, from blacks to whites, from Spanish-Americans to Puerto Ricans, from ghettos to suburbs. The teaching problem shifts from one subculture to another, while the pervasive social and cultural values carried through the mass media are absorbed by the young in their life in the American community.

The vehicles for these values range from Little League baseball and the Kiwanis Club to Sunday School and the Beatles. The pervasiveness and the emotional power of community institutions and

[4] Karl W. Deutsch, "The Coming Crisis of Cross-National and International Research in the United States," in *Newsletter*, American Council of Learned Societies, New York, Vol. XIX, Number Four, April 1968, pp. 2, 3.

the mass media are greater in affecting the attitudes of the young American than are those which he finds in his learning in school. In many instances, the school simply reinforces attitudes already gained from the total environment, since a central purpose of the public school is to enable the young to learn how to be an American, that is, the kind of American who adapts himself to the norms of behavior of the white middle-class American community. In fact the teachers themselves share the tastes and values to be found in the rest of the society; the school and society in white middle class culture form one homogeneous community.

It is also necessary to repeat what has been said so often about the massive effects on the minds and attitudes of the younger generation from the single medium of television. Whatever else can be said about the television phenomenon, it is true that the flow of information, opinion, and value-forming images from this single source is a primary educational influence on the young and that from this source, along with the weekly magazines and paperback books, a supply of general information about the world and its happenings is provided on a scale greatly in excess of the amount communicated through formal instruction in the schools. The statistics in most common use to illustrate this point are provided by the Reverend John M. Culkin of Fordham University, that the average American child from preschool through to the end of high school has seen 15,000 hours of television, as compared to 10,000 hours of classroom time in the same period, and that college students see twenty films for every book they read.

In part, this accounts for the rapid increase at an earlier age in the number of high school students who are sensitive to social questions ranging from the cultural habits of the hippy movement to the mistreatment of the Negro, and for the increased sophistication of a growing minority of college students and young political activists to the issues of domestic politics, war and peace, and world affairs in general. The formation of a youth culture with its own interests and values, separate from the older generation yet with influence upon it, can be traced to some of the cultural effects of the television medium and the opening up of questions, ideas, and examples of human conduct which in former years were unavailable to the young because the medium did not then exist. For a variety of reasons, the power of the medium has been used as an instrument for cultural conditioning and the reinforcement of American ideological and

social values rather than as a stimulus to fresh thought, social criticism, and cultural enlightenment.

In this context, other influences within education stem directly
from the child's life with his parents, from their relation to each
other, their attitude to the child, the emotional and cultural tone of
the family life, all of this forming the cultural currogate for his
growing up. We now know enough about the early childhood years
to know that the child's emotional set and his style of coping are
derivatives of the emotional and social relation with one or both of
the parents and are established, usually in a permanent way, by
the age of eight to ten. Although research conducted at Sarah
Lawrence, at Bennington, and elsewhere shows that the values of
college students do change under the influence of college teaching
when the college considers the personal growth of students as a
major concern, the political attitude and world outlook of American
students are mainly the same as those of their parents. Other research, particularly of the kind carried out by Philip Jacob[5] and by
Nevitt Sanford and the authors of *The American College*,[6] indicates that attendance at college has, except in the case of colleges
with a "peculiar potency," very little influence on the values the
students bring with them from the society.

Since it is the attitude taken toward the world which is decisive
in what one learns to think and to know about it, it is with the
creation of attitudes that the educator must be primarily concerned.
By attitudes I do not mean agreement or disagreement with specific
political or social doctrines or world views, but attitudes in support
of rational inquiry as against dogma and prejudice, independent
thinking as against acceptance of social norms, tolerance toward
opposing views as against ethnocentrism, the achievement of a
large view of world society as against a parochial view of one's
own.

In considering the education of the teacher and his role in the
society, it is therefore important to be reminded that during his
childhood education the school and college teacher in America has
been immersed in everybody's American culture; that in about
seventy percent of the cases the schoolteacher is a woman, and

[5] *Changing Values in College*, Philip E. Jacob; Harper & Brothers, New
York, 1957, 174 pp.
[6] *The American College*, ed. by Nevitt Sanford; John Wiley & Sons, Inc.,
New York, 1962, 1084 pp.

therefore more likely, in this culture, to adapt to current social and political norms than to challenge them; and that public school teachers in America are not regarded as intellectual and social leaders, but as the carriers of the conventional wisdom under the direction of those elected to school boards and appointed to superintendencies who represent that wisdom. Otherwise they would be unlikely to be elected or appointed.

There is a sizable and convincing body of research which confirms the fact that whatever else may be taught within the American public schools, one major effect of school attendance is to create an acceptance of the existing social order, of the American world view and its attendant national and international policies. After a thoroughgoing and sensitive review of recent research in the field, Mr. John Patrick, research associate of the High School Curriculum Center in Government at Indiana University, has this to say in summary:

> Perhaps the most acute educational problem reflected by political socialization research is the proclivity of our schools to approach the task of political socialization in a one-sided manner, especially in schools serving mainly lower or working class children. The schools reinforce and develop strong, supportive attitudes toward state and nation. Most American children learn well the lessons of conforming to the socio-political *status quo*. Certainly the schools may contribute substantially to national strength and stability when they impart supportive political orientations . . .
>
> However, certain consequences may flow from overemphasis upon conformity that are inconsistent with many of the professed objectives of American public schools and with certain democratic ideals. For example, overemphasis upon conformity appears to be associated with authoritarian school atmospheres where docile children are prized above active, deeply probing thinkers; where strict adherence to authoritative pronouncements is preferred over student inquiry into pressing, socio-political concerns; where strict obedience to rules is stressed to the exclusion of inquiry into the need for rules. This may contribute to some unanticipated and undesired consequences for adult political behavior such as alienation or cynicism, dispositions to passively accept authority, and tendencies to be intolerant of reasonable political dissent or non-conformity. Certainly social forces other than the school may contribute to these types of political behavior, such as the present quality of life in lower class homes and neighborhoods. But since the school's climate of opinion and educational atmosphere appear to be more influential in shaping political attitudes than does its formal programs of instruction, it is possible that an authoritarian school environment may subvert textbook and teacher prescriptions of democratic political values and that it may contribute to the hardening of

political beliefs and to a close-minded resistance toward alternative or unorthodox points of view . . .

Another factor that may contribute to the ossification of political attitudes is that commitment to political beliefs in early childhood precedes knowledge of relevant political information, that early learning is based on emotional attachments rather than knowledge. Later cognitive learning often serves merely to reinforce these early commitments, to provide rational justification for a closed system of basic beliefs rather than reflective examination of tentatively held viewpoints.[7]

Although Mr. Patrick is writing about political attitudes and how children are shaped for society, what he has to say has to do with the child's perception of world affairs. When education is considered as a total process, including but expanding beyond what happens in schoolrooms, it is obvious that the education of the American teacher gives him very little chance to learn about alternative or unorthodox points of view, either about America's position in the world or about the social and political attitudes of the people and governments of foreign countries. As a student, the future teacher is deliberately, and to a degree necessarily, taught to see the world and the world's affairs from an American point of view, and from the point of view of one who accepts the American political and social system, as well as the ideology implicit in it, as a system of unquestioned superiority to any other. For the most part, when the character and structure of other systems are considered, they are considered in contrast to the worth of the American.

It must also be remembered that the American teacher begins to be educated for his profession not just at the point of his admission to a teacher education program in a college or university, but in the elementary and secondary school and in the American culture at large. He is subject to the same community pressures and value systems as anyone else, he moves through the same curriculum and the same school life as anyone else, and his conception of what education is and what a teacher does and is, are images deeply embedded in his consciousness by the experience of being taught by the teachers in his school.

He then arrives at an institution for higher education, prepared

[7] *Political Socialization of American Youth,* John Patrick; A review of Research with Implications for Secondary School Studies, High School Curriculum Center in Government, Indiana University, Bloomington, Indiana; mimeographed, pp. 66–67.

Mr. Patrick cites 96 items of research findings, and supplies a definitive bibliography of materials drawn from recent work in the field.

for admission the day after he stops being a high school student and, in that sense, is indistinguishable from high school students, to undertake "cognitive learning (which) often serves merely to reinforce . . . early commitments." From my observations, whatever commitments he may have had in his younger days, at the point of college entry the high school student has not changed them in the direction of a wider concern for the world and its problems, not even in making a commitment to the vocation of the teacher as I understand the meaning of these words. That is to say he, or much more often, she, has enrolled in an institution which educates teachers either because it is close to home and provides a fairly inexpensive education leading to a job after graduation, in teaching or in another field, or because teaching is a sensible and secure career if one has no passion to be anything else. In the case of more than 60 percent of the women students in our research sample, teaching was considered to be a career suitable for an interim period before marriage and a basis for employment security in the event of widowhood, or during a later period when, with the family raised, it would be something to do.

Once the student is enrolled in a teacher education program, his curriculum and the methods of instruction, by textbook, lecture, examination, and grades, are essentially an extension of high school, with the same rewards and punishments, the same style of social life, and the same culture-bound intellectual atmosphere. The education student arrives with almost no developed intellectual interests. The first two years of general education, as prescribed in the curriculum for certification, followed by an academic major, from four to six professional education courses, and practice teaching, usually in the senior year, leave him little room for electing courses either in foreign cultures, world affairs, or in any other field, even if he wanted to.

From the point of view of the student, not only is his college education substantially like that of high school in method, style, and content, but the professional education courses in college draw on materials from standard elementary and high school practices and curricula with which the student is already familiar from having just gone through the schools themselves. In addition, his practice teaching is carried on in schools almost exactly like the one that he attended while young, sometimes the actual one he did attend. His teaching is supervised by teachers almost exactly like those who taught him in school. In other words, he travels continually over the same familiar territory toward a destination a few steps away from where he started.

THE INTERNATIONAL CONTENT OF THE CURRICULUM

If we put the question bluntly, to what extent are American teachers being prepared through their curriculum to understand and to teach about the nature of world society? The answer is, almost not at all.[8] Not more than three to five percent of all teachers, according to the best estimates available, have had in the course of their preparation to become teachers in the social sciences or any other area of the curriculum, any formal study of cultures other than their own, or have studied in a field which could properly be described as world affairs. This does not necessarily mean that they are ignorant of that kind of knowledge; teachers, like anyone else, can learn what they want to on their own time, through travel, independent study, special institutes in the summertime, and so on. But it does mean that since students who are preparing to become teachers very seldom possess an initial interest in politics, world society, or foreign cultures, they are unlikely to develop such interest either on their own or through their curriculum of teacher preparation.

Students who are going to be teachers do two-thirds to three-quarters of their work in the regular departmental courses of the arts and science curriculum. As far as the content of their education is concerned, whatever is true for undergraduates in general is true for teacher candidates, except that in the case of teachers, they are hemmed in even more than the others by academic requirements.

Not more than ten percent of American undergraduates have taken courses containing other than Western materials; two percent is approximately the amount of curricular time spent by high school students in studying cultures and societies outside the Western world. In many high schools there are no courses which deal in any

[8] Additional material having to do with curricular content is available in the EWA publications and other sources, particularly, *The University Looks Abroad; Education & World Affairs; Report on Program 1963–64; Coordinating International Programs & Activities at U. S. Colleges and Universities: A Directory; op. cit. Introduction*, p. 1 of Footnotes.

Also, *Teacher & Curriculum: Report of the Conference on American Education in a Revolutionary World*, U. S. National Committee for UNESCO, Washington, D.C.

way with world affairs or non-Western cultures. When that is transposed into its meaning for teacher candidates, the ten percent of
undergraduates with instruction in world affairs is reduced to well
below five percent, due to the limited opportunity for electing
courses outside the prescribed curriculum, and the fact that in only
two states are there requirements having to do with international or
non-Western affairs. A survey in 1965 of member institutions of the
American Association of Colleges for Teacher Education showed
that less than 20 percent of them offer education courses dealing
with educational systems of societies outside the United States, and
that the courses which do exist are usually worked out by interested
faculty members rather than by deliberate planning in the schools
of education.[9]

Another way of asking the question about teachers' knowledge of
world society is to look at the number of courses and units of study
in elementary schools and high schools which deal with non-Western
and world materials, and to ask whether those who teach the courses
which do exist have had any preparation to do so. There is as yet
no national survey which can answer that question, although a
fairly accurate answer can be given on the basis of what is already
known. For example, Dr. Claude Phillips, of Western Michigan University, in a study of the schools of one county in Southern Michigan,[10] has found that the 69 high school social studies teachers who
responded to his questionnaire were teaching 92 social studies
courses, of which only eight could be considered to have a world
focus—one in world geography, six in world history, and one in international relations.

Seventy-seven percent of the teachers said that they tried to in-
corporate materials dealing with the non-Western world in existing
courses from time to time, although less than half of them had done
formal study of any kind in relevant subjects. Of those who had, the
study consisted of either one or two departmental courses devoted
to a country or a continent. Five of the 69 teachers had had three or
more courses which focused on non-Western cultures during their
college training; only nine had done such work after leaving college.
Nearly all of them felt that they were not actually prepared to teach

---

[9] *The Professional School & World Affairs: The School of Education,* A Report from Education and World Affairs, p. 24.

[10] "World Affairs in Secondary Education," by Claude S. Phillips, Jr., *Michigan Journal of Secondary Education,* Vol. 7, No. 1, Fall 1965.

subjects beyond those dealing with America and the Western countries.

Judging from the present state of the teacher education curriculum, the situation across the country is approximately that shown by Dr. Phillips' survey, with exceptions in a few institutions where students of declared interest in foreign affairs, including Peace Corps Volunteers, have studied in the field in order to teach in high school. Dr. Phillips cites three barriers to the broadening of the curriculum for teachers: the narrowness of the undergraduate curriculum in higher education, the continuing emphasis on the physical sciences both in high school and in college to the neglect of the social sciences, and the conservatism of school boards, college and high school administrators, professors, teachers, and parents who have been educated in the traditional narrow curriculum.

In trying to break down some of these barriers, Dr. Phillips' own institution has now included among its undergraduate requirements in general education one course in a non-Western culture, has developed an undergraduate minor in area studies, including Asia, Africa, Latin America, and Eastern Europe with approval from the certification officers of the State Board of Education, and has installed a Master of Arts degree program in International and Area Studies for students with a traditional background in the social sciences.

When the education of teachers is analyzed in these terms, from the point of view of the teachers' opportunities for cultural and intellectual growth, new dimensions begin to emerge. The problem begins in the fact that the teacher's range of possible experience, intellectual, cultural, and social, is so severely limited by the circumstances of his education, and his personal experience is so circumscribed by the social and cultural milieu in which his life is lived, that involvement with the wider issues of international society, or even of his own society, is not natural to his temperament or to his outlook. He has not been asked to or expected to become involved with wider issues or to see himself and his country from a wider perspective, but only to learn what he is taught, from texts which raise few fundamental questions, by teachers who are older versions of himself, and of what he will some day be.

From the time he began his own education to the time he begins to teach others, the American teacher has been locked into a curriculum and a culture of standard American proportions. He passes through agreed-upon procedures for becoming a teacher, and his development as a person of broad intellectual interests and a rich personal life has seldom been enhanced by what has happened to him. An additional irony lies in the fact that when he is introduced to world history, to courses in international relations or courses in non-Western cultures, these too are taught in such a way that they seldom open up his mind to new perspectives or stimulate his thinking in new directions. The non-Western subject matter in the context of his curriculum for teacher preparation is regarded as more material to be covered, followed by more examinations to be passed. In his eyes, to include such subject matter in his education is not to open up a whole new image of what the world is like, but simply to add further items to the store of material available for passing on to his pupils when he too becomes a teacher.

SOME UNDERLYING CAUSES OF NEGLECT

It is not hard to see why this situation exists. The main reason lies in the fact that the education of teachers for service in the public schools has always been conducted in a local context and a poverty-stricken way outside the main stream of the intellectual and social forces of contemporary history. We have never brought to the task of educating teachers the full power of the American intellect or more than a minimum of our social energies and economic resources. It has been an area of neglect, scandalous neglect, when compared to the energies and resources devoted to the development of the automobile, the refrigerator, television, highways, bombs, space travel, or the education of scientists, engineers, fighter pilots, and astronauts.

It would be natural to think that the colleges of liberal arts in America, in view of their origins and the intentions of their founders, would have plunged into the education of teachers as a primary mission. Most of these colleges were started to give to their adherents, and through them to the public at large, an education in moral values and religious faith. The colleges wanted to produce graduates who, in one way or another, would propagate a certain kind of faith, centered in the Judaic-Christian tradition and in general referred to as the "values of Western civilization."

But as the colleges became more secular, they have adapted themselves to what the society wants—trained manpower for business and the professions—not educated persons capable of influencing society in the direction of enlightenment. Rather than continuing their own tradition of propagating a faith or, to put it another way, of introducing an element of moral content into the educational and cultural institutions of their society, they have given as little attention to the education of teachers as have the other academies and universities. At a time when the normal schools and teachers colleges were struggling to develop programs to educate hundreds of new teachers, the liberal arts colleges were developing into all-purpose institutions in which the liberal arts and sciences were considered to be a preparation, not to teach, but to gain access to the social and intellectual prerequisites for entrance into the educated classes. The difference in social prestige between the teacher institutions and the liberal arts colleges has increased as the years have gone by, and the disinterest of the latter in the mission of teacher education has continued into the present. The irony is that while the curricula and purpose of the liberal arts colleges have become more academic and less relevant to the needs of the student and his society, the students have in many cases been seeking a sense of purpose and relevance for their own education by becoming *de facto* teachers in the slums, the rural areas, in foreign countries, and among themselves.

In the meantime, the country's central intellectual resources for what has now become known as the knowledge industry have been mobilized in a relatively few major universities, research institutes, graduate schools, professional schools, industrial research units, and government agencies with their research branches. Higher education, at what it considers to be its best, has become an instrument for producing manpower for purposes other than teaching. Yet the quality of higher education depends for its future on the quality of the teachers it produces—teachers for its own graduate schools, for its undergraduate colleges, aside from the teachers in whose hands rest the preparation of the oncoming generation of future college students now in the primary and secondary schools. One would assume that even in terms of the narrower interest of the university as an organized institution, the problem of developing new teachers to serve its own needs would occupy a central place in university planning.

The contrary is true. There is at this moment no serious and continuing effort on the part of the universities to develop scholar-teachers for the undergraduate young and for the generation just behind them in the schools. Although there are in existence a growing number of All-University Committees on Teacher Education, concentration in planning and operation is still on the development of the research experts and Ph.D. specialists for the academic and institutional markets, leaving a teaching gap exactly in the middle of the whole educational system. When we look at the total quality of that system, it becomes clear that the achievements of the United States as a civilization and as a world power have been reached by the use of only a fraction of the latent intellectual resources which lie within the population. The only way to bring the latent talent into full play is to develop thousands and thousands of teachers who know how to seek out that talent and to foster it, and first of all, in the colleges, to teach those who will do the teaching.

When that problem is faced squarely, it becomes clear that the center of it all is in the undergraduate college of arts and sciences. That is where the teachers for the public schools not only learn the things they need to know about the subjects they will be teaching, but the attitudes they will carry into the school system and into the society. That is where the students who will go on to graduate school and into the academic profession not only learn the basic elements and preparatory materials for their later work, but learn to become the kind of students, and later, teachers, who are considered to be most acceptable by the standards of the academic profession.

If there is to be a break in the habitual patterns in which teachers are educated, if there is to be reform in the quality and scope of undergraduate teaching, it will have to be made in the present undergraduate college. If students going on to graduate school had a keen sense of their own identity as teachers and catalysts in cultural change, they would not put up with most of the restrictions and educational absurdities of the conventional requirements for the Ph.D. degree. If undergraduates preparing to become teachers became intensely interested in the quality and relevance of learning and teaching in the undergraduate college, they would not put up with the restrictions and triviality of much of their own education, and they would certainly approach their work as teachers in the public schools with a zest and a determination not to accept humdrum educational practices simply because those practices had the approval of the educational bureaucracy. The colleges and universities are the breeding ground for teaching, yet they have not begun to create the conditions in which teaching and the teacher are honored and rewarded above all else, in which scholarship, research, and teaching are linked together in the organic set of relationships they must have if the academic culture is to stimulate the intellectual interests of college students and the college faculty.

If we have not realized fully what a radical change in educational thinking and in the use of our national resources is now demanded by the new position of the United States in world society, this is understandable. We are less than thirty years away from the isolationism natural to the whole of American political thinking, and a little more than ten years away from the chauvinism and xenophobia of the McCarthy period. We have never actually left the McCarthy period. The main framework for policy decision and political alignments in the United States and abroad is still the dialectic of pro- and anti-Communism. Ideas, persons, and countries are still measured in terms of their relationships within that frame of reference. Ideas and persons are still subject to suspicions of disloyalty to the country if they deviate in the direction of full-bodied internationalism on major issues of war and peace. During the years when the responsibility of the United States in world society has been making sharply increased demands for enlightened world understanding on the part of our leaders, teachers, and citizens alike, the cultural and political climate in the United States has not been at all congenial to the development of lively ideas for political education, either in world affairs or in liberal democracy.

That too can be understood. We have never had a tradition in the United States of broad political education in which a liberal or radical movement is taken for granted as a normal and legitimate part of the culture. The radical, no matter what he has been radical about, but especially the radical in politics, has always been suspect. In later life he may be revered—Norman Thomas, David Dubinsky, Sidney Hillman, Eugene Debs—but when he is young, active, challenging, controversial, and dissident, when he takes part in serious political and cultural movements, he is more often reviled than respected. In the case of teachers who hold political views even slightly at variance with the norms of popular consensus, the teachers have been doubly suspect, since their role is considered to be that of Americanizing the young, not internationalizing or liberalizing them, or raising questions in their minds about the wisdom of the course of action pursued by their Government in foreign affairs.

The years of rapid change in America's world position from isolation to world involvement were years in which educators at home, without a political tradition, without being accustomed even to thinking in political terms about their own place in the society, have been inundated with the practical problems of expanding rapidly an inadequate educational system while at the same time reforming its content. So concentrated has been the attention given to the practical problems of funds, enrollment, buildings, personnel, and public relations, that questions about the world and where it is going have seldom been raised among working educators. They have not been accustomed to thinking about the relation of education to the world or to any large framework of social or political thought. They have tended to do what they have been asked to do, by the Government, by the public, by the foundations, by the state legislatures.

Reforming the science and mathematics curriculum in the 1950s, for example, was important, safe, praised, funded, and rewarded. It was therefore enthusiastically carried out. Meddling with issues in world affairs, reforming the social studies curriculum to make it more intellectually alive, politically relevant, and international, was risky, open to criticism, unfunded, and, in many local situations, prohibited. What reform there was in the curriculum in world affairs was based on the principle of arming young Americans with ideas with which they could protect themselves against Communism and could "strengthen the forces of democracy."

We have not yet begun to construct a philosophy for the development of new school curricula in the social sciences and humanities which are free from the biases of American foreign policy. The educators have not yet been able to make a clear distinction between the content of knowledge considered as a body of material to aid in the process of Americanizing children, and knowledge of world events and issues as a means of understanding America and oneself in a world perspective. Until that distinction is made and applied in the reform of curricula, the teacher is unlikely to receive a preparation for teaching which will enable him to rise above the political environment in which his earlier beliefs were formed.

THE GROWTH IN SIZE

In the meantime, the American schools have grown to an extraordinary number and size, 25,000 school systems, 50 million pupils, and 2 million teachers. This growth has its roots not only in the population expansion but in the increase in fundamental needs of the American communities and cities. The local school boards and their schools are the American instruments for getting certain things done which in other countries are done by other institutions. In the United States, school teachers are hired as substitutes for the family. It is only in recent years that there has been any direct relationship between the universities and the schools, and the relationship is still tenuous, even though most of the education of schoolteachers is conducted in college and university classrooms.

The normal schools, and later, the teachers colleges in the United States, were not invented by scholars. They were part of a citizens' movement to satisfy explicit educational needs, and they were linked directly to the society and to the schools, not to the universities. There has therefore been no public feeling that the elementary and secondary schools are intellectually or socially separate from the society. Parents have not considered the schools and teacher training institutions to be intellectual centers, but places where their children could be trained to become useful Americans, and could be given a chance to move ahead in their society. The present demands of the poor for education of a quality at least equivalent to that of the well-to-do is a continuation and a manifestation of that citizens' movement.

It is hard to remember that in most parts of the country, we are only seventy to eighty years away from the time when the idea was first accepted that teachers needed any particular kind of training before they started work. With the drastic teacher shortage in so many American cities, we may be returning to what could be a refreshing new beginning of the old plan of learning to teach in the schools by teaching in the schools.

It is less than eighty years ago, in September of 1890, that Joshua Crittenden Chilton, itinerant salesman of education from Michigan, bent on starting a training school for teachers somewhere in the United States, addressed the citizens of Denton, Texas, on that subject in the Denton courthouse square. After explaining the need for teacher training in Denton and in Texas, and describing the Pestalozzi pedagogy, Mr. Chilton, who had dressed himself as an educator—long Prince Albert coat, full beard and mustache, and a tall silk hat—called on "all who believe in higher education and who want to see our State in the very front of intellectual as well as material progress," to help start the Texas Normal College and Teacher Training Institute. "Then," says the historian of the event, Professor James L. Rogers of North Texas State University, the institution which descended directly from Mr. Chilton's Institute, "with his high aspirations stated, the new president took his small staff and student body up the stairs over the B. J. Wilson hardware store and classes began."[11]

Since that time, when public schooling in Texas had existed for only six years and there was only one school in the state for training teachers, the citizens of Denton and Texas have continued their support of teacher education. But it was their movement, and they were the ones who had to decide whether they wanted to spend tax money to train teachers. What began as Chilton's private venture in persuasion, the idea of a man who held no college degree but had been to a normal school in Michigan, has now gone through stages of development similar to other institutions across the country, from normal school to teachers college, from teachers college to university—always justifying itself to the public by reference to the needs of the citizens for teachers and for education. North Texas State has now become a university of 16,000 students, graduating approximately 1500 teachers a year, with a graduate student enrollment of nearly 3000, of whom nearly 500 are doctoral candidates. What began as a movement in which teachers in and from the schools taught new teachers how to teach, has become a movement in which faculty members in the colleges teach about teaching to students who have never taught. In a sense, it has been one long bootstrap operation, involving homemade boots and locally produced straps.

If the quality of intellectual effort is to some extent attenuated, and if an interest in international affairs is not yet a major concern in the education of teachers, at North Texas State or elsewhere, this can best be regarded as a phase of social growth in a citizens' movement, rather than as a failure in the good intention of educators. The growth in size of the institutions of teacher education has pro-

11 *The Story of North Texas,* James L. Rogers, North Texas State University, Denton, Texas, 1965.

duced problems common to such institutions, among them the problem of recruiting faculty members from outside the circle of professional educators, and the creation of a curriculum for educating teachers which goes beyond the normal school and the teachers college. But the growth has come in response to the needs of citizens not unlike those who supported Chilton in the first place—the need for a place where the advantages formerly held by the well-to-do and the privileged could be obtained for those who had little money and little preparation for higher learning.

It is also useful to remember that we can see in the history of the entire state college movement a direct and rapid journey back to the recent origins of teacher education. In the Pacific Northwest, the first settler who came to the present site of Western Washington State College in Bellingham arrived as recently as 1848, the first normal school started in 1896, the first B.A. degrees, marking the transition toward a teachers college, were awarded in 1933, with a change of name to Western Washington College of Education in 1937. By 1961 the shift to Western Washington State College was complete, with twenty-three departments and a continuing concern for educating teachers along with liberal arts students and those who would enter the other professions.

The speed of transition and the terms in which it was made are typical of the entire movement in teacher education. What is not as often recognized is the fact, demonstrated clearly in the case of Western Washington State (any one of hundreds of other institutions, in Wisconsin, Connecticut, Massachusetts, or Michigan, might serve in illustration), that the evolving teachers colleges are connected to the educational needs and interests of the state and its citizens and to the national interests as construed by the federal grantmakers and the foundations.

Some of the arithmetic of the connection in the case of Western Washington State College is this: Grants of $500,000 from the Ford Foundation for the graphic arts; $121,000 from the National Science Foundation for mathematics and the earth sciences; $2 million for a computer center; additional funds from various sources inside and outside the State of Washington for a speech and hearing clinic, a poverty program, a neutron generator, a Fresh Water Institute, and more than a dozen other projects in research and education. The College now has more than 6000 students, from its own state, twenty-seven other states, and thirteen foreign countries, all of whom have a chance to attend any of fifty major events in music and the arts each year and have a wide variety of curricular programs from which to choose, along with the curriculum for teachers, of whom there are approximately 600 graduating each year in addition to nearly 100 teachers with the M.A. degree.

The education student is now placed in the middle of a variety of other students and in a situation in which his intellectual interests can be extended beyond anything that was formerly possible. It will take more years than have been available so far to find the ways in which the total environment of intellectual opportunity can be best used to the advantage of the education student. Those ways are unlikely to develop until there is a great deal more clarity among the educators of teachers about the philosophy of education they wish to adopt. Having lost the basic insight of the rough and ready, practical and plain work of the normal school, the new transitional institutions need to return to the roots of their own tradition and to reestablish the principle that intellectual growth is a functional part of the process of learning to teach, and that it is a *result* of teaching and learning, not a prerequisite for undertaking them.

In American communities, there has been very little consciousness in the past that teachers should have more qualifications as members of a separate intellectual or scholarly community than anyone else who worked in town, read a lot, or liked to talk about books and foreign countries. Although there are those who deplore it or deny it, there has never been an intellectual élite in the United States charged with the responsibility for running the country's cultural and educational life. Nor has education been considered to be the province of the intellectuals, élite or otherwise. It has been considered as a game anyone can play—the American Legion, the Chambers of Commerce, newspaper editors, crackpots, politicians, parents, admirals, clergymen, businessmen, assorted journalists, anyone with something to say.

In fact, since the subject of education has become a matter of constant and dominant public attention, a whole new breed of competent and informed critics has created itself among parents, public-spirited citizens, businessmen, members of the professions, and, above all, among the members of the press and of the public affairs section of the television and radio networks. There are 1400 members in the 50 states of the National Committee for Support of the Public Schools, ranging from lawyers, labor leaders, doctors and par-

ents with considerable influence in their own communities, to national figures like John Hersey, George Gallup, Omar Bradley, and
the Committee Chairman Mrs. Eugene Meyer.

When one of the major weekly magazines or national newspapers
turns its attention to educational issues, it can call upon a research
staff of hundreds, along with reporters and writers who have followed closely the issues involved—teacher strikes, poverty programs,
teacher education, the attitudes of high school students—and whose
information, objectivity and insight are in many ways of a higher
quality than that of the professional educators whose work they are
reviewing and reporting. A great deal of the time, the educators
take their views and their information from what appears in the
major magazines and television programs, while conversely, those
educators who wish to reach the teachers and educators, as well as
the public, with their own views, prefer to write for the mass magazines rather than for the publications designed for circulation
within the teaching profession.

I find this a healthy and promising situation, and do not see in it
the sinister implications found by those critics of the mass culture
who feel that the intrusion of the public into fields belonging to the
intellectuals and professionals is dangerous to the future of the culture. Everyone *is* in it—the rioting Negro, the flaming segregationist,
the anxious parent, the cultural critic, the practicing educator—and it
would be dangerous public policy to allow either the teachers, as
some have argued lately, to claim the exclusive right to know what
needs to be done with children and to be left alone to do it, or to
allow any other sector of the total community, anti-intellectual or
otherwise, to claim the right to settle policy for education in
America.

However, the continuing open debate does raise certain problems, one of which is that if there is no sizable group of persons in
the schools themselves who, by commitment, vocation, and the talent to go with it, take a serious interest in ideas and in the larger
issues of American and world society, there is no place within the
educational community, or in the experience of school children
growing up, where fresh and relevant thinking in these matters is
an area of continual and intense concern. Nor are there sufficient
models in the schools for the young to emulate, of the active, in-
quiring, imaginative, large-minded scholar at work; there are too few
instances in the schools of man thinking and bearing witness to the

power and delight of the intellect. There are mainly practitioners of education.

Added to this is the fact that the majority of those who enter programs of teacher education are from middle income and lower income groups, for whom entrance into the teaching profession is primarily a form of social and economic advance. They bring very few cultural and intellectual interests with them from the background of their own homes and schools. Since they enter institutions where learning to teach is considered mainly to be a matter of learning to handle children in classrooms with a standard syllabus, and the academic subjects they have studied in college are studied in isolation from anything to do with teaching itself, they seldom have the opportunity to learn to understand what it means to be a scholar and a teacher in the full meaning of these words. What is missing is the idea of education as the liberation of oneself into new levels of intellect and emotion, of education as a means of achieving new capacities and insights which can then become part of the stream of contributions made by the human race in the development of the arts and sciences, societies and civilizations. The present concept of teaching in America contains no call to lend oneself to great enterprises, to become useful in the larger sense.

CHANGES IN AMERICAN SOCIETY

One difficulty presents itself to anyone who writes about American education: the educational system and the society in which it exists will not stand still long enough to be clearly observed and accurately described. Since the work for this book began, three factors have been introduced into the American society which affect deeply the character of the educational and social system and alter the perspective from which it can be observed.

The first of these is the profound unrest, nowhere more deeply felt than in the educational system, produced by the scale of American intervention and the ensuing violence of the war in Vietnam. The major sources of citizens' resistance to the war have come from the universities, where most of the initiatives in opposition have come from the students—through demonstrations against the draft, refusals to serve, opposition to university control of political action, opposition to American foreign policy. More than anything else, the war has opened a wide and, in some ways, an unbridgeable gap between the generations, with undergraduate and graduate young activists bitterly opposed to what they consider to be the reactionary and authoritarian attitudes of the older generation and its educational leaders. Beginning with the issue of the war, the opposition of the young has turned to questions of educational reform, priorities in the use of national resources, and demands for radical social change.

The second factor is the explosive and violent quality of life in the American inner cities, where conditions which have long required thoughtful and compassionate effort in education and social reconstruction have now become literally intolerable. The pace of change and the degree of danger to the national welfare have now become so greatly out of balance with the progress of reform that many of the educational remedies and programs which, even one year ago, seemed adequate as a beginning have now in this short space of time become irrelevant and obsolete.

The third is the marked shift in the thinking of the younger generation about its place in American society and the educational system, in part a product of the other two factors, in part a product of a cultural shift through the communication system of a mass society which can now communicate with itself hourly, can expose its own problems and developments to the world minute by minute, and can bring the world into the American community day by day, week by week, and month by month on a scale never before known. The struggle between the blacks and the whites in America has now assumed a new phase of actual and potential violence which promises to defeat the normal procedures for maintaining public order. It has its parallel in struggles of greater violence between insurgents and counterinsurgents throughout the developing third world.

For the first time there is now a cohesive movement within the younger generation of American Negroes who have found an identity and a political base in the conception of pride of race and comradeship in rebellion. The younger generation, both white and black, now has its own sense of identification with the underprivileged of the world, and with the insurgents of the third world who refuse to accept their place in a social order which they have no power to control. In one sense, this has broadened the conception of nationalism among a growing proportion of American youth to include a recognition of their national counterparts in other coun-

tries in the world. It has produced, by indirection, an internationalism of youth.

The effect of these changes has been to make it absolutely imperative that the educational system respond to what is in fact a
revolution in the attitudes and demands of American citizens, especially of those who until now have been neglected by the educators.
No matter what the level of concern has been in the past, no matter what has been proposed and advocated as a solution to educational problems which have so clearly become world-wide, a new
urgency of effort among educators must now be invoked to match
the urgency of the situation. If we are not to allow the speed of
change and of disintegration to continue to outrun the provisions
being made to accommodate the change, we are going to have to do
things in education during the next two years which we never
dreamed we could or should do, even two short years ago.

THE RESPONSE OF EDUCATORS

One way of reporting quickly the intellectual and social climate
of the contemporary teacher education movement is to say that on
few campuses are there educators of teachers who have recognized
in any specific way the existence or the significance of radical
changes within American society or in America's relation to the
world. There has been little discussion among the educators of
teachers of the implications of the war in Vietnam for American
society and its educational system, little awareness that a Negro
revolution was in progress, that deep-going changes were occurring
in the attitude of youth to education and society, or that American
foreign policy is internationally discredited. It is as if the institutional structures and preoccupations of the educators of teachers
have sealed off the reality of the very society they existed to serve.

The comment of a student in response to a question about the
level of student interest in international affairs sums up the general
situation:

"Disregarding topical interest in Vietnam, most students have
little or no interest in the outside world. By interest, I mean any
kind of knowledge of and thought about world problems—peace,
poverty, disease, economic status of many emerging and traditional
nations. Again the influence of courses is small in the area of foreign
cultures because even Western cultures are only touched on in gov-

ernment survey courses. Even these are taken by few who will
enter secondary school teaching."

Miss Martha Darling, a former member of the staff in international
affairs of the National Student Association, who conducted a survey
of student activities in world affairs in the Boston-Cambridge metro-
politan area, to whom the above comment was made, adds the following: "Nor are there major countervailing influences outside the
classroom to stimulate interest. The majority of foreign students
are reported to be few and quite Westernized and Americanized.
International, political, economic, and moral issues seem in a way
a little too serious for discussion—or irrelevant. More congenial are
subjects like 'How do you like the U.S.?', and the bits of information exchanged about national customs do not appear to be pro-
jected into an image of an international and interdependent
community . . . The education students spend much of their course
time with methods, measurements, and general educational mechan-
ics. Their future charges seem to figure in their education courses
more as objects of these methods rather than as the subject of
the teaching process; more as identical models or types described in child psychology textbooks than as individuals with
specific problems who are to be educated to live and function
and contribute to a world which grows closer together. On the whole,
the students in the academic majors seem to be more aware of the
implications of the international and national scene for America and
themselves."[12]

I have mentioned elsewhere the minority of student activists
whose educational and political ideas are making a difference to the
campus atmosphere. I should say at once that their numbers are
comparatively small, from 3 to 8 percent on the livelier campuses,
none at all on others, and that the major problem in education having to do with world affairs is the political lethargy of almost all
the education students, matched and complemented by a similar
lethargy on the part of their faculty members.

A theme has returned again and again to my mind as I have
been reviewing the enormous power and possibility for good
in our cultural resources—the new schools being built, the thousands
and thousands of new students being added to the university rolls
every year, the energies going into the Poverty program, the Na-

[12] Report to Harold Taylor, from Miss Martha Darling, January 1966.

tional Teacher Corps, the Peace Corps, urban education, Head Start, Job Opportunity Centers, the civil rights movement. It is the familiar theme: How can we turn the huge expenditures of intelligence, energy, and money being poured into the war in Southeast Asia in a new direction for peaceful reconstruction? We can now see evidence of a power undreamed of in any former period of American or world history. We have literally built whole new towns in Vietnam, taking sandy wastes and converting them into huge centers for service and supply, installing networks of roads, taking deserted coastlines and converting them into giant ports, converting jungles into airports, building an international transportation system.

The lesson, beyond all others, is very simple. When it comes to training, transporting, equipping, housing, and supplying vast numbers of Americans to accomplish a national purpose, whatever it may be, we have the capacity to do whatever we decide to do. Whatever else emerges from the present war, the scale of thought about what can be done in international education and peaceful reconstruction, if we decide to do it, has reached a proven magnitude which puts all previous thought of scale into obsolescence. We should be thinking, in our cultural and educational policies for internationalism, not of a few students here and a few teachers there, but of 25,000 to 50,000 student-teachers sent abroad each year for cooperative learning with their foreign counterparts, thousands of fellowships for volunteers to the teaching profession and the human services, millions of dollars for the support of volunteers to help in the reconstruction of territories destroyed by war. The young men, blacks and whites, who are fighting in numbers beyond anything we would have dreamed two years ago, have the will and the idealism to turn their efforts toward reconstruction when that becomes our national policy.

A new kind of G.I. Bill at the conclusion of the war could divert these energies into the teaching and helping professions, by providing the subsidies for veterans to build upon their experience in the villages with the people of Vietnam, and, with new curricula in the colleges and universities, prepare them for teaching and community development in Vietnam and Southeast Asia. Since the Defense Department operates one of the largest educational programs in the world, let us take the skills and talents already developed within that system for peaceful use, for teaching, for social reconstruction.

As the months have gone by, we have already seen the colleges and universities become the source of new political thinking and social change in education and cultural affairs, with a new constituency of the young who have created their own leadership among themselves, and have formed the basis for new political allegiances which run counter to those of the established national authorities—for education and for foreign policy. The break of the National Student Association with the Central Intelligence Agency was not only a political but a symbolic act. It marked the time when the younger generation broke with established Government authority, when the students, through one of their major organizations, refused to accept the leadership, control, and policy of a Government whose subsidies had determined the course of student policy in world affairs. From this point on, the political and social force of more than 6,000,000 students and 450,000 faculty members is a source of independent thought and action which will, in one or another way, affect the direction of American politics, education, and foreign policy. A wise and farsighted Government will consider this to be a potent force for good. A negative and anxious Government and educational leadership will ignore the existence and possibilities of this new constituency and will try to dampen its effects and to divert its attention into established channels.

Evidence that the liberal new thinking in international education exemplified by the passage of the International Education Act is in danger of such dampening is shown in the lack of Congressional support for the allocation of the necessary funds. A policy of internationalism in education cannot be carried out with the limited funds presently at the disposal of the colleges and universities, since in nearly every case they are already hard pressed to carry out the obligations of domestic programs to which they are already committed. As of the present writing, none of the funds in the total figure of $130 million for a two-year period authorized for the International Education Act in October of 1966 has been appropriated. Unless the weight of financial support demanded by the terms of the Act and the demands of wise public policy is applied to the situation now, we will enter the 1970s further behind than we have ever been, since we can count on the pace of increase in the need for a full program of international education to run even faster between now and then than it has in the past.

A PERSONAL NOTE ON EDUCATIONAL THEORY

During the course of the present study, not only was I forced to consider these wider implications for education of the changes occurring inside America and in the relation of the United States to world problems, but I was confronted with the fact that to study education from the point of view of the education of teachers raises a different set of questions from those involved in the study of education as that term is generally used. Although I could find no basic distinction between the principles of education most applicable to the nurture of intellectual growth of all kinds and the principles applicable to students being educated to become teachers, I was continually made conscious of one very important educational difference— the difference between possessing knowledge and using it.

I had recognized this difference before, and had thought about it, written about it, and was concerned about it, as any person involved in the study of philosophy must be, but had never specifically applied it as a theory in the education of teachers. Put simply, the point is that to teach what you know is the most immediate way to find out what it is you know, and to learn whether you understand it, or whether it is relevant, useful, interesting, important, accurate, or otherwise worth while. Every man has his own body of knowledge, made from the materials of his own biography, depending on where he was born and in what circumstances, on the variety of personal experiences he has undergone in his own and other cultures, and on the formal studies which the accidents of his academic history have provided for him.

In my own case, the formal studies were mainly in philosophy, history, and literature of the West. I am thus the representative of a culture-bound education later somewhat corrected by confrontation and involvement with other cultures and their representatives. The formative experience in education which led to my present views was gained in the lively atmosphere of an American land-grant university, and the even livelier atmosphere of an American experimental college, where the worth of an educational idea was continually on test and was judged by the degree to which it enhanced the intellectual and personal growth of persons for whom it was intended. As a student I carried out the academic tasks set before me in the Canadian and English systems of education, and I entered the profession of teaching without ever having learned to teach or having examined closely what it was that I knew which might be useful in the lives of others.

It was the first years of teaching philosophy to undergraduates in a relatively unselected student body at the University of Wisconsin that I learned, sometimes to my horror, the limits of my knowledge and the actual, usable content of the education I had received. Through teaching, and through the teacher's necessity of meeting the educational needs of students from day to day, I learned what it was I needed to know in order to make what contribution I could to the culture of which I was a part. I also learned what it was I was most interested in. Until that kind of testing was administered daily in the classrooms of Wisconsin, the body of knowledge which inadvertently was mine lay inert in my mind, certified by appropriate degrees, but uninvestigated and unchallenged by the demand that it be used within the culture.

My conclusions about education and about the kind of knowledge of most worth to the younger generation and to the culture at large have been formed almost entirely by that experience of teaching, and by the experience of administering education at an experimental college where we tried continually to develop forms of organization which could involve the student in his own learning. The central idea which has reaffirmed itself in my mind through the years is that the best way to learn something is to teach it. This applies to students as well as to teachers. The way to teach teachers is to have them teach—themselves, each other, and children in the schools. The best kind of teacher is one who has had a variety of experience outside the academic system, who teaches what he is most interested in and cares most about.

I must therefore confess to a strong practical bent in my thinking about education, one which leans more heavily on the value of direct experience with ideas, issues, people, and situations than on the regular apparatus of educational institutions. I hold to the central conviction that the scholar who divorces himself from teaching, who relies solely or principally on the insights and judgments of his professional colleagues, free from the necessity of justifying his scholarship in the teeth of its relevance, its intrinsic value or use in the lives of the young, is likely to find himself incapsulated in an academic cocoon which inhibits the growth of his mind and his scholarship. A book is an effort on the part of its author to express to others what it is he has found, and although it may be addressed to a special audience of those who already understand its terms of reference, unless he is able to make what he knows available in some measure and in some form to those who are not in his frame of reference, he suffers the fate of exclusion from his culture. A comparable fate awaits the novelist or the playwright who, having written from his own experience in the world, shuts himself up to write more, sees only other authors and writers, reads what each is saying about the other, and finds that he no longer has very much to say to the world, since the wellsprings of his experience have dried up. Either that, or he begins to write novels, short stories, or plays about his own writing problems, or critical pieces about other writers.

Something like this happens to teachers whose personal experience is limited by the kind of lives they lead. They spend so much of their time with each other and with children, inside and around educational institutions, that their capacity for fresh educational thinking becomes impaired. They become so accustomed to their own school and their own community, with so little chance to become directly involved with schools and communities completely unlike their own, that they tend to assume that what happens in their own environment is what happens and should happen everywhere else.

I found this to be true in a personal way in writing about education in America while serving as President of Sarah Lawrence College. I tended to write as if there were only two kinds of institutions, Sarah Lawrence, and the rest, without knowing very much about what actually went on in the other places. That is one of the occupational difficulties of any educator. His work keeps him in his own institution during the time the others are functioning, and he meets his colleagues on neutral grounds—at conferences, meetings, congresses, etc.—where each speaks and writes of education from the point of view of the institution with which he is associated.

On the other hand, to explain America and American education to those who are not Americans is one of the most direct ways to force oneself to come to terms with the content of one's own belief. This becomes necessary if an educator accepts the assignment, as was true in my case, to speak before the student bodies and faculty members of foreign universities about the philosophy of American education, or to discuss with foreign students and scholars issues in education and social change as they present themselves within American society.

I therefore place a central emphasis in the education of teachers in world affairs on various forms of confrontation between the members of world cultures, rather than on the unilateral presentation through texts and curricular materials of ideas and facts drawn from the study of cultures. If one addresses a foreign audience about American education, it is necessary to start from scratch, assuming that apart from some elementary facts about the geography and national character of Americans, most of them mistaken, nothing very much is known about the American educational system or its aims.

The experts in the audience have usually become experts by formal study rather than by direct experience within the American culture, and whether in Moscow, Leningrad, Teheran, Djakarta, Athens, Tokyo, or Istanbul, the speaker is forced to return to the essentials of his own knowledge of his own culture and its educational system. In the case of addressing an American audience or teaching Americans about American education, it is helpful to assume that they too are foreigners, and to present their society to them as if it belonged to someone else. The teacher who has never known what his society looks like to someone else can seldom see it as it truly is.

THE DEFINITION OF WORLD AFFAIRS

With these preconceptions and presentiments I was therefore not altogether surprised to discover when I began the present study that the words I used to explain its nature meant something so different to the students and educators with whom I talked, that unless I took great care, I was almost certain to be misunderstood. I mean misunderstood about the simple words like student, teacher, educator, world affairs, curriculum, teacher education, or the word education itself. The phrase, Education of Teachers in World Affairs, meant to most others Teacher Education, and courses in international relations and non-Western cultures. Non-Western culture was something studied as a counterpart to Western culture; teacher education meant something labeled, technical, and quite specific, already classified with an attitude taken toward it. It was something you did in order to meet state certification requirements, while you studied the regular college courses in the academic departments.

Various educators held various views about what was meant by international education itself. Among these views were:

1. Courses in international relations, stressing the role of the United Nations, international organizations, and the business of Governments dealing with each other.

2. Courses in political science which stressed the relation of the Western democracies to the Communist countries and the conflicts in ideology in post-colonial Africa and Asia—the political strategies involved in American foreign policy.

3. Courses in world history, world culture, and world geography, designed to broaden the scope of the student's general knowledge.

4. Area studies which stress the interrelation of the academic disciplines in exploring the history and characteristics of a given region of the world.

5. Comparative education, to explore the similarities and differences among national systems of education.

6. Special sequences of courses in foreign cultures, designed to prepare teachers to teach in a given area of the high school or college curriculum.

7. Courses in general education containing knowledge of foreign countries and their cultures outside the Western hemisphere.

8. World affairs courses emphasizing current events.

More often than not, no distinction was made between the need for such courses in the general education of prospective teachers and their use in the preparation of teachers who could themselves teach specific courses in international affairs, or world history, to elementary and high school students.

In the case of a large number of students and a considerable number of university faculty members, I found that teacher education was held in low regard, often with a formidable, if uninformed, disrespect. The negative attitude seemed in part to come from an unexamined assumption that "teacher education" was all one thing. It was what had been talked about and criticized in the public, it was what Admiral Rickover did not like, it was a standard program of professional courses, all of them unfortunately unavoidable. I can report as a primary fact that "teacher education" is, on the whole, not highly regarded by most of those undergoing it, or by those who stay out of it and hear about it from their friends, and by those who know little about it. When I turned from the interviews, meetings, conferences, and class visiting with the students and professors to the literature of teacher education, I found almost exactly the same set of assumptions in the literature about the nature of the programs. I could see the reinforcing effect of documents from the educating profession on the practices of the schools and colleges. The documents reflect the practices, which then gain legitimacy from the documents. Again, teacher education is classified as one particular kind of education, defined by its own terms.

In search of guidance toward improvement of the schools, the tendency of school men is to review a kind of national check list, of the sort provided by James Conant and others, of subjects, organization, numbers of qualified personnel, costs, etc., and to measure themselves against a national agenda of the things they should have and the things they should be doing. I had the feeling that for many of those with whom I talked, courses in non-Western culture, if backed by sufficient authority, would simply be added to the obligatory list. There is thus a one-dimensional quality in the concepts which dominate the literature, the research topics, and the agenda of educational action and reform. The tendency is to think of education as a closed system, with no relation to the political, social, economic, or world context in which education operates. The educational system is assumed to have its own parts, students, teachers, administrators, curriculum, all of them organized within the system in such a way that each part can function at a certain level of efficiency.

The present aim of the professional educator, as I learned about it from deans of colleges of education, professors of education, and from the articles and books which they and others in the field have written, is to make education more professional, to raise the level and status of professional education as a discipline to that of the major graduate schools, law, medicine, architecture, or engineering. Although some faculty members of colleges and departments of education with whom I talked felt comfortable with the idea that the study of education could be usefully carried on as a central concern in the social sciences and the humanities, most believed that unless education were treated as a separate study and as the province of professional educators and students of education, its content would be misconstrued and its essential place in the curriculum would be lost. The teachers' organizations and the professional educators together urge that teachers press for professional recognition and, with the accrediting and certifying agencies, urge that professional standards be applied to teacher education programs and to the performance of teachers in the schools.

Nor did I find a very different view in the documents, statements, and policies of the American Federation of Teachers, which, although militant and effective in political tactics for increased teachers' salaries and benefits, is possessed of no educational or social philosophy around which its members are organized. In common with the trade union movement in general, the Teachers Union is concerned primarily with economic advantage, and political considerations are relevant where organizing power is needed to achieve them. As far as teacher education and world affairs are concerned, there are no programs of broad consequence in effect among the union members, and it is fair to say that the American Federation of Teachers has no international education program and no present intention of creating one.

I am not arguing here the legitimacy of Union demands or of the organizational methods for improving the grossly inadequate salary scale of the American teacher. That scale is a matter of very great significance in classifying the teacher within the social and economic system, and in stultifying the influence of teachers in social and political change. I mean, rather, to point out that teachers are union members of a particular kind and do not usually identify themselves with the interests or the ideology of the trade union movement. Nor does their membership alter the conception of professionalism which the union is concerned to foster. The unions wish to improve the status of the teaching profession by increasing the economic and political power of the organization.

Within that professional framework, teacher education programs are designed to make certain that teachers can function within the existing system, can do what is required of them in their profession, and can make use of whatever methods and innovations are current in order to improve the effectiveness of teaching. This accounts in part for the current emphasis on innovation, most of it technical, having to do with programmed learning, the use of television, electric typewriters, movable classrooms, computerized classrooms, team teaching, systems of reading, and so on. No matter what may be the merits of the innovations, effectiveness is measured almost entirely within the closed system, by how rapidly and well the students learn the subjects they are taught, how well they meet the academic standards against which they are tested.

In this system, the most successful student also becomes a professional. If he is talented he learns the skills and habits sought by the system and its prize-givers, who number in their ranks the sponsors of the National Merit Scholarship Awards, the Presidential Scholars, the donors of university and college scholarships, prizes, fellowships, and other awards. With high grades and academic aptitudes, the right student can earn financial reward, social approval, and a place in the professions and executive classes later on.

The best kind of teacher for working within this structure is therefore one who is skilled and experienced in teaching a subject in which he has become professionally competent, not one whose values lie outside the structure and who takes a serious interest in world events and issues. The teacher's rewards are based on his ability to prepare his students to meet the criteria of their success. He therefore prefers to teach bright students with academic aptitudes, and there is a good deal of jostling for position within a given school in which teachers of proven ability seek to acquire students with scholastic aptitudes, with the rest of the students often distributed to those who, for one reason or another, are less able to achieve success in teaching the subjects.

Prestige factors then enter, of the kind which afflict the colleges and universities, where the highest prestige is reserved for those who teach graduate and postdoctoral students of proven talents. The average and below-average freshmen are taught by the new, inexperienced, and less prestigious faculty members and by teaching assistants. These are drawn from the ranks of the less prestigious graduate students who, usually for economic reasons, teach because they are not subsidized completely by the graduate fellowships awarded to their higher-ranking fellow students. This means, among other things, that the genuinely professional student has all the advantages, and the average student, comprising at least ninety percent of the high school and college student body, gets the least effective kind of teaching because he has not acquired sufficient professional skill to be recognized as a Good Student.

The best administrator in the schools then turns out to be the one who is able to organize his school or college program so that the best curriculum is taught to well-motivated and able students by good professional teachers. The administrator's prestige rests on the same extrinsic criteria—in the case of the high school, the academic achievement produced by the student body and how many students go on to what colleges. For the colleges, the question is, what academic achievements are produced by the students there, and how many of them go on to prestigious graduate schools, not how many become lively and interesting teachers. I found in a number of institutions which were formerly teachers colleges and are now multipurpose universities, as they prefer to be called, that faculty members were pleased to announce that many of their present students were *not* going to become teachers, having been so successful in their studies that they were going to graduate school in other fields.

I believe that this set of attitudes, so firmly fixed within the professional education establishment, toward teaching, toward students, and toward the aims of education, accounts in large part for the lack of initiative in the past among educators for tackling the social and economic issues in which educational intervention is so crucial—the problems of the ghetto, of the rural slums, of the impoverished and the neglected, and of the world order. The attention of the educators has been turned inward and directed to a set of questions which in the long run are technical and organizational, assuming that the student is a standard human entity, with individual differences measurable by educational devices, and that teaching as a standard process in which the teacher is defined by the functions he fulfills and not by the person he is. The *being* of the student and the teacher is therefore not a matter for educational concern. The main concern is in assuring the adequacy of the professional skills which student and teacher can acquire.

The new demands of a changing society press upon the educational system from the outside, with a strength which is increasing daily, forcing changes in the educational system which it has not prepared itself to make. The social legislation of the 88th and 89th Congresses, with the sudden release of funds in amounts never before available for educational use, has so changed the external situation of the educable population that educational changes are happening outside the formal system of instruction designed by professional educators. This accounts for the fact that the educational approaches of Head Start, VISTA, the National Teacher Corps, and the Peace Corps are mainly the result of planning by a new group of Government appointees in the field of social welfare and social science, with cooperation from educators, rather than as initiatives taken from inside the colleges of education, some of whom have been reluctant to change their ways, even when the demand for new approaches and new programs stare them in the face.

This also accounts for the fact that the concept of direct social experience and direct action in social and cultural situations, or field work in education, are foreign to the basic construct of the standard educational pattern. That pattern in teacher education has been designed for the white middle class in a society of the moderately well-to-do, not for the variety of cultures, economic and social groups, to which a democratic educational system must adapt itself.

One of the ways in which the pattern is reflected shows itself in the attitude to practice teaching, usually the only kind of practical experience for which the student-teacher can acquire academic credit. Practice teaching is literally that: an assignment in practicing teaching in a classroom with assigned materials to practice with, including a roomful of children. For this reason, many young people with an interest in teaching have gone outside the regular system of teacher preparation to find their own way to where the educational realities are—in the lives of children who need tutoring, who need interesting adult companionship, who need recreational and social leadership and the chance to gain a personal identity.

Similarly, it accounts for the fact that the majority of Peace Corps Volunteers who volunteer for teaching abroad choose not to engage in teacher preparation programs before volunteering, and prefer to learn the art in their Peace Corps training and in the reality of a teaching assignment in a foreign country. The idea of learning to become a teacher by first becoming a person of rich and varied experience in the live situations of society is not one which fits easily into the thinking of the professionals. It explains in part the absence of a full-fledged program in an education for teachers which takes into account the richness of phenomena in world cultures and world society.

The question then is: How are policies set in the entire system? Who decides what kind of education teachers should have? Who is responsible for the present state of affairs?

The public impression is that institutions called teachers colleges decide the teacher education questions, while scholars and clear-headed critics in the universities do their best to improve matters. The facts are otherwise.

Approximately 200,000 elementary and secondary school teachers are graduated with teaching certificates every year, having been educated at one of approximately 1200 institutions where teachers are prepared. Of the 200,000, around 40,000 or 20 percent of the total come from former teachers colleges which are now state colleges and universities. The rest graduate from the private and public colleges of liberal arts—around 45 percent—and the private and public universities—35 percent. A very small proportion of those starting to teach each year take a Master of Arts degree before beginning, 7 percent in the case of elementary and 10 percent in secondary schools.[13]

This means that whatever is wrong or right with the education of teachers, the policies are mainly in the hands, not of the teachers colleges (only 47 of which now exist) or of the institutions which were formerly teachers colleges, but in the hands of the private and public universities. On the other hand, the attitudes and values of the teachers of undergraduates in these universities are in many ways conditioned by the attitudes of the faculty in the graduate schools since, as I have been saying, the whole system is arranged in a hierarchical form as far as teaching is concerned—the lowest in the kindergarten, the highest in the postdoctoral seminar.

The graduate school of education therefore has its own responsibility and potential power to make decisions which can affect the whole system. It can, if it wishes, set the tone and in some ways the content of what is done in the undergraduate teacher education pro-

---

[13] Descriptions of the types of programs, numbers of teachers, requirements, etc., are contained in publications of the National Education Association, the National Commission on Teacher Education and Professional Standards, the U. S. Office of Education and The American Association of Colleges for Teacher Education; particularly *Teacher Productivity—1966*, AACTE, 1201 Sixteenth Street, NW, Washington, D.C.; National Education Association, Research Division, *Teacher Supply and Demand in Public Schools* (annual reports); *Manual on Certification Requirements for School Personnel*, National Committee on Teacher Education and Professional Standards.

grams, just as graduate school requirements reflect the general professional interest of the graduate school faculty members and therefore control the preparation of undergraduates.

I can report that the graduate school of education in the United States has now moved toward the idea that the education of teachers must be made more professional, that is to say, more directly related to the academic hierarchy and its values, less related to the idea that the task of the graduate school is to prepare teachers for service in the public schools. The university faculty members, working through committees, some holding joint appointments in schools of education and university departments, now have more power to decide about what the education of teachers should be than they have ever had before.

In general, they and the faculty of the graduate schools of education believe that the best way to prepare public school teachers is to admit students with a regular B.A. degree to a graduate school M.A. program, and to provide them with a year to a year and a half of combined school internship and graduate study in academic and professional subjects, yielding both the teaching certificate and the M.A. on graduation. The combination of these and other variations of the Master of Arts in Teaching programs has recruited a new cross section of B.A. students, many of whom had not intended to become teachers during their undergraduate years, while diminishing the number of public school teachers prepared in the graduate schools. Until now, very little has been done to include an international component in such programs, either through experience abroad or study at home.

The real thrust of the graduate schools of education is toward doctoral programs, designed to develop new kinds of school administrators and professional educators, for the public school, for the departments and colleges of education, and for research institutes in curriculum and educational planning. The influx of federal funds for research and experiment in all phases of elementary and secondary education has not only created sharply increased demands for research talent and new kinds of organizational and professional personnel in the regional educational laboratories and community development work, but also has made it possible for graduate schools of education, after years of financial starvation, to spend money on projects, research, and experiment which were impossible even to think about in former years.

The report of the Harvard Committee on the Graduate Study of Education,[14] although deliberately confined to the problems of Harvard, both sums up and indicates trends in contemporary university thinking about the role of the graduate schools of education. Theodore Sizer, Dean of the Harvard Graduate School of Education, points out in his introduction to the Report that schools of education have long been out of balance, owing to the tremendous pressures on them to produce the thousands of teachers necessary to man the schools. "It is not that there are not enough persons in the field; indeed there are more degrees of every description granted in this country in education than in any other.[15] It is rather that there are not enough absolutely first-rate people, either academically or in terms of commitment, to move the field forward. Sadly, education classes in most universities are drawn from a low academic level of the student-body, and from the best of this group (and from most of its males irrespective of quality) educational leadership is drawn. There are exceptions, of course; but the evidence of weak professional leadership and shoddy scholarship makes the general conclusion irrefutable. Service in the schools is low-status work, but it should not be. Scholarship on the problems of schooling is neglected, but it ought not to be . . . The following report is, really, an affirmation that university schools of education can make a significant difference not only in supplying raw material for the nation's schools but also the significant ideas upon which education must rest . . ."[16]

The Report itself follows out the implications of Dr. Sizer's introductory remarks, and the work of the ten committee members who prepared the Report is representative of both the method and content of policy-making by university faculty members who are addressing the problems of graduate schools of education across the country. After considering in turn the possibility of doing away with the School of Education, as at Yale, or turning it into a research institute, or reorganizing it on the basis of the regular academic

[14] *Report of the Harvard Committee on the Graduate Study of Education,* Harvard University Press, Cambridge, Mass., 1966, 125 pp.

[15] The fact that more degrees are granted in education than in any other field is beside the point. There are far from enough persons in the field, there are shortages in every sector, and the number of persons graduating in education, although large, is not within thousands of reaching the number of qualified teachers presently needed, to say nothing of future needs. The dimensions of this problem are described on pp. 139–43 of the present report.

[16] Ibid., p. vii.

disciplines, or using it exclusively for "the doctoral training of practitioners" or for model teacher preparation and service programs, the Committee calls for balance among the various scholarly and professional obligations of the School, for doing less work in preparing teachers through the M.A. and Master of Arts in Teaching, more work with doctoral candidates.

In its argument for balance, the Report is academic in the best, as well as the worst, sense of the term. That is, the Committee deals with the existing reality of the organization and resources of its University and the School, and in an intelligent and thoughtful way seeks to find the best means of using these resources for improving the quality of research and professional preparation of the students attracted to the School. In doing so, it has called upon a cross section of the best informed and concerned persons in the country for their views and for information about the activities of the institutions with which they are connected.

At the same time, the Committee exhibits no passion, it introduces no large conceptions, no central ideas around which new patterns of thought might form, and presents no view of education except to say that "Education is better conceived as an organizing perspective from which all problems of culture and learning may be viewed. To place the issues of professional practice within such a context is to relate it to the whole life of the university. The special task of a university school of education is to facilitate such relationship, and in so doing to benefit both practice and scholarship."[17]

In different words, the Committee is saying that it does not wish to own to a perspective according to which education, culture, and learning might be organized; anyone who wishes to do so can find his own organizing perspective, his own definition of education. The issues of education are to be related, not to the whole life of man, but to the life of the university and its intellectual and professional concerns.[18] When one considers how narrow are the patterns of

[17] Ibid., p. 72.

[18] In explaining why the graduate school of education should emphasize doctoral study and thus produce "the greatest potential for fundamental and long-term influence upon the field of education," the Report identifies the "most challenging current problem of professional definition, namely, the problem of working out a productive combination of fundamental studies providing advanced training for a new variety of careers in education practice, all to be

life in the academic and university community, and how limiting the intellectual life there, it becomes clear that the aim of the American graduate school of education in shifting as it has toward a major commitment of the kind described by Harvard is to leave the world at large pretty much as it is, except for the influence upon it which might be exerted by skilled professionals who bring intellectual acuity to bear on whatever problems their employers need help in solving.

There is no mention, in fact, of the world at all, no recognition of the changes in twentieth-century world society which demand reconsideration of the whole content and method of graduate, undergraduate, and public school education. The lack of explicit statement in the Harvard Committee Report does not mean that reconsideration is not taking place, and that individual faculty members and students are not taking initiatives in developing new conceptions of what is to be taught and what is to be done. Dean Sizer, for example, himself teaches a well-attended course in the comparative development of American, English, and Nigerian education; Robert Rosenthal has carried out important educational and research projects in the slum areas of Boston; individual tutorial projects have involved students in the social and cultural problems of the ghetto; the Harvard-Radcliffe undergraduates have developed a rationale and a volunteer program for education with a world point of view;[19] the School itself, with the aid of Government and Foundation grants, is carrying on educational development and research projects in Venezuela, Colombia, Mexico, Tunis, Bar-

informed by intellectual values, technical proficiency, and clinical awareness. We have here a challenge to strengthen the power and raise the standards of the profession, as well as to improve the quality of the currently expanding educational endeavor, by training able and intellectual professionals for key posts in schools, communities, universities, industry, government, communications, planning, and research . . ." Ibid. p. 24.

Here the aims of education are stated in a form which more clearly indicates the narrowness of the conception. The studies are to be informed by "intellectual values, technical proficiency and clinical awareness," all of them useful for training men and women to serve in key posts wherever they are needed, but not designed to develop men and women with a view of the world and of education which might help to enrich them both.

[19] *An Experiment in Education*, Radcliffe Government Association, Phillips Brooks House, Room 5159, Shepard Street, Cambridge, Mass. The student program *Education for Action* calls for a combination of educational study and teaching abroad and in rural and urban slums during two three-month summer periods, with appropriate studies on the campus during the regular terms.

bados, and a major curriculum-making project in Nigeria under a contract with AID.

But in the concept of education and society implicit and explicit in the Report, the world outside the university turns out to be only another element in the "organizing perspective," and the projects in foreign countries do not touch directly upon the lives and education and experience of those who will be teaching in the public schools, except as faculty members with foreign experience bring the elements of that experience to bear on the materials of the courses they teach. The conclusions reached by the Harvard Committee about the professional and academic prescriptions for work in graduate education coincide with those already drawn, or in the process of being drawn, by committees and faculty members of the graduate schools of education elsewhere in the country. In view of these common assumptions, it would be unusual for a school of education to concern itself with the development of an overall curriculum or program which was shaped according to a new conception of the nature of world culture and world society, or one which could assure an overall relevance to new philosophical, social, and political questions raised by the existence of what can only be called a world revolution. As far as education is concerned, the world continues to be one thing, the university another.

On the other hand, new opportunities for extending the range and depth of international understanding and experience on the part of professional educators lie in the specialized research institutes and academic departments of the universities where foreign cultures are dealt with, if only they can be linked to the educational issues and problems of the society itself. The situation at Harvard, as at Columbia and Stanford, presents a case in point. The Harvard Center for Studies in Education and Development is located in the Graduate School of Education, and with a staff of scholars and experts in a variety of fields—economists, sociologists, statisticians, historians, mathematicians, administrators, educators, with considerable experience in foreign service—carries out research and educational projects in Latin America, the Middle East, and Africa in the countries cited above. It is thus a valuable resource for the education of Harvard students of education who might otherwise not have access to teachers and scholars working so directly on the going problems of educational and social change in world society.

The experience of the members of the Harvard Center brings them close to agreement with one central point in the findings of this Report, that study and action having to do with the educational problems of the developing countries leads directly to a more sensitive awareness of the character and scope of similar problems in this country, or, conversely, research and action in the areas of educational and social change in the United States has direct bearing on the development of educational ideas and attitudes within the wider context of a world system of education.

In the language of the Annual Report of the Harvard Center for 1966–67:

> Seminars and increasing interchange with faculty members outside [the Center] have resulted from the necessity for relating the Graduate School's overseas interests and capabilities to its domestic ones. This communication has become increasingly important because of the growing realization that education problems are not primarily "foreign" and "domestic," but rather "common" and "critical" and differ more in place and time than in kind.
>
> The Center's several involvements make possible a wider employment of the faculty's expertise in identifying and solving educational problems which plague the developing world. In addition, involvement provides an important perspective to our own domestic educational issues and a greater possibility for making contributions to education which extend well beyond our own borders.[20]

It is possible that through centers of this kind in the future, with an inflow of foreign students and teachers, returned Peace Corps volunteers and others directly involved in field work and action research both in the United States and abroad, with the inclusion of graduate students as research and teaching assistants in the overseas projects, entire sectors of graduate schools of education can gain the advantage of wider experience in world education. What distinguishes Centers of this kind from those in area studies and international relations is that they come at the problems of developing countries and world society from a concern to analyze and plan for educational and social development, and the kind of knowledge they put together and disseminate is of direct relevance to the edu-

[20] Annual Report, 1967, Center for Studies in Education and Development, Graduate School of Education, Harvard University; to be published. Evidence in support of these generalizations is also to be found in the findings of the research published in *The University Looks Abroad*, by Education and World Affairs, op. cit., which examines in detail the operation of international programs on six major campuses, Stanford, Michigan State, Tulane, Wisconsin, Cornell, and Indiana.

cational growth of students of education. The Centers are therefore capable, if the proper arrangements are made for linking their work to the rest of the curriculum in education, of expanding to an international dimension the interests, usable knowledge and viewpoint of teachers and educators in the schools and in the colleges for teachers.

In the absence of Centers or Institutes, there are of course other ways of injecting a wider point of view into appropriate areas of the education curriculum. Too seldom do the schools of education consider the ways in which, without the support of foundation or government funds, existing budgets and programs can be converted to use as vehicles for international education. International programs most often occur in the universities when the interest of administrators and faculty coincides with the interest of the Government, or of foundations working cooperatively with the Government, in supporting special programs. At times during my visits to American campuses, it was hard to decide whether the programs were in effect because the Government and foundations wanted them there, or because they had developed through initiatives in the institutions themselves. It does not really matter in the long run which is true, as long as the interests truly coincide. But one thing is certain, the development of international programs in teacher education is, in comparative terms, so expensive that unless subsidies are provided from sources outside the present funds available to the colleges of education, it will be very difficult indeed to mount new international programs of substantial size and influence.

One frequent comment from administrators and directors of international programs in general was to the effect that if it were not for the Ford Foundation, the Carnegie Corporation, the Government, and a limited number of other foundations, there would be practically no international programs on the campuses, and that if that kind of support were withdrawn, many of the present programs would collapse. In the vocabulary of the initiates, the difference between hard money and soft money—the latter being that provided by grants, the former from regular university budgets—is crucial to long-range planning.

AN ALTERNATIVE EXAMPLE

An example of the way in which an association with Government programs can eventually affect the international education of teachers is to be found in the work of Ohio University in Athens, Ohio, over the past ten years. Government and foundation subsidies made possible new international programs in the beginning, with consequent effect on the content of work in world affairs throughout the university as a whole. In 1961 and 1962, for instance, two groups of approximately thirty teachers from seventeen countries came to the university, under the sponsorship of the International Teacher Development program of the U. S. Office of Education and the Department of State, for three months of study and experience at the university and in the Ohio community. Their presence had the effect of drawing the attention of the College of Education to a variety of ideas in world education, and served as a means of educating students and faculty at the College, aside from the education the visitors received in their turn. Three education programs, in Northern Nigeria, Western Nigeria, and South Vietnam, on contract with the Agency for International Development, are under way at the university, which has also conducted Peace Corps training programs for the Cameroons.

The College of Education has been closely involved in the work of the international programs, has more than forty of its faculty members abroad, with thirty-two presently teaching in the college who have had foreign interests and experience. Without setting down many details of the educational work of the College in Nigeria and South Vietnam, it may be sufficient to say that ten secondary schools in the latter country are working on pilot projects with Ohio faculty members, curriculum materials have been worked out for both South Vietnam and Nigeria, where in-service teacher education programs have been started, and teacher training institutions have been or are being organized, in particular a new multipurpose teachers college in Kano, Northern Nigeria, which was started from scratch in 1963.

Having built this body of experience within the College faculty and program, the College has now begun to turn its attention directly to the way in which undergraduate and graduate students of education can extend the international range of their work, and has proposed the establishment of an Institute of International Education in the College itself. The Institute would find ways of using the work overseas and the special competence of faculty members throughout the whole University to affect the education of teachers. The intention of the proposal, which is backed by the administration of the University as well as by the College of Education, is fourfold:

(1) . . . "to make teachers more proficient in teaching about the world," (2) to develop educators with special competence to serve in educational projects abroad, (3) to prepare educators for positions in the United States which require a knowledge of the world's educational systems, (4) to act as a study and research center for American and foreign teachers."

The kind of intention and program represented by the Institute of International Education proposal at Ohio University is characteristic of work going on elsewhere, although I could find in operation no very satisfactory solution to the major problem of creating links between the education of undergraduate and graduate students and the foreign service programs of Colleges of Education and their faculty members.

SOME ANALOGIES WITH THE PROFESSIONAL SCHOOLS

In reviewing the work of graduate schools of education, I found that they had most of the same problems as the other professional schools in internationalizing the curriculum and introducing the component of practical experience as a central element in the professional training itself. The publication by Education and World Affairs of a series of studies of international education in the professional schools has drawn attention again to the fact that the role of the American professional—the doctor and public health administrator, the engineer, lawyer, the agricultural expert, the business executive, the educator, the architect, among others—has taken on an international dimension by the very conditions of professional service, because "the functions they serve must be performed in all societies."[21] The analogies to schools of education which appear most relevant are those which occur in architecture, for example, where the parallel between designing new environments and new educational systems is very clear, and the interrelationships obvious. There are other parallels between schools of education and schools of public administration, or of law, with its necessary blend of the theoretical with the practical case-study approach, or more particularly of medicine and public health, if education is considered to be a profession concerned with healing the diseases of ignorance, curing

21 See Introductory statement by William W. Marvel, President, Education and World Affairs, in each of the publications on the Professional School and World Affairs, op. cit.

mental and intellectual deficiencies, enhancing emotional and social growth, and creating conditions for the optimum development of the human being.

I have often thought, as I have looked at the practices of the schools of education and the educators responsible for undergraduates, that if the medical analogy were taken seriously, educators are acting toward their students (patients) as if a patient coming for treatment, having announced his physical symptoms and ill health, were told to go away and come back when his deficiencies were cured, that only then could he be admitted for treatment. Transposed into professional education, the analogy continues, and the student of education is told that he must study academic subjects having little to do with the problems he will encounter in the lives of his students or their society, and that after at least three years of academic isolation from the life situation of those to whom he will minister, he is then allowed to see them, most often in the classroom (operating room or clinic), and to work with them (operate on them) as a way of learning his profession.

We can be thankful that the medical profession has begun to move in recent years in the direction of furnishing more direct experience with patients in the beginning years of medical training, and in the direction of research and education in the psychiatric and social aspects of medicine, combining in one program the study of mental and physical illness, the study of environmental effects on the human organism, and the consideration of educational and economic problems in the lives of those whom the profession serves. That is the direction in which the professional education of teachers must move if it is to remain relevant to the needs of contemporary world society.

Or, to put the issue in purely educational terms, the professional schools of education, both for undergraduates and for graduates, have moved toward isolating the student from direct experience with children, their parents, and the problems of the social order. In the meantime the needs of the children, the students of education, and the social order have all been creating demands in the opposite direction.

One of the most interesting documents in the field of medical education, with several implications for the professional education of teachers, is the report of a special committee on curriculum of the Harvard Medical School, issued in the spring of 1966.[22] The report reflects not only the views of the Harvard Committee but a growing dissatisfaction among medical students and medical schools across the country that the curriculum is too rigidly organized, with insufficient freedom of choice among subjects for study, too little opportunity for taking care of patients in the earlier years of training, too little attention to maintaining the "motivation of most beginning students to help suffering humanity," too little attention to making "teaching the greatest of all educational experiences for the teacher."

Among the recommendations of the Committee are that, rather than postponing student experience with patients until the third year, the students should begin in the first year to interview patients as part of the training program, that work in the behavioral and social sciences should supplement the work in biological science during the second year, that practical experience be the emphasis of the third year, and that in the fourth year the students should choose courses, with the help of faculty advisers, from an elective curriculum covering all the divisions of the medical school offerings. "To teach the details before the motivation to learn them exists, is pedagogy doomed to failure," says the Report, in advocating fewer lectures and more time for small group discussions and "problem-solving exercises."

All of these recommendations apply with equal force to the professional school of education, and one could wish that among the educational planners in this field, at Harvard and elsewhere, there were more persons with the views and strength of educational conviction demonstrated by the medical staff of the Harvard Committee. Once professional education is considered from the point of view of the person who will use it and the person on whom it will be used, the argument for greatly increased flexibility in curriculum and an increased emphasis on the fusion of practical with theoretical studies is already made. The flexibility is necessary to accommodate the diverse talents and interests of those who are preparing to be teachers, including returned Peace Corps volunteers, foreign students, inexperienced high school graduates, those gifted in lan-

[22] *Report of the Subcommittee on Curriculum Planning,* Harvard Medical School, May 1966; mimeographed, 23 pp. The continued reference to Harvard is not intentional, but made necessary by the fact, in this instance, that the Medical School Report states more succinctly than any other the point of view in reform which I am concerned to support.

guages, mathematics, or literature, as well as those who are teaching the teachers, especially, in the context of the present study, those who have had experience abroad.

Too often the faculty member with foreign experience returns to his high school or college of education and, because of the rigidity of the curriculum, teaches standard courses in the present curriculum rather than developing new courses of his own which can use his international experience and talents to the best advantage of his students and of his own intellectual development. Too often the sheer existence of particular courses in the departmental system of the college of education demands that these courses be taught and no others, and that persons whose own training may not have prepared them for imaginative development of new course materials in the assigned area are simply put to work in order to fill the assignment. If we are to have interesting new work in international education, or in anything else in the professional education of teachers, we are going to have to give serious and continuing attention to the intellectual interests of the individual faculty members, and, through a vastly increased national subsidy for study and travel, turn them loose to develop new interests and new content for the courses now frozen into the teacher education curriculum.

The demonstration of what can be done when there is enough money to do it has been carried on almost exclusively in graduate schools of education which have agreed to prepare specialists who can carry out duties connected with Government service abroad, in international organizations, professional research, and institution building in foreign countries. In general, the school of education becomes an agency under contract to produce certain kinds of professionals rather than an international center for the development of new modes of education and internationalism. Consequently the effect of the subsidies for international education is seldom felt in the American undergraduate curriculum, in the preparation of teachers, or in the main stream of graduate work in American education itself.

THE SOURCES OF INITIATIVES

The original impetus for making new programs has come from a combination of Federal subsidies, usually through AID projects, foundation grants for advanced professional work of the kind at

Michigan State University, Columbia, Harvard, and Stanford, as well as grants for area studies centers which have extended their course offerings to graduate and undergraduate students. The result has been, as is the case in other fields, that the major institutions with existing resources and capabilities have received the major grants, have built the strongest programs, and have worked most directly with Government, foundation, and national educational bodies in supplying the need for professional scholars and educators in the international area. The spread of new materials in foreign cultures and new courses in a wide range of international subjects throughout the entire curriculum in the major universities has come as a result of the subsidized Institutes and Centers and the presence on the campuses of qualified experts in foreign fields.

Beginning in 1956, when Michigan State appointed the first Dean of International Programs in the United States, the trend toward the development of such programs has grown until there are now executive officers, either Deans, Vice-Presidents, Coordinators, or Directors of International Programs, in more than one hundred universities. In some instances the progress toward a curriculum, usually in the graduate departments, in which work in foreign cultures is integrated with the general curricular design, has been extraordinary.

However, in very few instances has there been serious effect on the actual content and style of the education of public school teachers, relatively few of whom are educated in graduate schools or in the universities where such graduate schools and international programs exist. Of the forty institutions from which the largest number of secondary and elementary school teachers graduate each year, only four, in the case of elementary school teachers, and twelve in the case of secondary school teachers, could be classified as universities in which substantial work is being carried on in the international field either in the School of Education or in the graduate schools in general. As I have already pointed out, even in the case of major universities with a generous supply of courses in the international area—languages, foreign studies, and world affairs—the standard program of teacher education allows little room for electives, arouses little interest in world issues, and involves a minimum of opportunity for enlarging the education student's view of the world.

It is not widely understood, inside and outside the universities, that the mere existence of prestigious graduate schools with special work in world affairs does not mean that teachers either have access to them, or that their influence reaches into the school system, the undergraduate curriculum, teacher education, or the community. The teachers, I have observed, are the last people to be thought of where education is concerned. It is a trickle-down theory—that once area studies, non-Western centers, international research, and the preparation of professionals for service overseas are established on a campus and in consortia of campuses, the word will trickle down to the teachers, and eventually to the students in the schools. More often, nothing trickles, because the graduate center is sealed off from both the undergraduates and other sections of the institution.

What is needed is a theory of a completely different kind, which starts from a recognition of the educational needs of the children and their teachers in the schools and moves toward the invention of new educational plans and materials for meeting both, using the resources of the colleges and universities to fulfill the plans. It is a matter of making direct links between resources already available among experts in the university and the work of the colleges of education and the public schools.

Since few of the faculty experts in foreign cultures and world affairs are interested in the schools or in their teachers, present initiatives will have to come from teachers and from *their* teachers in the colleges of education. The people who are working at expanding the international sector in teacher education have usually become involved in the work after seeing at first hand what was missing in the programs of the schools and the undergraduate curricula. There is therefore a double task for scholars who are concerned to supply what is missing—to stay in touch through their own research with the best in contemporary scholarship, while remaining close to the reality of teaching in the schools and colleges of education.

To undertake this double task is no less scholarly or intellectually respectable an enterprise than that of the rest of the academic community. It is simply a matter of using one's own scholarship to enable the teachers to improve theirs, and the particular virtue of the materials thus produced for students and teachers lies in the fact that they come from scholars whose experience has included a direct acquaintance with foreign cultures and with the needs and conditions of the schools and institutions where teachers are educated.

In spite of the fact that there are many ways in which the specialized scholarship of the academic faculty can be enriched by direct work with educators in the schools, there is a serious gap between the faculty members of colleges and departments of education and the members of the arts and science faculties of the universities. I found little of the intellectual hostility of one group toward the other that I had been led to expect by having heard so much in advance about the quarrel between the academics and the professionals. Most of the time I found an attitude of amused tolerance toward the professionals on the part of the liberal arts faculty, and signs of defensiveness on the part of the professionals.

But more than anything else among the liberal arts faculties, I found a lack of serious interest in the problem of teaching and teacher education, along with a sense of certainty that in any case such problems could be solved by fairly simple means. Put the students through a regular academic program with a major field of study, keep them away from education courses and schools as much as possible, let them teach a little in their senior year, and they are ready for a career in the public schools. The all-university committees on teacher education, with a preponderance of liberal arts faculty in the representation, usually held to this view.

After a series of seventeen meetings will all-university committees, I came to question the idea that this kind of committee should be the major group responsible for the education of teachers on any campus. Whereas in former years there was a central focus of attention by the teacher educators on the preparation of teachers, no matter how limited in scope that attention may have been, now the responsibility, when spread over an entire university, dilutes the attention as well as the responsibility. When everybody is responsible for everything, nobody is responsible for the core of the matter—that is, the continual and intensive effort to keep the education of teachers relevant to the cultural and intellectual demands of a changing society.

In attempting to correct a one-sided arrangement by which teacher education was formerly the province only of professional educators, the new arrangement now involves a group of people who are themselves more interested in the separate disciplines they represent and in making certain that students carry on work in these disciplines than they are in rethinking the entire problem of how best to develop interesting and internationally informed teachers for the schools.

The problem is wrongly construed by the separation between practice in the art of teaching and the content of the liberal arts, between a body of departmental subject matter to be assimilated and a set of practices and methods by which it is to be communicated to school children. As far as world affairs were concerned, most of the faculty members simply reported which of their courses were available if students wanted to elect them, what offerings in foreign languages and cultures were in the curriculum. I found that the university committees have failed even to question the premises on which their own teaching and system of instruction is based, at a time when undergraduate teaching has been denounced as an open scandal by scholars, critics, and students who have examined it in studies and experienced it in person. Membership in a university faculty and certified competence in a given academic discipline is no guarantee of educational insight or even of the capacity to teach or to understand what teaching means. Yet these are the criteria used to determine committee membership.

Over the past twenty years, the critics of teacher education, mainly from the universities, have concentrated their fire on the lack of preparation of teachers in subject-matter fields, on the superficiality and redundancy of the instruction in methodology, and on the lack of intellectual content in the education courses. The reforms in teacher education have been responsive to these criticisms, but they have been responsive within the same narrow frame of reference as the criticisms. That is to say, the professionals have assumed the academics are right—that the way to produce better educated teachers is to have them take more academic courses, the way to improve professional education courses is to make them more academic. Accordingly, neither the academic man nor the professional educator has been giving concentrated attention to the practical arts of teaching and learning, or to the relevance of what is learned to the actual world.

In many cases, this has reduced the college of education to impotence as far as taking action and making educational policy is concerned, since by definition the academic life of its students is in the hands of the arts and science faculty and educational policy is made largely by those who are not themselves educators of teachers and do not wish to be. The situation is worsened by the fact that, having turned over their students to others and having kept only the vocational side of the student's preparation for themselves, the colleges of education seldom even see their own students until the junior or senior year, after the necessities and duties of general education and the academic majors and minors have been fulfilled.

On the other hand, the students of education, who at least by declaration of intent are in college in order to become teachers, have no opportunity to be with children and to learn what it is like to be a teacher or to practice the art in any way until three years after they enroll. This is to put the college of education into a situation comparable to that of a music school whose students are turned over to another institution for academic education for three years to be given courses in everything else but music, and then are allowed to play an instrument and study music in their senior year.

It is also true that when an all-university committee makes the policy for teacher education, it brings with it the educational biases of the academic mind, a mind afflicted with the idea that only through academic study is anything of importance learned. The fallacy in this view is at the root of a great deal of bad education now being pressed upon the American undergraduate, especially when it fails to prepare him intellectually for taking part in the political and social movements so crucially important to the progress and improvement of education itself. The undergraduate curriculum of the universities has become the wasteland of the academy, at a time when this is exactly the territory which the fledgling teacher is ordered to traverse. What students need is not more subject matter of the kind they are now getting and in the way it is now given to them. What they need is a chance to put together a body of knowledge for themselves, on the basis of what they discover for themselves. They need to create something from the wellspring of their own actions, something about which they feel so deeply that they want to teach it to others. They need a chance to act on the world, not just to exist in it.

Although I would enjoy nothing more than to take the time and space here to describe, analyze, and decry the quality of teaching and content in the undergraduate curriculum of the American college and university, I have done this elsewhere, as have others, and I confine myself here to a brief repetition of what is generally known by students and other observers with direct experience of what has been going on in the colleges from day to day.

Having attended upward of seventy classes of various kinds during the course of the present study—classes in education, the social sciences, and the humanities, from large lecture courses to discussion groups led by graduate assistants—I am prepared to say again that the system of lectures, examinations, grades, academic credits, and textbooks imprisons the student in an impossible situation in which his capacity for intellectual growth is inhibited, his imagination stunted, and his initiative impaired. Where there are occasional superb teachers, capable of turning the system to good use, the students are presented with a chance to learn, by example and precept. They do so, with admiration, respect, and delight. It matters less what may be the exact subject matter such persons teach—Western, non-Western, national, or international—than that they lead the student to a capacity for self-education by whatever means, that they lead the student to a commitment to use his intellect, his talent, and his personal resources to advance the level and extent of his own knowledge and that of the people around him.

What troubles me most is not merely the absence of powerful and enlightened teaching which can move and shake the younger generation into a new mood of intellectual and cultural concern, but that under the present circumstances the school, the college, and the university are losing all capacity to influence the lives and commitments of young people. The young seek, wherever they can find it, the kind of teaching which does have an effect on their lives, and if they cannot find it in the schools and colleges they will find it elsewhere.

". . . if the university does not educate, others will," says William Arrowsmith in his rousing, devastating, and beautiful statement about teaching in America. "Education will pass, as it is passing now, to the artist, to the intellectual, to the gurus of the mass media, the charismatic charlatans and sages, and the whole immense range of secular and religious street-corner fakes and saints . . . What matters is the integration of significant life and knowledge, of compassionate study and informed conduct."[23]

This is what matters to those students who have already begun

[23] *The Future of Teaching*, William Arrowsmith; address to the Annual Meeting of the American Council on Education, New Orleans, October 13, 1966, American Council on Education, Washington, D.C., pp. 3, 8.

to question the relevance of their education to the lives they hope to lead, to those who have already become involved in social action, who cannot stay tranquil while the big injustices perpetuate themselves. The path they can take into a larger understanding of the world and into an understanding of how best to act upon it to secure its welfare does not lie through the orderly syllabus of a general education course, with or without a dash of foreign content. It lies through informed experience with the cultures which surround them in their own society. What the academic men do not understand is that to educate students to become teachers who understand the world and can teach honestly about it, it is first necessary for them to become sensitive to the character of their own lives in this particular society. Otherwise they have no way of understanding the nature of anyone else's life. It is then like trying to explain modern art to someone who has never seen a modern painting.

I would therefore make one major generalization about the present state of teacher education, one which is implied by much that comes before and will come after. What is presently lacking among educators is a concern for the commitment the young are capable of making to teaching, not simply to a profession or a career, but as an act of devotion to the cause of learning and to the welfare of children and their fellow man. If they see around them in the colleges the cynicism of teachers who care little for the art of teaching, whose own true lives are lived elsewhere, or whose talents ill equip them for the task they have accepted, the young are unable to respond and unlikely to create their own conceptions of what it means to be a teacher. If they see in the four years ahead of them in college no large horizons, no anticipations of delight, no promise of an opening up of their lives, but only duties to be borne and trivial tasks to undertake, they are unlikely to find the inner energies through which to infuse their own education with a sense of purpose. The curriculum, whatever it is, must start with the intention of creating a situation in which the student can honestly commit himself to what he is asked to do, and what he is asked to do must in some way illuminate his understanding of what it means to be a teacher. His motivation for learning matters very much indeed, since it determines how he learns and whether he learns. Those who do not know how to arrange an education for teachers which makes them want to teach, should not meddle with education.

SOME SAMPLES OF PROGRAMS

It would be natural to expect that in the institutions where teachers are being educated, the larger ones, graduating from 1000 to 2000 certifiable teachers a year, would be likely to possess the resources in faculty and educational initiative to move into the field of international education. This does not prove to be the case. Sometimes the very size of the student body seems to prevent experiment or initiative of any kind, since standard curricula designed for large numbers of students are regarded as unavoidable and necessary, and often the large number of faculty members, confined sectionally to their own departments, all of them busy getting their students through the requirements, seems to paralyze initiative of all kinds.

What makes the difference in those cases where new work had begun in nonprestigious institutions[24] is the presence of a small group of faculty members, students, and one or more administrators who, as a result of their own interest in world issues and the education of teachers, have simply started programs of their own, with the permission of and, in some cases, the support of their institutions. It is encouraging to note that wherever there is serious interest in the reform of teacher education through adding a new cultural dimension to the experience of teachers, there is usually an interest in world education. Institutions which look outward to the social issues of American life, and which are concerned to bring the forces of education to bear on them, are prepared to look further out to the issues in world society about which students should have knowledge and understanding. The impact of the national concern for dealing with disadvantaged children through education has had the effect of inducing a greater concern for political and social issues of all kinds. Once education is conceived as a process of human development, and once the development of human resources for service in the society is considered to be a major function of the College of Education, the attention of educators is likely to turn in the direction of international and world problems.

[24] I cannot think of a better word. I do not mean to divide institutions between those with and those without prestige but to refer to the fact that those who do not already have what the grant-makers want, can seldom obtain grants to get it.

Some of the most valuable work, too little noticed in the past, has been going on in the smaller colleges of the Midwest, both private and public, usually through initiatives taken by local faculty members and administrators. In those cases where the American Association of Colleges for Teacher Education has involved college presidents and faculty members in even the limited ways made possible by a series of four- to six-week travel-study projects abroad, or by internships for foreign educators in American colleges, things have begun to move—with international arts festivals, symposia on world issues, work camps in Africa, exchanges of faculty members and students with foreign universities seen in the attitudes toward reform of education in the direction of internationalism.

Two examples are relevant.

Wilmington College, in Wilmington, Ohio, a private college of approximately a thousand students, was designated by AACTE as one of eleven institutions to carry out pilot projects in international education, with a grant of $500, matched by $500 from the College. The money was to be used to bring visiting Fulbright scholars and foreign experts to the campus for short periods to teach in a number of areas—education, language, geography, history, political science. Through collaboration with other AACTE member institutions, with the Regional Council for International Education, centered at the University of Pittsburgh, and the Cincinnati Council on World Affairs, speakers and teachers in foreign studies have come to the campus, Wilmington students and faculty have joined seminars on Africa, the Far East, and Latin America held nearby. As part of the pilot project, President James Read visited Kenya in 1964 and arranged for the Assistant Director of the Kenya Institute of Education, Mr. John Osogo, who is responsible for the development of curricula in teacher education schools in Kenya, to spend six months at Wilmington as an administrative intern, visiting elementary and secondary schools, schools for special education, the Ohio State Board of Education, and other college campuses.

Other faculty members have taken study trips to Israel and to Egypt; students carry out independent study projects abroad as part of their four-year programs, in Latin America and in Europe; at other times students spend a junior year at the European-American Study Center in Basel, Switzerland, where the Center is supported by the Regional Council for International Education. The College has also begun an institutional affiliation with the University of Nicaragua aided by a grant of $1000 from the U. S. Department of State to help with the exchange of tape recordings, books, curricular materials, as a prelude to more extensive exchange of students and faculty members in the future.

Among other items are included:

An eight week travel-study project for twenty-five students to go to Africa for interviews with educational and political leaders, visits to schools and colleges, and two weeks in an African work camp.

Establishment of an International Education Center for American and foreign students, with discussions of educational systems, foreign cultures, world issues, etc.

A Speaker's bureau on the campus for foreign students to speak to community groups and to college and school classes.

An International Festival, now in its eighteenth year, brings artists, speakers, and art objects from foreign countries for a five-day celebration.

A contract has been signed for a Peace Corps project involving eighty students who will enter Wilmington College as freshmen, and combine a five-year degree of Bachelor of Arts with two-year Peace Corps service abroad, teaching and working in agricultural development. From my observations during a visit to the College, Wilmington provides an unusual example of the way in which a small institution with a serious interest in the education of teachers has, with extremely limited financial resources, injected a spirit of internationalism into its entire program. Further progress depends almost entirely on the provision of sufficient funds to extend the work already going on.

Earlham College in Richmond, Indiana, with 1136 students in 1967, began ten years ago to build into the four-year curriculum new work in foreign cultures; it was the view of the President and a small group of faculty members that the students should have a wider range of knowledge of the world than the usual courses in the liberal arts and sciences. Although the College does not specialize in the education of teachers, many of its graduates enter the field. The Earlham faculty designed a self-supporting study-abroad program which fitted the curriculum of the Richmond campus, by which students in groups of fifteen to twenty-five go abroad for study in a summer and fall term, under the supervision of an Earlham faculty member. During the nine years of its operation, students have lived with families and studied in France, Italy, Germany, Austria, England, Denmark, Finland, the Soviet Union, Spain, Mexico and Japan. The College has regular language programs in Spanish, French, German, Russian, and Japanese.

The Japanese development is especially interesting as an example of local initiative in foreign study. It has been done in partnership with Antioch College, which has one of the most enterprising foreign-study programs in the country, and with the International Division of Waseda University in Tokyo. Earlham, without funds to appoint a complete new faculty, organized a long-range plan to develop the talents of faculty members already at the College, and over a period of annual programs, with seminars, visiting specialists, reading assignments, and independent research projects, ending with ten weeks of study in Japan, has been able to install courses in Japanese culture which range from the language itself to Japanese history, political science, art, music, drama, philosophy, and education. In addition, performances by foreign artists, discussion groups, lectures, convocations, meetings, and annual Institutes of Foreign Affairs deal with life in China, India, Japan, Malaysia, Indonesia, the Middle East, and Africa.

During a four-year period, the College was involved in the development of a comprehensive high school in Kenya on an AID contract, and at one point, as an independent project which they organized themselves, eight Earlham students spent a summer in a work camp to build and repair school buildings in a remote area close to the border of Tanzania. Again, it is clear that with limited funds and campus resources, the transposition of a small college, or a large one for that matter, from a local concern with a limited curriculum into an institution with the flavor of internationalism is not only possible but practicable.

THE GENERAL CONDITIONS

However, in the most of the larger institutions, the number of faculty members and administrators directly interested in the international education of teachers is relatively small and the programs seriously underdeveloped. Few faculty members have read the available literature. Still fewer have applied the conclusions to be found in that literature to the possibilities for the education of teachers. In one case, when I asked a group of twenty-five members of a college of education faculty if there had been any changes in the education curriculum to match the changes in world society, the question was asked, Why should there be?

On many campuses I found myself answering a flow of questions from faculty members and administrators about what was happening in international education, and what ideas and programs were in operation elsewhere. There were many questions about the Government agencies, most of whose programs in international education and cultural affairs were little known on the campuses, including the work of Congress in preparing and passing the legislation of the International Education Act. There was little indication that the Act itself, with its implications for educational change, even when known, had been taken with the seriousness it deserves. Most of the questions about the new legislation and its provision for a Center for Educational Cooperation had to do with whether there were possibilities for grants to organize new programs and, if so, what form these programs should take in order to match the provisions of the Act.[25]

The diffidence and lack of direct interest in the international education of teachers can be traced to several sources.

In the first place, the idea of general education is now so deeply embedded in the university curriculum and university thinking and the standard pattern of requirements for the first two years and for the B.A. degree so firmly fixed, that it is hard for anyone in the universities to think his way into other notions about how to spend the student's time during the first two and the last two years of college. Since the history of Western civilization in one or another of its versions is considered essential for all, that area of the curriculum is already pre-empted, with little room for other cultures. It is considered sufficient that courses in international relations, foreign cultures, foreign languages, and world affairs are offered by the departments as electives which students of education can take along with everyone else. The fallacy lies in assuming that education students are interested in taking them, or have any reason to take them as preparation for teaching in schools where there is very little demand for teachers with an international outlook.

Even where there are area studies programs and large research

---

[25] This situation may have changed somewhat since the above was written; the regional conferences arranged across the country by the Department of Health, Education and Welfare have been reported to have had positive effects in arousing interests and in informing the colleges.

institutes in foreign affairs, these are designed for graduate students and for those undergraduates who intend going on to graduate school and into careers other than public school teaching. With the present disjunction between the graduate school and the undergraduate teaching programs, and the separation of the college or department of education from the main body of the liberal arts college, very little coordination or flexibility exists in arranging curricula for teacher candidates.

It is also true that teacher candidates, owing to the scholastic aptitudes they bring with them to college, are much less likely to be the winners of scholarships or fellowships in the open university competition, and in general have less money to spend on their education than other students. They are therefore less likely than others to take the initiative in trying for a Junior year abroad or to vary in any way the pattern of curriculum which they know will deliver them safely into a teaching post at the end of four years. In consequence, they make few demands of their own for study in foreign affairs, and go unnoticed by the faculty members in the field.

Finally, the conception of study of foreign affairs and international relations held in the academic community is one which is essentially unrelated to the needs or interests of undergraduates, even when the undergraduates are interested in world society and its problems. The courses are constructed as background for an understanding of how scholars in world affairs deal with the problems in their field, not with the way men and women live their lives, or with the way the conflicts of moral and political decision in American foreign policy are related to personal and cultural factors in American life. Grayson Kirk states the case for the conventional work in international studies in the following passage:

> . . . it is necessary to consider just what a student of international relations attempts to do. His objectives are many and varied but most of them can be grouped under five main headings. These are: (1) analysis of the various forces which influence the foreign policies of the principal states of the world; (2) critical examination of the method which states use to carry on their business with each other, and the instrumentalities which they have established for that purpose; (3) assessment of contemporary economic, political and legal relations among states, and the trends which they reveal; (4) study of the means by which conflicts among states may be adjusted; and (5) consideration of the legal and moral principles which

should govern intercourse among nations . . . The focus must be on inter-governmental relations and all things which affect them.[26]

If the focus must be on intergovernmental relations and all things which affect them, there is very little of interest to students in this dreary procession of analyses, instrumentalities, trends in relations, and consideration of legal and moral principles presented by text-books and lectures in the world affairs classes. Courses of this kind are generally of little value to the student who is becoming a teacher and who needs to gain a sense of the reality of life in another culture, of the reality of existing conflicts between ideas and ideologies, and to learn something which he can teach to children.

WESTERN AND NON-WESTERN CULTURES

What then is being taught to teachers? What do the courses in general education, both the Western and the non-Western courses, intend to accomplish, what purpose is to be served, for example, in the study of foreign languages?

The study of a foreign language, if carried on in the context of the life and culture of the country whose language is learned, can be a serious and enriching intellectual experience. It is an entry to a new world. When it is taught outside that context, as the preparation of a "language teacher" who is then employed to teach the language to students meeting "language requirements," it is a sterile exercise which adds nothing to the world dimension of the student's education or of American culture. If the language learned is never used either to talk with or to come to know the people who speak it, if it is never used to enjoy the pleasure of direct access to a foreign literature and culture, it is literally useless, except for gaining credits on a transcript. It is like studying plumbing as a way of understanding oceanography.

Yet the study of foreign languages in the American school and in the education of the American teacher is usually carried on in isolation from the cultural context which gives such study its true meaning, and too often it is assumed that the mere addition of foreign languages to the curriculum is a blow struck for internationalism and against parochialism. Even in the Spanish-speaking areas of the United States, usually those poorest in economic and educational

[26] Grayson Kirk, *The Study of International Relations in American Colleges and Universities* (N. Y. Council on Foreign Relations 1947), p. 8.

resources, the rich cultural heritage of the Spanish-speaking children is either eroded or ignored by an educational system which insists that the children speak English, while in nearby well-to-do schools for English-speaking students, learning to speak Spanish is an artificial exercise without a cultural base.

In a similar way it is assumed that requiring all students, as part of their curriculum in general education, to take a course in Western culture or Western civilization, usually a survey course in an anthology of famous books and authors, is a means of deepening their awareness of their own cultural heritage by relating it to its origins in European thought and culture. It then follows that the way to broaden the student's understanding of his wider heritage is to add a course in non-Western culture, through a policy of equal time for the rest of the world, a little of each for all.

What is actually needed is a radical revision in the conception of culture and in the conception of what truly educates. If we genuinely cared to have our students and teachers understand the nature of Western civilization and Western culture, or of world culture, we would immediately stop thinking of culture as entirely composed of what is set down in famous books, and we would begin to think of it as the way in which various peoples on the world's continents have tried to come to terms with the conditions of their lives, how they have organized themselves, through their arts, politics, customs, religions, social systems, and personal values to live their lives to the end.

When we begin to do that, we find in the history of our own culture the roots of the world, roots so deep in the past and so intertwined that we can see the world as one. Then we establish the continuity of our world in the West with the world anywhere, and we do not need to add units of non-Western culture to balance a parochialism which, if our teaching were sound and deep, would never have existed.

At one liberal arts college with an interest in educating teachers, I found an extreme case of the Western Culture syndrome during a series of all-college discussions of the reform of the present curriculum. In a lively meeting of the college Curriculum Committee, except for a physicist and a biologist present, to a man the faculty representatives, including one from the Education Department, assumed without question that what was needed for teacher preparation, as for anything else, was a program of the regular academic subjects in their proper order, and that a required course in Western culture for four consecutive terms was *the* central integrating intellectual experience for every student.

Not only was there no response to the idea that this experience should be broadened to include other kinds of materials from other civilizations, but the flat statement was made and defended that the educational center for all Americans was a knowledge of Western culture. The students, on the other hand, at subsequent meetings asserted stoutly that the four-term sequence in the Western humanities was the essential of their education, since it gave them the humanities as an antidote to science; since the great works of the Western past were so much greater than anything in the present, the chronological sequence of Western thinkers was also necessary before the present or the outside world could be approached. The students refused the notion that a freshman student might be better off in beginning his education in literature with poetry by Robert Lowell or Andrei Voznesensky than with Homer. Their grounds were that Homer was a better poet and belonged to the Western classical tradition. No matter how I tried, I could not convince the students that a sensitivity to specific works of art, either in one's own or another culture, was the first essential to an understanding of art, in the past or the present. They preferred to stay with the standard Western classics, learned in the correct order.

There was also serious resistance to the notion that experience in society or in life had anything to do with the liberal arts. The liberal arts and life in the society must be kept separate. In their view, the real purpose of the liberal arts college was to take people out of society, since society is a corrupting influence. The humanities, they believed, must be kept separate from the social sciences since the humanities deal with values and the social sciences are descriptive and deal with facts. Both faculty and students were thus opposed to the idea that direct experience in teaching children and in community action is a primary source of learning to recognize and to develop systems of values. Practice teaching was one thing, liberal arts and the humanities were another.

In a brilliant paper on this and related topics, Richard Morse makes the central point. "Our non-Western specialists are important to us," says Morse, "not because they penetrate Oriental mysteries or predict Caribbean surprises but because they angle into subject matter freshly. They recognize no pecking order or compartmentalization of scholarly disciplines, no walls between Great Traditions and popular or folk-loric ones. This produces a good deal of cant about 'integrated' and 'interdisciplinary' programs. But it also shows up our 'Western' specialists as performing largely curatorial functions."

"The real use of non-Western studies is in the emotional and intellectual shock they give. If this shock were now being provided by American studies—that is, if our students were experiencing their own culture as *foreign*—the situation would be propitious *ipso facto* for non-Western studies to find their proper curricular nest without elaborate strategies and apologies. To put it the other way, only when American culture is so experienced will we know that non-Western studies have found their nest."[27]

We have a right and a duty to make similar demands on the rest of the teacher's curriculum. The purpose of studying psychology, whether as a professional course or as a liberal art, is to enrich the student's knowledge of the qualities and character of human nature. In this, the study of psychology is no different in purpose than the study of literature, philosophy, anthropology, or theater. The idea that there is one kind of obligatory psychology which is necessary for the teacher to know before teaching, and another kind of psychology (equally irrelevant as it is now taught) for liberalizing the college student, is as absurd as it is harmful.

Even a quick summary of the content of textbooks in psychology used in the instruction of teachers to teach must show that most of what is said is irrelevant, and what is not irrelevant is to some degree misleading. The basis for the study of psychology as far as teachers are concerned lies in the reality of the child and in what the future teacher can learn from being with children, helping them to learn, sympathetically, unobtrusively, and carefully taking account of who they are, how they behave, and what the problems are with which they need help. The psychology contained in the textbooks has little meaning to the student of teaching until he knows what the psychologist is talking about. The textbook is a

[27] Richard Morse, *The Challenge of Foreign Area Studies*, in Supplement to the Spring 1966 issue of *The Educational Record*, published by the Council on Education, Washington, D.C.

substitute for experience when it should be a supplement and a guide to experience.[28]

Aside from the question of relevance, the content of the psychology courses presented to students who will teach is too narrow in its treatment of human nature. Not only do the texts reduce human nature to a series of banal traits, measurable characteristics, and scientific categories, but they do so on the basis of a fairly narrow conception of human nature, for example, the characteristics of the adolescent, by which the adolescent is defined in terms of an abstract American of a certain age group whose characteristics are measurable and can be accurately described.

Mankind is assumed to be American. To be told about or to read about the characteristics of an American adolescent may or may not be useful to the teacher or to anyone else, but these characteristics do not define the human being at a stage of his development, if by human we mean *human*, and not the local American product. A course in psychology designed to prepare students to teach, or to inform the student about human nature, would do both things at once and would draw upon the original sources of psychological insight and descriptive analyses of children and adolescents in a variety of cultures. It would not provide equivalents of the Gesell and Spock baby books for the practical use of the teacher-practitioner. The practical things are best learned in practice. The theories of psychology and the descriptive materials are best learned in relation to that practical experience.

I do not intend to go all the way around the curriculum in order to make this point in each instance. It is enough to say that if we are interested in enlarging the teacher's conception of the world through the kind of preparation we give him to teach, then there must be a radical shift in the content and approach now existing both in the professional courses in education he must take and in the courses in the liberal arts and sciences. The shift is necessary, not only for teachers but for everyone else, since the question of the education of teachers is simply a testing point for the education of all those who are learning to enter the culture. College graduates, if they have been truly educated, should all have something to teach to someone wherever they may go. There is no more interesting subject than the philosophy of education, no more fascinating area

[28] A more extended discussion of the texts and course material currently in use in education courses is to be found on pp. 200–14.

of knowledge than the history of education, whether these be called professional subjects or by some other name. When they are taught to students who themselves intend to teach, they should be rich in the materials of the world, full of the sense of life, since they have to do with the way people struggle with ideas and conditions in order to make some kind of sense out of the conditions which surround them.

That is precisely the opposite of what general education courses deal with, and it is time that the mythology of general education be examined closely to see whether its myths are related to the educational realities. The idea of general education occupies a central place in all educational planning for the liberal arts and sciences, and is now, more than anything else, an administrative convenience rather than a useful educational principle. I raise the question here, since in most of the curricular suggestions for the the infusion of internationalism into the education of undergraduates, potential teachers, and nonteachers alike, the proposal is to use these "traffic courses," that is, the courses through which all student course-taking traffic is directed, as the road to salvation. The general proposition is that since all students have to take two years of whatever is contained in the general education courses, that is the place to add some foreign and non-Western content. A similar argument is made for adding foreign studies to the other courses in the requirements for academic majors and minors, since they too are part of the traffic pattern.

Originally introduced in the 1940s and early 1950s as a national antidote to the disease of narrow and specialized courses and the fragmentation of a badly working elective system, the programs of general education have failed in their intention to develop broadly educated persons by confusing the idea of breadth of knowledge with the idea of an attenuated academic coverage of organized materials. The practical effect of introducing the programs has been once more to shift the emphasis away from the individual teacher and his creative imagination in developing his own courses, to a standardized set of materials in a curriculum made by others. When general education courses have failed, they have done so because an insufficient number of first-rate scholar-teachers with fully developed interests in teaching freshmen and sophomores have been available to conduct them. The rewards for the college teacher lie within the departmental system, with its specialized forms of scholarship which are more profitably applied to the preparation of students for graduate work in given fields. Few faculty members possessed of the conventional ambitions wish to throw in their lot with the inhabitants of a territory which grants no academic advancement and little intellectual stimulation.

As a countermeasure, the emphasis should be placed on the development and recruitment of scholar-teachers whose particular interests lie in the field of world affairs, foreign cultures, and international issues, preferably those who have had experience in study, teaching, and travel abroad and for whom the development of new courses in the field of their interests would be a means of extending their own scholarship as well as the dimensions of knowledge for the freshmen and sophomores. In the effort to make certain that each student has had a broad exposure to the major fields of human knowledge, educators have failed to notice that the way to achieve a breadth of mind and a capacity for intellectual growth is to achieve a depth of knowledge in one or another sector of the available curriculum. Out of the study of a foreign culture in depth comes an understanding of the breadth of variety in other cultures, that is to say, one achieves a breadth of mind. From study in depth comes a capacity to apply the experience of knowing a great deal about a few things to the study and exploration of what is not yet known. That is the road to liberal, rather than general, education.

THE NATIONAL SHORTAGE OF TEACHERS

One final dimension of the teaching problem, the biggest dimension of all, must now be added—the dimension of sheer size in the number of teachers required for the entire educational system. The problem is complex and far-reaching, more complex and farther reaching than is publicly recognized, even among those most directly concerned with the education of teachers. It has to do not merely with the annual provision of thousands of teachers for service in the public schools, and with the continuing education of the approximately two million persons already teaching there, but with the question of who will teach the teachers, and who will teach those who teach them. The question of who will teach an understanding of world society is subordinate to the question of who will teach at all.

Who will teach the 1.5 million students in the junior colleges, and the additional one million students who are expected there in the next five years? From what source will come the presidents, deans, and academic leadership of this, the most rapidly expanding sector of American higher education, at a time when more than 300 four-year colleges and universities are already in search of presidents?

Who will teach the additional four million college students, among the nine million predicted by the U. S. Office of Education for 1975?

President Johnson, in his message to Congress on Education and Health in February 1967, summed up part of the arithmetic when he presented the arguments for passage of the Education Professions Act of 1967. "Our work to enrich education," said the President, "finds its focus in a single person: the classroom teacher. . . . Next year, more than 170,000 new teachers will be needed to replace uncertified teachers, to fill vacancies and to meet rising student enrollments. Moreover:

> There are severe shortages of English, Mathematics, Science, and elementary school teachers. [I might add to the President's list not only the shortage but the comparative *absence* of teachers of world affairs]
>
> More teachers are needed for our colleges and junior colleges
>
> Well trained administrators at all levels are critically needed
>
> New kinds of school personnel—such as teachers aides—are needed to help in the schools
>
> By 1975, the nation's schools will need nearly two million more teachers.

To help meet this growing demand, the Federal Government has sponsored a number of programs to train and improve teachers. These programs, though they have been effective, have been too fragmented to achieve their full potential and too limited to meet many essential sectors of the teaching profession . . ."

The passage of the Education Professions Act has had a positive effect, but it is too limited a Bill to help with more than part of the problem. The estimate is that by 1970 we will need to fill 35,000 new full-time teaching positions in the colleges and universities, with graduate schools now producing 21,000 Ph.D.'s a year, at least half of whom will enter nonteaching professions. Of the 75,000 students currently completing their preparation for teaching in the elementary schools, only 60,750 will actually assume teaching positions, and of the 166,400 students completing preparation to teach in the secondary schools, only 77,988 will begin teaching, leaving the schools far short—approximately 50,000—of the 170,000 needed for 1968.[29] This leaves aside the education of teachers for special assignments to disadvantaged children, those who can carry out educational research, counselors, social workers, subprofessionals, specialists in reading and other fields.

But we must also ask, who will then teach the rapidly increasing number of graduate students in the arts and sciences, in medicine, law, architecture, engineering, social work, the performing arts, and the fine arts? Who will supervise the work of the increasing number of postdoctoral students drawn from every sector of the scientific and scholarly community?

These questions cry out for answers at a time when the entire array of social services in the United States and abroad are making new demands for educated men and women to deal with crucial areas of public welfare, the employment services, mental health, community development, race relations, civil rights, poverty, urban planning, international agencies, and a dozen other fields.[30]

The kind of educated persons needed to man these posts on a national and international scale can come from no other source than the universities and colleges, particularly from those which have already taken a serious interest in education in its full dimension, universities where there are colleges, schools and departments of

[29] Later figures, based on 1967 fall enrollments would increase the shortage by a minimum of another 25,000.

[30] Dr. Herman Niebuhr, Jr., Director of the Center for Community Studies at Temple University, has discussed one part of this problem in a paper, *Training as an Agent of Institutional Change.* "The 1957 administrator (in the human services field) looked for adequate numbers of trained personnel at the professional level, for he still labored under the illusion that public assistance really should be populated by Master's level counselors; that an adequate number of psychoanalysts would solve the mental health problems of the nation; and that fully qualified Master teachers was the high road to the school's success. At least some of these illusions have washed away for the 1966 administrator. He still wants the graduate-level professionals, but he now knows that mass delivery of services takes place at another level. Yet there is no mechanism other than the College of Education for the preparation of human and community service personnel at the undergraduate level, and there are almost no non-professional preparatory programs at the high school level."

Training as an Agent of Institutional Change, prepared for a Conference on the Critical Need for Trained Personnel to Man the War on Poverty, July 1966, sponsored by the U.S. Office of Economic Opportunity; mimeographed.

education flexible enough to consider the idea that the teaching and the professions of the human services are closely intertwined. A new and broad definition of education, to conceive it as a means of aiding the process of human development in all its dimensions, is a first prerequisite for dealing with the new responsibilities placed upon contemporary educators.

Until now the assumption has been continually made that we in America can do everything we want to do, and all at the same time —fight a war in Asia, expand the social services, take the leadership in world affairs, solve the problem of poverty, give the Negro his due, increase the range of the creative arts, expand our cultural life, lift up the developing countries, extend the system of democracy, and build a great society, all with the same people, at a time we have not paused long enough to educate more of them or to assess the finite resources of our present manpower. We seem to have forgotten that the existence of intelligent, skilled, enlightened, and highly educated persons is the primary base on which all of our plans, projects, and national welfare rest, and that if we launch new projects entailing huge sums of new money in any one dimension of our national or international life, either in the military or any other sphere, we drain off our educated men and women, leaving the schools, the colleges, and the universities with the same problems they had before, but in greatly intensified form, without the resources in manpower and finances to solve them.

My earlier comments on the continuing neglect of teacher education throughout American educational history referred to the roots of that neglect in the preoccupation of the universities and their supporters with other matters, mainly research, scholarship, and professional services to various patrons other than the citizens and their school system. In spite of everything that is said about the new role of the university in America as the source of intellectual and social power for meeting the country's needs, there remains a disjunction between the major university as it functions and the deeper spiritual, social, and intellectual needs of the society it serves.

The disjunction reveals itself most clearly in the neglect of teaching. It is the imperviousness of the university to the needs of its own students, its institutional attitude toward the accumulation and dissemination of knowledge, its corporate character, its role in the knowledge industry—this is what arouses the antagonism, the criticism, and at times the contempt of observant and informed students who witness its character at close range. With the bulk of university energies reserved to meet the market for professional manpower, what energy remains is allocated in a diluted form to the education of students and to the development of teachers, for the public school and for the colleges and universities themselves.

If the university were as seriously concerned with the creation and dissemination of knowledge of world affairs as it continues to claim to be, it would think of its students as a subject of primary and intensive concern, since they are the link between the university and its wider constituency in the total culture. The students are in fact the major agents of social and cultural change, they are the ones who can, if taught, take ideas out of the academy and transform them for use, through their lives within the society and within the professions and vocations which serve society, especially the profession of teaching. Otherwise, the ideas remain inert and unused, either inside or outside the academy. At the present time, the education of students is not being taken seriously, at precisely the time that they are beginning to take themselves seriously. What the universities ignore is the fact that the only thing they do which could not be done just as easily elsewhere—research, publication, accumulation of knowledge, constructing libraries, laboratories, theater—is teaching young people. The heart of the university is in its undergraduate college, and any university which bestows the bulk of its energies and favors on its professional schools is likely to find itself with no heart and nothing but an academic mind.

The answer to the question, Who will teach the teachers to be international, has to be sought within the present academic system.

Where are they and who are they?

First, the graduate school professors teach Ph.D. candidates in the graduate schools, who then become teachers in the undergraduate colleges and begin to move back up the hierarchy to teach in the graduate school. This leaves a shortage in the undergraduate college for potential teachers and nonteachers alike.

Second, the professors in the graduate schools of education concentrate on doctoral candidates, who presumably will teach the teachers in the schools of education. There is a shortage here of qualified persons trained in the social sciences and humanities rather than in the educational departments of the schools of education.

Third, the supervisors of practice teaching must be trained both in school teaching and in the disciplines related to education. There is a shortage here.

Fourth, the high school and elementary school teachers supervise the student teachers in their classrooms, provide advice and counsel, and occasionally run seminars for groups of teacher candidates. There is a shortage here, and many universities have serious difficulty in finding places in schools for their student-teachers.

Fifth, there is a present shortage of teachers in the schools themselves and, as indicated above, it is bound to increase in the next two years unless something quite drastic is done.

Sixth, none of this includes the need for teachers to serve abroad, in increasing numbers if international plans and programs now contemplated are to be carried out.

At the same time, the pull of upward mobility in the teacher's career is constantly away from the public schools, and the combination of lower salaries and lower status for teachers in the schools, added to the proliferation of opportunities and demands for service further up in the hierarchy, means that the most talented persons are the ones the schools lose first. When the universities recruit their faculty members, they not only seek them from each year's new group of Ph.D. graduates and from other universities, but from the most promising and talented faculty members in the state colleges, which, with lower salaries to offer, then recruit from other state colleges and compete for the new Ph.D.'s. As the need for junior college faculty members and administrators increases, they are recruited from the state colleges, the colleges of education, and the high schools. In the competition for teaching talent, it is therefore difficult for all but the most devoted high school, junior college, and state college teachers to remain committed to service within their own institutions where they are needed most. It is as if everyone were looking over his shoulder to see where everyone else is going.

SOME POINTS OF INTERVENTION

To change and improve the situation, there are certain points of necessary intervention. I am referring here not only to international education for teachers, but to the basic problem of creating a national effort in the improvement of teaching itself.

In the first place the colleges and universities as a whole, particularly the liberal arts colleges, must face up to the responsibility they have shirked and turn major efforts into the development of teachers for every part of the educational system, starting with the improvement of the quality of teaching in their own institutions.

The colleges could reform their present curricula and teaching methods to make the practice of teaching a normal part of the education of all their students. They could allocate at least twenty-five percent of their scholarship resources and loan funds for the recruitment and education of teaching candidates, bringing to their campuses for internships in teaching a nationally and internationally selected group of graduates with the B.A. degree, whose time would be divided equally between teaching undergraduates and studying toward an M.A. degree in the area of the curriculum in which they were teaching.

The study of education could be put where it properly belongs, not only in the colleges and departments of education, but as a regular component in the liberal arts curriculum, in the social sciences and the humanities; courses in the history of education would become as natural a part of the curriculum as physics, or the conventional courses in the history of Europe. Comparative studies of educational systems, considered in the context of their economic and social setting, could become a normal part of the work in anthropology, sociology, political science, and economics.

The high schools could organize teacher curricula in the junior and senior year with practice teaching and tutoring in the elementary schools with their own students, who could then be prepared to begin serious work in education in their freshman year in college.

The private schools could organize teacher preparation and education curricula, with practice teaching by their students inside the school—seniors teaching freshmen—and in the neighborhood elementary schools.

Undergraduate social science and psychology students in the universities could study educational and teaching problems as a regular part of their course work in the liberal arts.

Graduate students in the universities could assist in teaching freshman and high school students as part of their work in the social sciences and humanities, not merely as graduate assistants but as students of society through the study of schools in society.

In all these areas, foreign students, both graduate and undergraduate, could be enlisted to help in introducing new materials in foreign cultures into the stream of day-to-day teaching in the universities they attend and in nearby schools.

The graduate school of education is a major point of intervention. If the graduate schools in the arts and sciences concentrate on developing a new kind of practicing scholar with a serious commitment to the field of education, this could provide a main source of more and better teachers to teach the teachers. It is clear that, as of now, there are relatively few such people in the graduate schools whose entire attention is given to the education of teachers, and fewer still who have had either the experience abroad or the formal education to be able to teach in world affairs, foreign cultures, or international education. The most immediate way of remedying that situation is to make the relation between the College of Education and the graduate faculty of the university much more direct, to make joint appointments of experts in foreign affairs, foreign cultures, and related fields, to plan joint curricula with the other departments and divisions of the graduate faculty.

It should be perfectly possible to introduce a substantial component of the study of education into the work of students in area studies programs already existing, so that graduate students of education could not only work with the existing materials of the social sciences and humanities available in area studies, but could combine that work with a central concern for the educational history and problems of the region under consideration. The major change to be made, however, is in the development of a serious commitment on the part of all the components of the graduate school, in education or out of it, to the education of teachers.

THE STATE COLLEGES AND UNIVERSITIES

In the meantime, the crucial point of intervention for change is in the institutions where most of the public school teachers are actually being educated—the state colleges and universities, former teachers colleges, the urban universities, the liberal arts colleges—where there is already a commitment to the education of teachers, especially in the state colleges in which one out of every five students in the country is enrolled. The state colleges and the universities which have grown out of them have the advantage of being relatively free from a heavy concern with graduate education, many of them do not offer the Ph.D., and they have not yet had a chance to become fully set in their academic ways. It is therefore possible to develop a point of view within such institutions which links them directly to the problems of society, both national and international, and to the social and educational innovations represented by the National Teacher Corps, Head Start, VISTA, Job Opportunity Centers, Community Action programs, and in the world dimension, the Peace Corps, and the wider extension of the land-grant conception of service to the needs of all citizens. Institutions of the size and character of Ohio University, with its connections to education projects abroad; Southern Illinois University, with similar connections; Wayne State University, whose College of Education includes a Center for Teaching About Peace and War; Western Michigan University; and San Francisco State College, are natural resources for the development of new concepts and programs which can concentrate on the education of teachers who consider the world to be their campus.

The smaller state colleges and universities are the places which have been most neglected in the consideration of major research and action grants for the expansion of international education. As in the case of federal and foundation grants for research in the natural sciences, the funds have gone to institutions already strong in their graduate work and already well situated in the accumulation of faculty members. Many of these state institutions have no resources of their own from which applications for grants, new international projects, and new ideas for education may come. In part this is because, as I have already pointed out, they have been so wrapped up in the problems of expanding their day-to-day work to educate the large number of students they already have that they do not possess the time, the energy, or the outreach necessary to gain the attention of those who grant the funds.

Most of their state college administrators have not had wide experience in the world of grant-getting, either from foundations or the Government, and are not as expert or as sophisticated as those with more experience and better connections. None of the language and area studies centers established with Government subsidy under Title VI of the National Defense Education Act has been located in any of the 235 institutions of the American Association of State Colleges and Universities, even though these are the institutions which could make most use of them and which could have the most direct effect on the education of a large sector of the country's teachers. What is usually referred to as the humble origin of these institutions works against them when it should be working for them. Having sprung from the normal schools, from academies, teachers colleges, polytechnic colleges, agricultural schools, and seminaries, they are institutions where students and faculty members with experience in world affairs and knowledge of foreign cultures are most needed and can be put to the most direct use in the education of teachers.

In 1966, in a survey of the 191 member institutions of the Association of State Colleges and Universities, 36 replied that they had no non-Western courses, 96 replied that they did, and of the 96, 74 indicated that they had no overall coordinating committee for international education. Of the 59 who did not reply, other evidence indicates that few of them offer courses outside the conventional Western subject matter. In other words, nearly half of the 191 institutions were in the category of those offering no opportunity to students to study the world outside the West. Only 10 percent of these institutions offered scholarships for foreign students; in the total of 625,000 students attending the member institutions in 1965, there were just 163 foreign students from non-Western regions on scholarships at 19 colleges.[31]

At other teacher education institutions where there are committees and administrators in programs of international education, some of them having to do with AID contracts, there is little effect on the education of teachers in the institution as a whole. The particular interests of particular students and faculty members in a foreign language or a foreign area is confined only to the section of the institution they inhabit, where the population is extremely small. It is not hard to understand why this should be so, in view of the lack of funds for increasing either the number of faculty or of students with an interest in world affairs and international politics and education.

The students, as has been noted, are quite unlikely to bring such interests with them when they come, the faculty are already embedded in a curriculum which is both shaped by and which shapes the

---

[31] *International Education in the Developing State Colleges and Universities,* Fred F. Harcleroad and Alfred D. Kilmartin, a Report of a Study conducted for the American Association of State Colleges and Universities, 1785 Massachusetts Avenue, N.W., Washington, D.C., November 1966, 42 pp.

state requirements for teaching certificates, the institutions are seldom reached by federal or foundation grants, and there is no visible place from which new energies in the formation of policies for international education can come. Except, that is, from the initiatives of faculty members, administrators, and students who care so much about the issues involved that they simply start things moving within the limits of their present budgets.

These are what I have found to be the main dimensions of the problem of educating American teachers in an understanding of the world at large and in gaining a knowledge of its cultures, social systems, people, and character. I think of the teacher's education, the whole of it, in world affairs, or in art, or science, as a way of enriching the quality of his life, not as a way of preparing him to make a living by instructing children, running a school, or lecturing to young adults. The deepest criticism which can be made of the present system of teacher education is that it does not touch the life of its students, it does not arouse in them a delight in what they are doing, it does not engage them in action through which their own lives may be fulfilled. Its general effect is to tame their intellectual impulses and to fit them for duties in a school system.

I argue for a wider dimension of world thought and feeling in the education of teachers, for their sake first of all, then for the sake of the children and their schools, then for the sake of the improvement of the educational system and the country. That is the order in which the efforts must go. It is the quality and range of the teacher's mind and character which determine the degree of his influence and the form his influence will take. By working out ways in which his education may bring him face to face with cultures, ideas, values, facts, and people outside the range of his ordinary experience, we can make a difference in his life and in the quality of the gifts he brings to teaching. By doing so, and by giving enough teachers a chance to think in the bigger terms of world affairs and world issues, we should be able to enliven the entire educational system at a time it badly needs enlivening. Aside from anything else, that seems to me to be a good enough reason for introducing the world and its affairs into the education of American teachers.

2

Colleges for Teachers

The art of teaching grew up in the schoolroom out of inventiveness and sympathetic and concrete observation . . .

WILLIAM JAMES
Talks to Teachers

What we need to do first if the American teacher is to be brought into the main stream of contemporary culture and world affairs is to create a radically new conception of what a college for teachers should be. A college or university which took the education of teachers with the utter seriousness the matter deserves would take the world as its campus and move the world into its curriculum and into the life of its students. It would create a model of how liberal education can best be carried on, by treating the liberal arts as a body of knowledge and experience to be used in the lives of its students and, through them, in the lives of the coming generation.

A college of this kind would be a staging ground for expeditions into the world, a central place where the student could prepare himself, through study and teaching in the arts and sciences, to understand what he will find in the world beyond the campus and how to continue to learn wherever he goes. The time spent on the campus would be a time for doing the things which can best be done there, or can *only* be done there, because the campus contains science laboratories, a community of scholars and teachers, libraries, art studies, a theater, dance studios, music rooms, instruments and players, meeting rooms for seminars and classes.

The time spent away from the campus would extend the student's education into a variety of settings, through a mixture of teaching, community service, field study, writing, observing, social research, work with children, with the student considered as an intern in society and its institutions, learning from the experience that society can give him. The student would be testing for himself that what he was learning from his college—through books, discussions, ideas, the values and instruction of his teachers—squared with the reality of his own experience in the world. In preparing himself to be a teacher, he would then possess a central motive for learning, since everything he learned would be in some way relevant to the use to which it would some day be put. Like the poet or the philosopher, he would think of his total experience as a means of enriching and deepening the content of his art.

In fact, preparing to become a teacher is like preparing to become a poet. The preparation begins in a decision to become something, in a commitment about one's life and the purpose for which it is to be used. Once the commitment is made, every available kind of human experience for the teacher or the poet becomes a source of learning. Everything becomes a possible source of knowledge, a means of extending the boundaries of the imagination, sensibility, and intellect, a way of extending and strengthening the original commitment. In the case of the poet, the ultimate expression of that commitment is in the lines he writes. In the case of the teacher, the ultimate expression is found in what he leaves in the lives of others.

What I wish to propose is the idea of a college for teachers deliberately designed to enlist the energies of its students in teaching themselves and others—in a real sense, a students' college. The practice of the art of teaching, along with the other arts, would be continual, since instruction would be carried on through self-education, independent study, joint research projects, seminars, discussions, field work, study guides prepared by the faculty and students together, experience with children, community development work, study abroad, film-making, work in the schools. The college classroom would then be conceived as the place to which the student brings the fruits of his own efforts to learn and to teach, there to receive help and instruction in what he is learning from the members of the college faculty. His motivation for learning is sustained by the practice of learning and teaching; he wants to learn more in order to teach, just as a musician wants to learn to play his instrument in order to be heard. Then the problem of learning how to learn and learning how to teach can be seen, through the student's eyes, as two parts of the same process.

If the question of how the teacher can learn to understand the nature of world society and to become sensitive to its character were only a matter of adding appropriate courses in foreign culture and world affairs to the college curriculum, there would be relatively few problems in arranging things satisfactorily. The content of the teacher's curriculum must obviously be broadened to include new materials drawn from the cultures of the world, and important work is already going on to achieve that end—in the graduate schools, educational research centers here and abroad, through UNESCO, international educational agencies, foundations, and curriculum planning of all kinds.

But the problem does not end there; it merely begins, and it begins with the quality, as well as the content, of the intellectual and personal experience available in and around the institutions where teachers are presently educated. It goes on from there to the question of how the teacher can learn to create an intellectual and cultural life of his own, and move into the larger dimension of a world beyond the one to which his cultural origins are bound to confine him.

In looking for new kinds of institutional arrangements and contexts in which these questions can find answers, I have returned to the old-fashioned idea of teachers colleges or, to put it more accurately, colleges for teaching, and to the idea that learning to teach is the ultimate liberal art. I note with regret the mass movement of educators away from the idea of colleges for teachers and toward the concept of the multipurpose university. I would prefer to reform the multipurpose university than to give up or diffuse the central function it used to serve. The movement toward this kind of institution has been an inevitable part of the growth of American higher education, and it does give both the institution and the student more room to move, both inside and outside the field of education. But in achieving greater flexibility, it is beginning to abandon its own heritage in favor of what seems to me to be academic respectability rather than intellectual or cultural vitality. In meeting all kinds of purposes, it tends to lose sight of its central purpose—the advancement of teaching and therefore the advancement of learning.

I am strengthened in these convictions by the views of William James, whose ideas about education came not only from a genius for speculative thought, but from a deep love of teaching and of the teacher's art. James broke many philosophical precedents, but among the most important of them, he broke the precedent that the mind of a great scholar in philosophy and psychology should remain aloof from the practical problems of education and teaching. He was, in fact, the first philosopher after Emerson to concern himself directly with the problems of the teacher-scholar in reaching a wider audience of laymen and teachers than those ordinarily assembled in university classrooms. In 1892 he gave what he referred to as "a few public lectures on psychology to the Cambridge teachers," later collected in one volume as his *Talks To Teachers*.[1] In the first of these talks he was concerned "to dispel the mystification" about psychology as a guide to the practice of teaching: "I say moreover, that you make a great, a very great mistake, if you think that psychology, being the science of the mind's laws, is something from which you can deduce definite programmes and schemes and methods of instruction for immediate schoolroom use. Psychology is a science, and teaching is an art; and sciences never generate arts directly out of themselves. An intermediary inventive mind must make the application, by using its originality . . ."

"The art of teaching," said James, "grew up in the schoolroom, out of inventiveness and sympathic and concrete observation . . . in teaching, you must simply work your pupil into such a state of interest in what you are going to teach him that every other object of attention is banished from his mind; then reveal it to him so impressively that he will remember the occasion to his dying day; and finally fill him with devouring curiosity to know what the next steps in connection with the subject are . . ."[2]

Although few teachers can manage to do with their pupils all that James suggests, few could deny the two major premises on which his reasoning rests, that "the art of teaching grew up in the schoolroom, out of inventiveness and sympathetic and concrete observation," and that to apply the principles of education and psychology to teaching, "an intermediary inventive mind must make the application, by using its originality."

[1] William James, *Talks to Teachers on Psychology; and to Students on Some of Life's Ideals*, W. W. Norton, 1958.
[2] Ibid., pp. 23, 24, 25.

These premises are basic to the construction of plans for improvement in the education of teachers. Present plans tend to ignore the fact that the art of teaching grew up and is growing up in the schools and in the American communities, through a combination of inventiveness and concrete observation. Whatever may have been wrong with them, the teachers colleges had a fundamental and serious aim and were directly connected in the pursuit of that aim to the life of the community, the schools, the parents, and the practice of education. What was lacking in them was a direct connection with the major intellectual and cultural developments in contemporary society, for reasons inherent in the history of the citizens' movement out of which the teachers colleges came. They evolved *from* the normal schools rather than replacing them, and were staffed mainly by practitioners of education rather than by scholars with school-teaching experience, or by teachers with a full background of scholarship. Under the general American assumption that taking courses and getting degrees is the path to becoming educated, those who wished to take higher degrees and to enlarge the range of their knowledge and careers took courses from other practitioners. The course-taking is still going on, and accounts for the continuing criticism of teacher education by the university scholars, now joined by a growing number of serious students.

But the reform of the system is not served by deserting the heritage of the teachers college, nor by separating academic study from direct experience with teaching and learning in the communities and schools. The reform, as must always be the case in the long run, receives its impetus as well as its insights from the living situation of the society and the new demands the society has a right to make on the instruments for education designed to serve its needs. What seems to me to have happened is that with the shift of the center of gravity for teacher education from the actual problems of the school in society, the professional educators have lost touch with the roots of their primary talent, and have tried, without a philosophy of education clearly in mind to guide them, both to accommodate themselves to criticism and to emulate the academic habits of their critics.

THE ACADEMIC INTELLIGENCE

In response to questions raised in conversation and correspondence during the study, a student at a large and academically sound urban university in the East described the student-teacher's academic environment in this way:

> The great mass of students at X University I see as middle-class, rather conservative (meaning afraid to take risks or a stand about anything that might lead to remarks on a report card), provincial (their experience being limited to X University and its environs), and conformist. They are also nice, well-meaning, and academically intelligent. I define academic intelligence as an intelligence brought to bear strictly on an academic problem raised in a course and related to the grade. I saw little use of the intellect to explore and to clarify individual identity, the world, morality, philosophy, the arts, in relation to the individual. I saw little attempt at exploration of the problems of man and his world, of peace and technology, of the self within society. Certainly there were students who were concerned with important problems, but in general I would say that their total impact on the campus was small, though at different times it varied; their impact on their friends was significant. Concern with world, moral esthetic problems was the concern of a small minority.[3]

As the college programs for students preparing to be teachers have become more academic, and the academic intelligence has become more highly prized than more useful forms of intellect, students in many parts of the country and in an increasing proportion of the student body have turned to other forms of experience than the academic for their own educational fulfillment. During the early 1960s some of them sought that experience in the civil rights movement, in which they learned to combine a concern for social justice with action programs for voter registration, demonstrations on behalf of the Negro, and, above all, for teaching—Negro history, constitutional rights, social structure, the arts, and elementary school reading, writing, arithmetic, and mathematics to those who had little or no formal education.

These college students learned about education by teaching, and in the absence of textbooks, visual aids, classrooms, or previous instruction, they formed their own methods, prepared their own texts, and planned their own curricula. Although some students dropped out of college and university to teach and work full-time, most of the work was done in the summertime. When students with this kind of experience returned to college, they had learned not only to understand the nature of their own society and to locate themselves in a social structure which was working in their favor, but had learned an extraordinary amount about themselves and their education, much of it of very great importance to an understanding of

[3] Letter to Harold Taylor.

education and how best to conduct it, for themselves or for anyone else.

As the civil rights movement grew in size and strength on the college campuses during the early 1960s, and more and more students were caught up in education and action programs on behalf of the Negro, the student movement extended its range beyond protest into action, beyond civil rights into international affairs and the issues of war and peace. Students who returned to their campuses from experience in the rural and urban slums found the courses in social science and humanities irrelevant to most of the social and intellectual interests they had acquired in the midst of their own society. Having seen the effects of poverty and educational neglect on the lives of Americans, and having become more sophisticated about what a society is and how it functions, they saw the world society in terms similar to their own, and began to make the connection between the causes of social conflict and injustice in America and the causes of social disorder and conflict in the world at large.

They also found that in the way their own education was organized, with its emphasis on the academic intelligence, none of the issues which truly concerned them in national and world affairs were the subject of analysis, discussion, or treatment in the courses they were taught. Their dilemma was real. Either they subjected themselves to the courses in order to graduate, thus spending time and intellectual energy in ways inadequate to meet their genuine intellectual and moral concerns, or they would have to drop out of college in order to become educated.

The way out of the dilemma for many of them was to create centers of intellectual and social action of their own on the campuses, a way taken by the students in 1964 on the campus of the University of California in Berkeley. There, students who had had experience in direct social and political action in the civil rights movement, supported by those who felt a sense of outrage at the administrative rules governing their rights as citizens and students, engaged in organized action to change the rules and the educational system.

The effect on other campuses of the Berkeley events has been recorded in a growing body of literature, and there now exists a substantial student movement concerned with the problems of educational and social reform, as well as with problems in international order. The teach-in as an instrument of protest combined with instruction was an invention of that student movement and a means of making international affairs a matter of serious concern to college students never before involved in such concerns. The disclosure that the Central Intelligence Agency had been covertly supporting the U. S. National Student Association international programs of former years had the effect not only of shocking the educational community, but of increasing students' awareness of the importance of the role students have played, are playing, and can play in international affairs.

Coincident with the rise of a student movement with international interests and an interest in educational and social change, came the impact of the social legislation of the 88th and 89th Congresses, and the release of funds for educational improvement on a scale never before known in America. As far as college students were concerned, the main effect of the legislation was to give them a range of opportunity for service in the public welfare which matched their eagerness and willingness to take their education beyond the academy and into action.

Even before the legislation provided funds for new programs in which the educated young could become involved, fifty to one hundred thousand had already undertaken as volunteers to tutor children in the rural and urban slums, a number which has now increased to nearly 250,000 across the country and has resulted in the formation of a student-run Tutorial Assistance Center, organized and administered by the National Student Association with a grant from the Office of Economic Opportunity. When the National Teacher Corps was first announced, 13,000 students applied for admission, thousands more have served and are serving in VISTA, Head Start, Job Opportunity Centers, youth projects, volunteer service at home and abroad, and in the Peace Corps.

THE STUDENT MOVEMENT TOWARD AUTONOMY

In other words, outside the formal system of the university and the system of teacher education, a whole new body of young people has become involved in programs which put their intelligence and idealism to work in the service of education, where they are learning to educate each other and the members of their society, either without formal university instruction or in programs of instruction directly related to the educational and social problems they are trying to solve. The citizens' movement has been renewed by the students who have made a new kind of citizens-teachers college for themselves by working directly with children, parents, and the people of the community. They learn as they go along, taught to be teachers by meeting the demands of the community for more and better education.

In Brooklyn, New York, for example, a new kind of college, sponsored by the students and faculty members at Pratt Institute and named The Central Brooklyn Neighborhood College, has been established "because we (the students and faculty) feel that existing educational programs in Central Brooklyn do not prepare students for college and do not expose them to the variety of skills and professions open to them." Staffed by volunteers, most of them students, the college asks for no tuition fees, entrance requirements, tests or grades; there is a great deal of tutoring, courses are offered in poetry, dance, drama, Afro-American history, small business operation, journalism, in whatever areas of interest to be found in the students who are enrolled. Headquarters are in a storefront in Brooklyn, classes are held wherever there is space in the community, and a job placement bureau and an educational center are part of the school.

This is the ideal context for learning to teach, since the volunteer teacher must make his own way by offering his own curriculum, thus having to learn a great deal more about what he is teaching. He is also in a situation in which, if he does not teach well, he is likely to be deserted by his students. The National Student Association has plans for a similar college to be staffed entirely by student volunteers, with a curriculum based on the tutorial system.

In the meantime, a movement inside and parallel to the programs of instruction and teacher education of the universities has been developing through the efforts of students who have volunteered to teach courses for and to each other, on approximately ninety campuses from San Francisco State, Wayne State, the University of Michigan, to City University in New York.

"Make Your Own Course," says a poster distributed by the Committee on Participant Education at the University of California in Berkeley; "Is Your Interest History or Chemistry? The War in Vietnam? Medieval Literature and Philosophy? A Poetry Workshop? The Cultural Effects of Media? Are you willing to take responsibility for your education? All you need are ideas and a willingness to pursue them. The above are just examples of possible course subjects. The method of learning may range from individual study to seminars, from group research to regular classes. The teacher may be a faculty member, a grad student, or you! Credit (if you like) may be arranged through the Board of Educational Development. It's up to you."

THE NEW GRADUATE STUDENT

One of the unnoticed and for the most part unanalyzed developments in the field of teacher education has been the new interest in education taken by graduate students, mainly in the social sciences and humanities. These are students who during their undergraduate years were involved in the civil rights movement, in social protest, demonstrations, teaching, political action, and educational reform. Many of these students have continued into graduate school, in Berkeley, the University of Michigan, Wisconsin, San Francisco State, and elsewhere, have become graduate assistants in university courses, and have built their own education and graduate research around the issues and interests which engaged them during their earlier years. They are not career-minded in the usual academic sense, but belong to a new breed of politically sophisticated and socially conscious intellectuals who intend making their careers in the colleges and universities, but who are seriously interested in effecting social and political change through their work as teachers and research scholars.

Many of them have been associated as undergraduates with the National Student Association and with Students for a Democratic Society, (SDS), an organization which has caused a good deal of negative comment and alarmed action by administrators on some of the campuses where chapters have been formed, but which is one of the most intellectually alive and socially aware organizations in the field of contemporary politics. The SDS students have been highly militant in their protests against the war in Vietnam, as they have in their protests and action programs against the draft and against many other Government policies.

The response of educators and administrators to their activities on most campuses has been very much like the response of the administrators and politicians in Berkeley to the activities of the Free

Speech Movement, to resist the demands rather than to understand their nature, to take administrative action rather than to deal with substantive issues. The actions of the students have been considered by the majority of educators not as a demonstration of their serious interest in world affairs and education, but as evidence of irresponsibility and troublemaking among the young. The SDS chapters usually provide whatever political controversies and militant intellectual leadership which exist within the student body, and quite often are the only source of such leadership to be found there.

In other instances, as in the case of the Columbia University SDS chapter, a hard core of student activists has taken direct action involving seizure of campus buildings, deliberate violation of university rules, conflict with the police.

On the other hand, on many campuses there is almost no student political leadership, but instead, a small group of students, wistful and concerned that they have no issues to raise, protests to make, or international causes to support. On one campus the students reported to me that the only issue which aroused a college-wide concern was the question of wearing shorts to the dining room.

One of the centers of student action from which SDS first grew was the University of Michigan in Ann Arbor, where there has been for many years a tradition of liberal social thought and political action, partly due to the context of state politics in which militant unionism has its own political representation, and partly due to the high quality of work going on at the University in the political and social sciences.[4] Students from Michigan, in the late 1950s and early 1960s, were active in the civil rights movement and in university reform, with a continuing series of criticisms and demands for educational change circulated on the campus through the university newspaper and among students with specific ideas about how university education should be conducted. In their criticism and ideas about the mass university, they anticipated the Berkeley students and, through study groups, research papers, and campus political action, sought changes, some of which were made, in the conduct of university education and university policy.

[4] The Center for Research on Conflict Resolution, staffed by University of Michigan faculty members interested in national and international problems ranging from race conflict to disarmament, has been a source of energy and talent to encourage the work of undergraduate and graduate students in world affairs.

STUDENT INITIATIVES IN INTERNATIONALISM

One of the student-faculty groups formed during this period at Michigan was called the Association for Commitment to World Responsibility, and along with a careful, detailed, and imaginative research study of the rationale, design, and feasibility of a United Nations University, also furnished some working papers on the idea of a student Peace Corps for service abroad. In the Presidential campaign of the fall of 1960, John F. Kennedy spoke in Ann Arbor, and during his speech urged the students to make their own contribution to American society by volunteering from one to three years of their lives in some form of public service needed by their country. Alan E. Guskin, a graduate student in social psychology and a member of the Association, became the leader of a group of students who, basing their ideas on research they had already been doing on education and world problems, urged the then Senator Kennedy to make good on his speech by committing himself to the formation of an agency in the government which would give American youth a chance to serve the world wherever they were needed. It is generally agreed that the work of Mr. Guskin and his friends in pressing Senator Kennedy into action was responsible for the fact that Mr. Kennedy made his famous Peace Corps speech in San Francisco in November of 1960, and that the speech took the form that it did.

When the Peace Corps began, Mr. Guskin and Judith Guskin, his wife, were among the first persons to be appointed to the staff in Washington. They returned in 1961 to the Michigan campus to join the Peace Corps Volunteers being trained for service in Thailand, where they both served as instructors at Krungthrep University in Bangkok, returning from there to posts in the research and evaluation side of VISTA; they are now working with the Florida State Migrant (Farm Worker) Program, of which Mr. Guskin is Director.

I cite these facts about the students at Michigan and the connection of Mr. Guskin to research and action projects in education and world affairs to illustrate what I mean by the importance of the undergraduate and graduate student in the development of educational programs. The studies carried on by the Association for Commitment to World Responsibility were not done in regular courses of graduate or undergraduate work at Michigan, although in terms of their high quality of research they could have been. They were done as an expression of the serious interest, talent, and commitment of students involved in their own education.

Their research was not published in educational or social science journals, although again, it could have been; it was distributed to interested and concerned people, among them persons in public life, the universities, and politics. Through the research the students educated themselves and a good many others. As a part of a new movement which is growing in size, these students represent a new kind of young scholar of whom there are hundreds across the country, whose interest in education stems from a critical awareness of the weaknesses in their own and the belief in the need for radical reform in the whole educational system. The career Mr. Guskin has been following since 1960, into the educational system of a foreign country, and now into projects of social and educational change in this country, is one similar to those being followed by a growing percentage of others, whose talents have already developed to a maturity which, in many cases, is beyond that of the educators in charge of programs for student-teachers.

It is from these sources in the graduate schools that we are going to be able to recruit the world-minded college teachers we need for the reform of the undergraduate curriculum and for the creation of new teacher education programs in world affairs. In fact, a good many of the graduate students are ready, before graduation, to take full responsibility for teaching groups of undergraduates who intend to become teachers and to work with them on individual study plans and field work. Rather than assigning this kind of graduate student to graduate assistant's work, they should be invited, on salary, to teach for one to two years with others among their ranks, and to combine their own and their students' research into educational questions and world affairs in the preparation of new materials for use in the colleges and schools. This could be arranged, for example, during the period of the undergraduate's practice teaching with arrangements made to try out some of the new materials dealing with world questions in the high school or elementary school to which the student-teacher was assigned. This would be of great benefit to the graduate student in linking his work directly to the public schools, as well as to the work of undergraduates and the college curriculum.

A present group of graduate and undergraduate students at Michigan, following in the tradition of the Association for Commitment to World Responsiblity and the earlier work of SDS on the campus, have formed the Radical Education Project to carry out an "independent education, research and publication program . . . devoted to the cause of democratic radicalism and aspiring to the creation of a new left in America."[5]

Over the past year, the Project has produced a series of student research papers on foreign and domestic policy, power politics, labor, community schools, the universities, and other topics, which are in use by student and faculty groups on campuses in the Midwest, along with a series of study guides for students in the field of political and social science. These have been used in some cases by faculty members to reorganize their own courses, in other cases by students to teach each other and to conduct their own seminars.

Among the topics on which the Project has been working during the present year (that is, preparing more materials, holding conferences, etc.) are: The University and the Military, College and University Teaching as a Profession, Youth, The Social Sciences and Social Problems, Disaffection in the United States, Contemporary Educational Theory and Practice. Their work, related in varying degrees to direct political action, is matched in comparable form by other students on other campuses, both inside and outside the SDS organization.

The difficulty for American education in taking advantage of the contributions to teaching and learning which student activists are capable of making is that there has been little understanding among the educators of the need for a radical student movement both in politics and in social change. So little accustomed are most educators to the idea of student political action and student dissent, on and off the campuses, that when it occurs they are ill prepared to deal with it except by looking for ways in which it may be muffled or repressed. Most educational administrators are more concerned about the effect of serious student political action on public opinion than they are on the validity of the action itself, more con-

[5] *Brief Report on the First Year's Activities of the Radical Education Project,* June 1967. Radical Education Project, 510 East William Street, Ann Arbor, Mich.

cerned to find channels for the control of dissent than to find ways
in meeting the criticisms on which it is based.

CONSERVATISM AND THE SOCIAL SCIENCES

Another source of conservatism in education for social thought
and action lies in the organized academic society which functions
within its own professional organizations, departments of the universities, and subculture, particularly in the political and social
sciences. The underlying causes of the remoteness of the academic
subculture from public issues in social thought and social action,
including its remoteness from the acting world of the student, have
been described and analyzed elsewhere, more particularly in Clark
Kerr's Godkin Lectures at Harvard, *The Uses of the University*.[6]
I will not repeat the descriptions here, except to say that the
subjects of research in the social and behavioral sciences are established more by academic convention and hierarchical leadership
than by their relevance to the major issues confronting world society.
Although the peace research movement has made some gains in
recent years and the impact of the protest movement of the Negro
and the poor have turned more academic attention to the educational issues involved, the operating principles of the major academic bodies and organizations bear more resemblance to the
policies of the American Medical Association than they do to the
Society for the Psychological Study of Social Issues.

What I am concerned about here is the way in which the system
of graduate education in the social sciences, particularly in sociology, anthropology, social psychology, and political science, can gain
new momentum and new social direction from the energy flowing
between the undergraduate education of activist students, graduate
education relevant to the interests of young activists, and the going
system of academic appointments, teaching and educational organization. The process of change in the education of teachers to give
it international social relevance will come from underneath, from
the ferment produced among the socially conscious and intellectually aware members of the young generation who have formed
their own groups and are carrying on their own action programs.
It will come from the new high school and university constituency

6 *The Uses of the University*, by Clark Kerr. Harvard University Press, 1963,
Cambridge, Mass. 140 pp.

which is creating its own style of politics, and in some cases is supporting its own candidates for public office.

There are already some signs of the effects of undergraduate and graduate school activists on the organized profession in the case of the sociologists, who now include among their ranks some of the new generation of graduates with the doctorate degree whose intellectual interests are in the field of social change and reconstruction. The academic and intellectual credentials of the new group are impeccable in conventional academic terms (as were those of most of the students in the Berkeley protest movement) and they have given a certain legitimacy to radical and liberal social thought which in past years has been absent from academic circles. Having moved from the status of student to that of college teacher and research scholar without changing gears or changing sides, these young scholars have formed new groupings inside the profession of sociology, and, among other things, occasionally turn their research talents in sociology to work on the sociology of the university community, with analyses and exposures of the process of power and change within the educational system.

Many of those who do so learned their trade outside the regular courses and research of the university graduate school, through projects of the kind I have described at Michigan and elsewhere, and are now in the process of making what was in former years a series of extracurricular ventures a regular part of the method and content of higher education. As yet, few of them have turned in the direction of international education and the social science of world development, but as their interest in the prevention of war and the achievement of creative social change increases, it is clear that more and more of them will concern themselves with world problems in an educational context. The listing of research topics and publications of the Radical Education Project may soon become the listing of courses in university catalogues.

STUDENTS AND THE TEACHING PROFESSION

In the meantime, owing to the gap between the academic system and the reality of the world in which students live, most of the American student body, and particularly those preparing to become teachers, remain politically inert and socially illiterate, while the small minority of student intellectuals and activists work out their own ways of expressing their dissent, ways which too often fail to achieve the genuine goals of social change and educational reform with which most intelligent educators agree.

I know at first hand what students who are trusted and encouraged in their efforts to think and act in radical terms can do in organizing political and social action projects which serve a serious purpose. For one thing, they learn that it is not enough simply to assert a view of one's own either to have it considered as a radical view or to gain the assent of others to its validity. More than anything else, they learn to take things seriously, and to understand the necessity of hard intellectual work in the formation of a point of view which can stand up under attack and make sense to those whom one is trying to persuade.

But it is in the field of education itself that the students have most to offer to those who are willing to trust them and to give them the responsibility they deserve. In my view, the powerful social and intellectual force which exists within the new generation of students has been greatly underestimated even by those educators who have taken the students seriously. Most educators and the public have tended to think of student activists and those concerned with civil rights and world affairs as a general nuisance, a motley group of radical dissidents, draft dodgers, or young rebels who will soon get over it.

On the contrary, what we have is a new and significant national asset. In fact, the core of the student movement is composed of a serious and informed body of young people who act out of a sense of personal commitment to each other and a sense of compassion for those who have been blocked from a place in society. They care very much about the quality of their own lives, are critical of the philistine values of a television society, and are sensitive to the effects of their acts on the lives of others. They are responsible critics of the society and its educational system, and the best of them have a political sophistication and social energy which is in advance of many of those appointed to educate them. In short, by their acts of engagement, their work in society, and their intellectual commitments, they have shown that they are already teachers. They have taught themselves to be.

But, as I have conferred with hundreds of them during visits to the campuses, I have found a curious paradox. The motivations and interests which brought them into a direct confrontation with the problems of world society and of American life are exactly those which turn them away from the teaching profession. Within their ideas, their talents, and their social idealism lies a formidable force for educational change of exactly the kind the country has been calling for. Yet most of them do not intend to be teachers.

When asked for reasons, they say two things. They say that they refuse to spend what they believe to be wasteful time in taking education courses which in their judgment are without serious intellectual content or relevance to their own experience as teachers and tutors. They want to work out their own methods and curricula directly with children and teachers in and out of school, with such help as they can get from educators who welcome their questions. They then say that even if properly certified and installed in a teaching post, they would not be able to teach about the world with any sense of integrity, because the system—the school board, the principal, the other teachers, and the community—has a set pattern of political, social, and educational attitude to which they have to conform, and by conforming they would lose their personal identity and their fulfillment as teachers.

To which I have replied, then how do you hope to reform either the society or its educational system if you refuse to act either in or on its educational institutions? I have usually won the argument but lost the candidate.

Until we create programs in the undergraduate and graduate colleges of education which can speak to the concerns of these students and give them the satisfaction of learning to act in the world and using their lives in a cause which has meaning to them, we will not engage the most promising of them in the teaching profession. We have been going about it backwards. When we should have been creating an education which could enlist their energies, we have been organizing a system which bores them to death and asks very little of them.

EDUCATION FOR STUDENTS

During my visits to the campuses, I seldom came in touch with educational plans which based themselves on the idea of involving the students in teaching and learning, of evoking the kind of enthusiasm for teaching which the students have begun to generate among themselves without benefit of required curricula or instruction. Yet here is the primary resource in talent and intellectual energy upon which programs for the education of teachers should be based. I need not repeat again the truism, now so widely circulated, that the present system of higher education puts the student almost entirely in a passive role. The young activists refuse to stay in that role; they challenge it on all sides but find themselves frustrated in their desire to act within the framework of existing institutions, especially those designed for the education of teachers. That is why they are forming their own enclaves inside the institutions, and gaining their direct experience with teaching and learning in the real situations of their society outside the colleges.

If, under these circumstances, we analyze the resources for change in the style and content of teacher education, we find within the younger generation a flow of energy and a body of ideas now available, in a way unknown in previous periods of educational history, for use within the colleges. The collective faculty body is conservative in character, as all collective bodies are eventually bound to be. The faculty is tied to certain preconceptions about the necessity of organizing knowledge and instruction into departmental categories. Yet the collective faculty bodies, through their committees and departments, are in control of educational policy. The administration is in the hands of administrators whose major responsibilities are for the most part noneducational; they administer policies agreed upon by the bureaucracy of the faculty. The major educational power of administrators lies in the funds they can obtain for particular projects, and in the appointments they make to the academic sector of the institution, although even here their authority is limited by the faculty procedures governing appointments, both administrative and academic. The existence of a lively and enterprising body of students, varying in size and quality from campus to campus, interested in improving the quality of their education and their society, is, therefore, in my judgment, the main source of power for improving the quality of teaching and learning in the institutions of higher education.

The question I am raising is: How can this source of power be developed for use in the education of teachers, especially in the enlargement of the teachers' view of the world? What are the practical applications and possibilities?

THE PEACE CORPS AS A TEACHERS COLLEGE

The most immediate application of the concept of student power has already been made in the development of the Peace Corps. Although it did not start that way, the Peace Corps is a teachers college in world affairs where the combination of practical experience in teaching, and immersion in and knowledge of a foreign culture is a preparation for the Volunteer to teach in the schools and colleges of the United States. It is not the whole of a preparation, but it can be, once the two years of Peace Corps service is made an integral part of a five-year undergraduate or three-year Master of Arts program in a cooperating college or university. The five-year program has already started in an experimental form at Western Michigan University, at Wilmington College in Ohio, and elsewhere, and the possibilities of Peace Corps service with a three-year graduate degree in education are wide open for experiment.

"We have seen the Peace Corps right from the beginning," says Harris Wofford, former Associate Director in the Peace Corps,[7] "as a kind of university in dispersion, and some of us have even thought it was a model for a new kind of education which, although it has been tried by many people around the world and in America, had never taken the sort of quantum jump it was possible for us to take when we started our program in Washington. I would like to describe the Peace Corps today as a teachers college, since all Peace Corps Volunteers in one way or another are teachers. Half of them literally go to teach in classrooms, the other half are out teaching in the community—birth control, agricultural extension, public health, community development.

"What is the novelty?

[7] Conference on World Education, Warrenton, Virginia, December 9–11, 1966, convened in connection with the research on which this book is based. The full text of Mr. Wofford's statement is published in the Proceedings of the Conference, along with statements by others on teacher education, world affairs, and international education. Mr. Wofford, a member of the Advisory Committee for the research, was associated with the Peace Corps from its beginning, and served as Director for Ethiopia, and as an Associate Director in Washington before leaving in February 1967 to become President of the State University of New York in Old Westbury. There Mr. Wofford is at work designing a college with the help of students and a number of interested educators, schedules to open with an experimental program involving 100 students in the fall of 1968.

"First, we were and are a new source of teachers as well as a source for new teachers. Not many of the Volunteers had ever thought of teaching before they joined the Peace Corps. The largest proportion of the Volunteers are liberal arts graduates. Many of those who are exposed to teaching in the Peace Corps decide that that is what they want to do with their lives, or with the next part of their lives, and many more would decide that way if we had better opportunities for them to teach in challenging situations when they come home.

"We have been trying to find new ways of learning to teach, above all by *teaching* . . . The division between teacher and student is blurred because the definition of a good Peace Corps Volunteer includes possession of the spirit of learning. If the Volunteer does not have the learning spirit, that fact is going to be discovered in the difficult assignment in which he is engaged. People are going to sense that he has come to do good against them. In the Peace Corps you have to learn from those you teach, you have to learn by doing, and it is not only learning by doing, but learning by going. Migration, people on the move, going into a radically new setting, with the possibility of trading the old life for a new one—this is part of the energy and motivation in the Peace Corps kind of education, just as it was for those who migrated to Israel or, in earlier days, to America."

THE IMPACT OF THE PEACE CORPS ON EDUCATION

In retrospect, the Peace Corps can be seen not only as one of the most important developments in American foreign policy during the postwar period, but as a crucially important contribution to the development of American education. It would not have been even remotely possible to have mounted in 1960 an international teacher education program involving 14,000 persons a year in fifty countries supported by millions of dollars, through the resources, either intellectual or financial, of the American colleges and universities. Yet that is the program that was mounted by the United States Government.

Since the beginning months of the Peace Corps in 1961, when no one, either in the Peace Corps or the universities, was very clear about how best to train volunteers for service abroad, a body of knowledge and experience in education has been accumulating within the Peace Corps through its research and evaluation and through the ideas the Volunteers themselves have brought into the program. Each year of operation has been a test of the validity of the political, social, and educational principles on which the Peace Corps is based, a test applied by the Congress, by the governments and people of the countries in which it has operated, by the American public, by the educational institutions, and by the Peace Corps staff and Volunteers themselves. The fact that the Peace Corps has grown in strength and educational maturity during its six years of existence is a tribute to the quality of its volunteers, the quality of its administration, but perhaps most of all to the validity of the principles on which it rests.

The first of these is the political integrity of the Corps membership, without which there would be no point in having the program at all. By political integrity I mean the freedom of every volunteer to serve the needs of the country to which he goes, without an obligation to the United States Government either to defend its foreign policy, to propagandize on behalf of the United States, or to report to American Government agencies on political matters in the country of residence. This has meant some restriction on the political activities of the Volunteer in the country of residence, since intervention or involvement in the internal affairs of the host country would entail one or another kind of political antagonism, from the right, the left, or the center.

This has also meant that over the years since 1961, particularly since 1965 and the escalation of the American intervention in Vietnam, student activists and others, both in the United States and abroad, have questioned the integrity of the Peace Corps and have linked service in the Corps to the support of U.S. foreign policy. For many of those in Peace Corps service this has meant a degree of personal embarrassment and, in some cases, the feeling of being morally compromised which affects American scholars and other Americans abroad who disagree with the foreign policy of their Government but are branded as its supporters simply by accepting its assignments in education and social service.

The only possible solution to that kind of problem is to hold fast to the principle of serving the needs of the host country in education and social welfare without reference to American interests or ideology, and devoting oneself to the idea that personal service in a humanitarian cause is one of the strongest and most direct ways of

building an international community as a counterforce to war and
the use of force and violence in political and social change. Without a continuous reassertion of the meaning of the concept of peace
as an integral part of the name and activities given to the Peace
Corps, there is no point in continuing the Corps itself.

The problems and dilemmas of maintaining a purity of motive in
an organization of this kind point to another principle, one which
has for the most part gone unnoticed by educators, the principle of
self-correction leading to continuous change in educational policy at
home and abroad. The Peace Corps selects highly qualified, well-
educated, and intelligent young people, gives them an unusual degree of responsibility and freedom to carry out a complicated and
highly significant set of tasks, and then relies on their judgment,
criticism, evaluation, and talents for the continuous operation of the
program. This means that, unlike most educational organizations,
corrections within the educational system are the direct responsibility of those who are undergoing the education. The experience
of the Volunteers, who would be called "students" in other circumstances, is the basis for planning the educational program itself.

The organization therefore learns incomparably more about itself
as it functions from day to day than any other kind of educational
institution. Aside from the views expressed by foreign officials, Congressmen, educators, and its own staff, each year approximately
seven thousand two-year graduates emerge, all of them with ideas
of what can and should be done in educational and social change,
all of them with access to the administration of the Peace Corps
program, even to the point of being recruited into the instructional
and administrative staff. It takes several generations of students,
even in the experimental colleges, for educational institutions to
change. In the traditional institutions, it takes forever. In the Peace
Corps, the change happens year by year, both in the shaping of
Peace Corps goals and in the operation of its programs.

However, as it has grown so fast and learned so much, the Peace
Corps found itself in an odd situation. On the one hand, it has become, without having set out to be and still without being recognized as such, a powerful educational institution, powerful in the
outreach of its programs into the world, powerful in the effects it
has had on those who have entered its service, sophisticated in the
knowledge it has accumulated about education in action. As a con-

tractor for educational services, it had begun by asking the educators to supply the training programs through which the Volunteers might best learn to serve. The programs that resulted in the early days were almost entirely a projection of the academic conventions with all the deficiencies and weaknesses inherent in the conventions.

Having seen these in operation, and having learned through research and the direct testimony of reliable witnesses about the irrelevance of many of the programs to the purposes they were to serve, the Peace Corps staff could only conclude that there must be some better way, and that they would have to take the initiative in finding it. On the other hand, the Peace Corps had not been asked by Congress to build an educational institution but to send Americans abroad to be helpful, and although the officers had become educators by default, as well as by interest and concern, they could not very well start a Peace Corps University. What they could do, and what they did, was to furnish a critique of conventional education out of the materials of their own history, and to establish a working relation with educators in colleges and universities where there were people who understood their educational problems and responded to their style of educating.

After a meeting with a group of such educators in July of 1965[8] to discuss the future of the Peace Corps educational programs, a Task Force was appointed to work out plans for what might be done. The report of the Task Force, in February of 1966,[9] is a document of serious importance for American education and of particular importance and relevance to the education of teachers.

The conclusions of the report are based on the idea that preparation for Peace Corps service should not be looked upon as short-term training, but as a full process which begins in school and college, is intensified in full-time training before the Volunteer goes overseas, and reaches its climax in the two years of service and in what follows after. Getting ready for service in the Peace Corps and then engaging in its service are in themselves an education which pre-

[8] *The Peace Corps in an Educating Society,* excerpts from a discussion at the Brookings Institution, July 22, 1965. Dr. James Dixon, Chairman. Peace Corps, Washington, D.C. 64 pp.

[9] Peace Corps Education Task Force Report, February 1966, Peace Corps, Washington, D.C. See also Peace Corps Education Task Force Discussion papers by Sister Jacqueline Grennan, the Rev. Theodore Hesburgh, John R. Seeley, and David Riesman; and "The Future of the Peace Corps," by Harris Wofford, *Annals of the American Academy of Political and Social Science,* May 1966.

pares the Volunteer to continue his education and his life at a higher level than would otherwise be possible.

The recommendations of the Task Force for the full-time training programs assert that the training schedule should include only a very few lectures by academic experts, should leave a great deal of time for individual study, research, and seminars with returned Volunteers and foreign participants, and should include "considerable periods of community action, practice teaching, or other work —in radically unfamiliar environments; in slums or rural areas or Job Corps camps in the mainland United States in other cultures such as Puerto Rico, the Virgin Islands, the State of Hawaii, Mexico, Quebec or Israel or in the host countries themselves—with some programs taking place entirely in these locations."

The report calls for the use of foreign students and returned Volunteers and others from the host country to be full members of the faculty for the training programs, and that rather than having separate courses in the conventional academic disciplines, the curriculum should involve the study of problems in American and foreign societies on a comparative basis. More than anything else, the Report called for the involvement of colleges and universities on a continuing basis with the Peace Corps, including some responsibility for the continuing education of the Volunteers while they are overseas and when they return to the United States. The beginning of preparation for educational and community service abroad should lie in the entire program in high school and college, through work with foreign students and returned Volunteers, through the study of foreign languages and foreign cultures, through field experience in teaching and community action. The person who serves America abroad, in other words, should be an example of the best that the whole system of American society and American education can produce. In serving America abroad, such persons are being prepared to serve America at home.

A NEW FRAMEWORK FOR THE EDUCATION OF TEACHERS

Looked at as a design for the education of teachers in the field of world affairs, the Task Force recommendations, many of which have been and are being carried out, provide a new framework for education applicable equally to the Peace Corps and to the entire body of practices in the American colleges and universities. By a kind of

historical accident, going back to some of the political events preceding and following President Kennedy's election to office, the
country has been presented with a national and international instrument for educating teachers which had not been contemplated
by educators in the form of a Peace Corps, but which has now come
to take a place in the forefront of experiment and change in American higher education. In one sweep, a philosophy of education has
been formulated whose roots lie deep within the history of American
democratic thought, linking American society to the going concerns
of contemporary world society, and developing workable methods,
backed by Congressional funds, for putting the ideas into practice.
In doing so, the Peace Corps concept has involved the colleges and
universities and other components of the educational system in a
national and international endeavor of high purpose and serious
significance.

Here is the structure, considered not as the Peace Corps *per se,*
but as an instrument for the education of teachers. The structure
consists of:

1. An organization and a staff in Washington, supported by
Congress and the executive branch, with funds adequate to
meet its needs for educating approximately 7000 teachers in
world affairs each year.

2. A national recruitment program for teachers which produces
approximately 44,000 applicants a year.

3. An enlightened selection process, continuous throughout the
training program, which chooses approximately 7000 qualified
persons annually for foreign service.

4. Provision of two years for foreign experience, much of it in
teaching, preceded by a training period which varies from three
months to two years, sometimes to three years, and which could
be fully integrated with a four- or five-year college program.

5. Administrative connections with foreign educational institutions, governments, and persons in forty-six countries, in addition to connections with American Government representatives
in those countries.

6. Direct connections with students, teachers, and community

workers around the world; connections with similar domestic and international programs abroad.

7. An approach to education which gives a wide degree of freedom and responsibility to the student, and relies on the energies, talents, and resources of the volunteer to create new forms of education and service, according to existing needs.

8. A structure of motivation which stresses the satisfaction of service rather than of material rewards or status, and provides compelling reasons for the study of foreign languages, foreign cultures, the liberal arts, and world society, both as a means of entry into new areas of experience and as a means of preparing oneself to serve others as a teacher.

9. A contracting agency for the development of new programs for the education of teachers in world affairs.

Considered in terms of this structure, as an educational instrument, apart from its relation to American foreign policy, the Peace Corps provides the best available model now in existence for the education of teachers in the field of world affairs.

There is already a sufficient body of research on the content of experience and the educational results of Peace Corps training and service to identify the place it occupies in the American educational system as a whole.[10] The emphasis in the research findings is on the way in which entrance into an alien culture by those committed to aiding its growth and welfare creates certain educational demands and requires certain personal attributes for the successful completion of the mission undertaken. Success is measured by how well the alien culture is served by the Volunteer, the Volunteer's intelligence is measured by the degree and quality of use he makes of it in ministering to the educational needs of a community he must understand.

Accordingly, the rules of the educational game are changed, and

[10] One of the best of the recent research publications is a book edited by Robert B. Textor of the School of Education at Stanford University, which contains chapters by university scholars associated with the Peace Corps and by returned Volunteers on problems, results, and implications of the Peace Corps work in thirteen countries. In addition to its own reports, the book contains a useful bibliography of other research. *Cultural Frontiers of the Peace Corps,* edited by Robert B. Textor, with a foreword by Margaret Mead; MIT Press, Cambridge, Mass., 363 pp.

the academic intelligence must be fused with a social sensitivity; ability in the teacher must include cultural proficiency and a capacity to tolerate ambiguities, paradoxes, and uncertainties, and to undertake educational initiatives. These are qualities not often sought in their students by those who teach teachers, nor are the qualities introduced as primary concepts in the thinking of those who plan for the education of teachers. Yet these attributes are crucial to any serious understanding by students of cultural differences and world affairs. Throughout this chapter and throughout the book as a whole, I have for this reason stressed continually the concepts of cultural immersion, social sensitivity, and cultural empathy in the education of teachers. I have argued that no matter what the teacher's specialty, from non-Western cultures to mathematics, and no matter what population of students the teacher is teaching—poor, rich, black or white, ghetto or suburbs, foreign or native—experience within a culture other than one's own is an essential ingredient in the development of teacher-scholars able to deal with the ongoing demands of teaching in America.

The evidence piles up that when the student-teacher and the teacher in service have had the advantage of work in community development and in teaching, within the context of the aims and practices of the Peace Corps, VISTA, and comparable programs, marked gains become visible in the teaching capacity and cultural proficiency of the participants. Ever since the psychologists and anthropologists began to turn their attention to the cultural and psychological implications of educational systems, the relation between cultural and intellectual factors in intelligence and human skill has been a central item of inquiry. But that relationship has not found its way into the working areas of educational reform. In the specific matter of education in world affairs, the establishment of the Peace Corps as an instrument of American foreign policy and cultural diffusion marks a turning point in both the theory and practice of teacher education. It has demonstrated in action the effect of cultural immersion on the growth and development of the teacher.

THE LESSONS OF THE PEACE CORPS

The intention of the Peace Corps, stated in the original Peace Corps Act, is to create and promote understanding on the part of the

Volunteers, of cultures, values, and ideas other than their own. Not to possess such understanding would make it impossible for the Volunteer to achieve the objectives for which the Peace Corps was established. Partly through the selection process by which cultural sensitivity, or at least a capacity for such sensitivity, is a determining factor in the admission of candidates to the program, partly through the content of the training curricula, and mainly through the actual two-year experience of working one's way through the problems of adapting intelligently to another culture, the achievement of cultural proficiency has been a distinguishing characteristic of the vast majority of those who have completed their Peace Corps service. The possession of this attribute is closely related to the idea of democratic man, at home with every kind and condition of human being, and is central to the ethos of a democratic society. To be in the position of having to cope with people and situations, often in a hierarchical or feudal society whose attitudes are repugnant to one's own, and to carry through an educational or social mission in circumstances hostile to one's own sense of how things should be done, is a direct means of coming to terms with oneself and learning to sustain one's integrity while accomplishing an assigned task.

The lesson for the educator of teachers is simply that the development of this kind of proficiency and quality of character, whether to be used in foreign service, in teaching in the American ghetto, or in acting as an American citizen, is best achieved by making it one of the major criteria by which a teacher and his work are judged, along with "knowing his subject," and being able to teach it to others.

Considered in this and other dimensions, there are certain educational results which can be listed in the achievements of the Peace Corps, each of which has serious implications for the theory and practice of teacher education as a whole.

(1) Experimental programs in short-term preparation for teaching should concentrate on matters which have direct relevance to the service to be undertaken—for example, knowing the social, economic, political, and cultural characteristics of the society in which one is to serve as a teacher. The way to learn about them is by direct experience combined with fresh materials and documents in the literature of social science and the humanities, with emphasis on the role of the student in collecting his own knowledge and putting it

into usable condition. That is what has given the successful Peace Corps training programs their strength.

(2) Willingness to give to the student-teacher responsibility for independent action and decision, for individual initiative and autonomy in style and content of teaching and learning is a necessary element in the development of capable teachers, when teaching is conceived as cultural diffusion and the development of usable talents, knowledge, and skills in those being taught. The success of the Peace Corps Volunteer, since it is measured by how much he contributes to the personal and social welfare of those he has been asked to help, depends in large measure on the imagination and initiative he is willing and able to take in the situation in which he finds himself. His own feeling of accomplishment is therefore a necessary ingredient in the measurement of that success, just as it is a necessary component in the educational program which precedes his period of service. Since he is a volunteer, since he is in the program by commitment and choice, he invests himself in the success of his own efforts and in the success of the program itself and the aims it is designed to serve.

In learning to adapt to future situations which his teachers and he both know will be relatively unstructured, his preparation for service must give him experience in dealing with a variety of unstructured problems for which he must find his own solutions. On the other hand, since some of his duties abroad may be quite specifically structured—he may be asked to teach a specific and highly organized syllabus, or to serve in a Government post whose duties are clearly circumscribed—he must learn how to take initiatives and contribute his talent within a precise frame of reference.

The lesson here for the education of teachers is obvious. The motivation for learning depends on the commitment of those who enter a career of teaching, and the strength of both the commitment and the motivation depends on the opportunity the entrant is given to serve the cause to which he is committed. Unless he feels that what he is asked to do in his education gives him genuine responsibility and preparation for further responsibility ahead, his motivation is weakened, if not destroyed.

(3) As was the case in the development by the military services of crash programs for language training during the Second World War, the Peace Corps has developed a high degree of sophistication

in short-term intensive periods (300–400 hours) of language instruction, and has a great deal to contribute to teacher education in this field. Since possession of an ability to work in the language of the host country is an essential for the objectives of the program, there is a direct, self-evident, and strong relation between learning the language and using it, with a consequent strength of motivation for the learner usually lacking in the conventional college language courses.

Additional strength is given by the fact that language instruction is so often conducted by teams of natives from the host country, who are eager to serve as instructors, and that the cultural content of the rest of the training program is so closely linked to the concepts and linguistic patterns of the language itself. Students in programs of this kind can see, sometimes for the first time, the intricate and subtle connections between the language and the characteristics of the culture out of which the language grew.

Faced with the problem of providing instruction in languages for which no previous texts and materials had been prepared, the Peace Corps called upon expert linguists for the kind of analysis modern linguistics can now provide, and has built new materials, methods, and programs which have proven to be very effective and which can be transposed into the college curricula whenever they are needed.[11] In this they can be helped by the returned Volunteers, many of whom have become interested in language training and language teaching through their own experience in the field. The body of experience and knowledge is available to those language teachers, linguists, and educators who wish to make use of it.

(4) Through the appointment of Country Representatives to supervise the programs in the host country, the Peace Corps has developed a new breed of foreign service officer whose duties have in a large sense to do with education and social change, rather than with conventional diplomatic representation. Additional appointments of Associate Representatives, usually former Peace Corps Volunteers, make it possible to continue the education of the Volunteers while they are in service, through seminars, consultations, informal research projects. In the case of those Representatives who have had

[11] The Peace Corps now provides instruction in 120 languages, many of which were unknown in this country before the Peace Corps began to teach them.

research experience in the social sciences and university teaching experience before appointment, an interesting new form of ongoing education becomes possible, with direct relation between the foreign service and the universities from which the Volunteers have come.

This means that the education of teachers in world affairs could begin with the appointment of faculty members on American campuses to serve for one year at a time on Peace Corps missions abroad, to coordinate the continuing education and practice teaching of the Volunteers with the work they have done before service and will do when they return home. Over a period of five years it would thus be possible to build up a sizable cadre of professional educators who are equally at home in the educational life of their own country and that of a foreign culture. At that point we will begin to have the leadership in this kind of teacher education which until now circumstances have prevented.

(5) The policy of the Peace Corps in making appointments to its staff in Washington and abroad of young Volunteers who show themselves to be particularly qualified for the work, regardless of their age or place in the academic or Peace Corps hierarchy, has implications for an improved use of teaching and educational talent among the teacher candidates on the American campuses. Most of the appointment policies in the colleges of education and the colleges and universities in general involve a slow and sometimes painful series of apprenticeships by graduate students who are faced with a long series of academic requirements, many of them irrelevant to their intellectual or educational interests. An application of the Peace Corps policy to American campuses would make teaching appointments from the ranks of those who showed that they had the talent and knowledge, regardless of their academic status and age, especially in the case of the shortage areas of teachers with foreign language training and teaching experience abroad.

It will be clear that the sum of these attributes is one which can have wide consequence for the development of a new body of teaching talent in the United States over the next ten years, at exactly the time that this development is most needed. There are now 18,000 returned Volunteers; by 1970 there will be 50,000; by 1980 there may be as many as 200,000. Just as we have found that the flow into our educational system of Fulbright scholars who have studied in foreign countries has given us the nucleus of talent for research and teaching in the colleges and universities, we will find that the return of Peace Corps Volunteers into the public schools and colleges as teachers, community workers, and scholars, aside from their impact on the culture and on the society, can give us the nucleus of leadership and ideas for expanding the whole conception of international education.

The difficulty at the moment is that the educational system has not yet adapted itself to the importance of collaboration with the returning Volunteers or with the Peace Corps itself in such an expansion. There is not yet a full realization on the part of educators that what started as a Peace Corps has become an educational movement with a record of tangible results in the production of new teachers and agents of social change.

Nor is there yet a full realization of the degree of disillusionment in the younger generation with the policies of the older generation—its educators and its Government. Those who have returned from their experience of foreign service in the Peace Corps bring with them a direct knowledge of the way in which American policies in domestic and foreign affairs have created an image of the United States as a powerful, imperialistic, weapons-minded country, betraying its stated ideals by military adventures and reactionary social controls. Those who remain at home have become more and more opposed to Government policy on all fronts, from Vietnam to Harlem. The idealism which found its expression in Peace Corps Service even two years ago has now been directed in many cases into projects and programs of opposition to the Government, and among the young radicals and liberals there is a general feeling that any form of Government service is in some way a betrayal of one's personal integrity.

Already the expansive spirit of the Peace Corps of the early days has been slowed, fewer qualified applicants are volunteering for service, more and more Volunteers abroad are restive under the criticisms leveled at them for serving a Government which administers mass violence in Asia. If ever there were an indication of the success of the volunteer conception of Peace Corps service as a way of educating teachers, it is the fact that this kind of service develops an antagonism to war and a critical spirit toward reactionary Government policies.

SOME EXTENSIONS OF THE IDEA OF
VOLUNTARY SERVICE ABROAD

There is, however, a whole new variety of Peace Corps arrangements which can be adapted to the existing schedules and curricula of colleges and universities. One pattern is the fifteen-month arrangement, in which the Volunteer begins with one summer of Peace Corps training on a campus, with foreign teachers and students recruited from host countries in an exchange Peace Corps role, along with returned Volunteers with experience in the host country, and selected experts from American college faculties to lead seminars and supervise student research. This is followed by a year of college work, usually the senior year, including practice teaching or community involvement, with a planned curriculum of studies in a foreign culture, language, and related disciplines, with a final summer of training in a cultural setting close to the one to which the Volunteer will go, in some cases conducted in the host country itself. An example of this pattern can be drawn from a Dartmouth program, in which the Volunteers spent the first summer in a training program at Dartmouth, the second in French Canada, with their senior year in between, before going to French Africa for their two years of Peace Corps service.

What this suggests for the regular, or non-Peace Corps, teacher education program is to recruit foreign students already in this country, along with returned Peace Corps Volunteers and faculty members with foreign experience, into a summer term for Sophomore and Junior student-teachers similar to the Peace Corps training. Follow this with a college year in a specially designed curriculum which includes practice teaching, using in the schools some of the materials drawn from the previous summer program. Then a second summer term spent abroad, through arrangements of the kind which can be made by the Experiment in International Living, Operation Crossroads Africa, or the American Friends Service Committee, for study, community service, practice teaching, ending with the teacher's certificate and the B.A. degree.

In other words, we can apply the pattern of the Peace Corps experience apart from the two years of service abroad, to speed up, improve, and intensify the education of the teacher for service in this country. The Peace Corps can serve, through its administrative organization, to help recruit the teaching talent for such projects from the ranks of its own Volunteers and their counterparts abroad, to teach American teachers in special campus programs of the kind demonstrated by the Peace Corps model.

Beyond the fifteen-month approach is the possibility of a full five-year B.A. program which mixes the methods already described with two years in a planned curriculum of studies in a foreign culture and language, along with the regular academic subjects and practice teaching, then two years of Peace Corps service overseas, followed by a final year on the campus, and the award of the teaching certificate and the B.A. degree at the end of that time. Western Michigan University has already begun a program of this kind, as have Franconia College in New Hampshire and Wilmington College in Ohio.

One obstacle to the spread of the Peace Corps degree lies in the fact that the host countries need Volunteers with skills and maturity more developed than those possessed by American college juniors and seniors. It is possible that as these experiments continue, there could be a mixture of summer terms in training programs during four years of college, followed by a final term in the host country and two years of service, with practice teaching and study supervised abroad by Peace Corps personnel or by an American faculty member who travels abroad for that purpose, with a six-year M.A. degree and a teaching certificate at the end.

There are, of course, dozens of variations, not yet tried, around the central idea. One could imagine a program in which, as a freshman, the student who wished to become a teacher through the route of the Peace Corps could work out an individually planned curriculum, with the help of a faculty adviser, in which community work, practice teaching, assignment to a Peace Corps summer term, either in this country or abroad, study of foreign language and the culture of the country of assignment, along with the regular college subjects, would prepare the student to take the B.A. degree with his teaching certificate, and then to go abroad fully prepared for his assignment.

Or, starting at the other end, with the B.A. Volunteer who has had either a fifteen- or a three-month training program before service, it is possible to arrange a relationship between the Volunteer and a sponsoring college through which the Volunteer would use his teaching experience abroad as a focal point for the study of the culture and educational system of the host country, would send back reports of his work to a faculty member at the home college, would receive recommendations about his teaching ability from educators in the host country assigned to work with him, and receive the teaching certificate and consideration for a teaching appointment to a school on his return to the United States.

As the Peace Corps continues to develop, it is clear that certain of the host countries will extend their present requests for Volunteers with special skills in technology, medicine, agriculture, and other fields rather than the B.A. general degree student, and that collaboration of colleges and universities can evolve curricula designed to produce those skills along with the B.A. degree. The Wilmington College Peace Corps B.A., for example, includes work in agriculture, using the facilities of the College Experimental Farm and the talents of the faculty in this field, without interfering with the liberal education of the students.

In other colleges, the interest of the liberal arts college in developing teachers would not necessarily be deflected by including summer programs for study and work in medical or technological fields. The need for teachers with technical skill and knowledge is growing by leaps and bounds for service in the vocational schools and the junior colleges in America. A three-year M.A. degree, related to the two years of teaching and service in the Peace Corps, with training before, during, and after the service overseas, would be an ideal preparation for a new kind of teacher with experience in world affairs, for the junior colleges, for the high schools, and for social welfare posts. Other possibilities exist in the case of doctoral candidates, for whom a three- or four-year doctorate in education, coordinate with Peace Corps service, would be ideal.

When the comprehensive, all-year-round Peace Corps education centers begin to operate on college campuses, where a continuous series of training and education programs can be carried on, there will be a new kind of association possible with members of the faculty where the centers are located. Not only will it be possible to appoint faculty members from foreign countries to work in the center alongside foreign students and returned Volunteers, but faculty members not presently associated with the Peace Corps can be recruited for teaching at home and working with Volunteers abroad.

That is to say, faculty members who have had a hand in preparing the Volunteer for teaching or community duties would remain in touch with the Volunteer through correspondence, could supervise research and study projects, and could go abroad on assignment to lead seminars, help the Volunteers with their teaching, or serve on the Peace Corps staff for two years or for shorter assignments during the summer, or while on sabbatical leave, as part of the contract of their college with the Peace Corps. The host countries are now asking for Volunteers who have greater skills and experience than the present young B.A. graduates; in some cases, the countries are really asking for fully professional agriculturalists, engineers, medical technicians, and others of similar talent.

At the same time there is an obvious need for the continuing education of the young Volunteers while they are in service, both in getting help in their teaching and in having a chance to talk to and work with a person who could help supervise a research project; for example, in some case studies of children and families in the community where the Volunteer is serving, or the preparation of new texts for elementary school children, using incidents and narrative from the Volunteer's experience. This would make it necessary to increase the number of people sent abroad by the Peace Corps under the label Volunteer Leaders, who are asked to supervise various parts of the Peace Corps program abroad. Some of these could be a new kind of traveling professor who would go where needed to do what was needed, as a tutor, adviser, teacher, scholar, and educator.

If and when this happens, we will have a full chance to build the education of teachers directly into the curriculum of the colleges through collaboration with the Peace Corps, since faculty members, appointed because of their special qualifications and interests in world education, teaching, and community service, will be able to gather around themselves more and more students whose interest in world affairs will grow as they discover the range of studies and experience open to them in Peace Corps teaching and service abroad.[12] At the present time there are few incentives to persuade students to come into teaching programs in world affairs, except the negative incentive that if you are interested you will have to take more courses and possibly study a foreign language. The idea that signing up to become a teacher means breaking through to a new

[12] The University of Missouri has already begun an M.A. program in community development which includes Peace Corps training and supervision by Missouri faculty members of the Volunteer in the field. Michigan State University has a Master of Arts in teaching which is built around Peace Corps service, both before and after the student goes abroad.

kind of life, undertaken with serious and interesting people in foreign countries, is one that has not yet been introduced to the American student. Now it can be, more and more often, both in the Peace Corps and outside it.

The existence of close collaboration between the colleges and the Peace Corps, especially those with continuing Peace Corps Centers, will have the effect of pushing the liberal arts colleges into a much greater concern for teaching teachers and for the liberal tasks of working on the social problems of American society, since these are the concerns the Peace Corps has in mind. In the case of the teacher education institutions, it will have the effect of raising the level of concern for the liberal arts and sciences, since the quality of study of foreign cultures and languages, the direct relation between studies in social science and the problems of the society, are both necessary elements in the preparation of Peace Corps Volunteers. The work of the college or university in teacher preparation for service abroad, when carried on in collaboration with the Peace Corps, will be scrutinized and judged by people from outside the field of education who care about good teaching and international education but are not in the grip of the academic and professional criteria which tend to warp the judgment of the professional educator.

My hope is that with the extraordinary apparatus the Peace Corps now has for raising the level of teacher education, its officers will not make the conventional mistake of combining forces only with colleges and universities which already have the resources and the prestige to produce the support the Peace Corps wants, and that they will not turn away from teacher education institutions which at the moment may not have exactly what is needed but which, in the long run, are the basis on which the reform and improvement of teacher education rests.

An illustration of what I have in mind can be drawn from the experience of Northern Illinois University in De Kalb, Illinois. Near the beginning of its transition from a teachers college to university status, Northern Illinois contracted to prepare the first group of Peace Corps Volunteers for service in Malaysia. At that time, like most of its counterparts elsewhere in the country, the University had little concern with problems in world affairs, either in the development of curricula or in the preparation of teachers and others for whom knowledge of a foreign culture or language would be a prelude to a career in international education.

The necessity of carrying out the recruitment program for staff to train the Volunteers for Malaysia, the necessity of developing a Malaysian training program for which there were no precedents, and the success of the first efforts in putting well-trained Volunteers into the field meant that a body of knowledge, faculty members, and interest was collected on the campus, out of which new programs for Malaysia and other countries in Southeast Asia grew. This meant that it was possible, and natural, to start a Southeast Asia area studies program, for undergraduates as well as graduates, and to staff it in part with former Volunteers who returned to Northern Illinois for graduate work based on their service overseas. The University now has an institutional commitment to education in world affairs, and the basis on which to build a full international curriculum in the future. There is no reason that other institutions of similar size and educational history should not move in this direction either on their own or in collaboration with the Peace Corps and other universities, agencies, and organizations on a national or international basis.

When the actual effects of involvement with the Peace Corps begin to show themselves on a larger number of campuses, through returned Volunteers studying there, through cooperative programs with the Peace Corps itself, or through the general infiltration of the idea that teaching is a rugged profession in which the men are sorted from the boys, the idea of the teacher as an employee of the school board, neutered, passive, accepting, and unaware of the bigger issues of the world, is going to change radically. There is no real distinction to be made between work in community development and work in teaching. They are both forms of teaching. That is not commonly known in America, where we separate everything. The difference lies only in the possession of certain kinds of information and skill, none of which is difficult to acquire if you are interested in acquiring it.

EDUCATION AND COMMUNITY SERVICE

That is one of the most important contributions the Peace Corps has made to the study of international affairs. International affairs, considered as the manipulation of ideas, rhetoric, and situations by governments is one thing. It is studied incessantly in colleges. International affairs studied as the effect of certain conditions in which various nation-states find themselves, and the change in those conditions by persons who deliberately educate themselves to change them, is a different kind of thing. This is the area in which the Peace Corps has chosen to operate, again, not so much by original design but by the ideas of those who collected themselves and were collected around the original idea. What I mean to say here is said directly by Frank Mankiewicz, former director of the Latin American Peace Corps program, in describing the problems in Latin America with which the Volunteer is asked to deal.

> A lower-class man in Latin America believes that he himself is power-less, and his neighbors are powerless, to do anything about their environment. People talk about themselves as abandoned or forgotten. They have lost the belief that they can accomplish anything for themselves. There are exceptions here and there in countries which have undergone some kind of premature revolution. But in most countries, although elections are held and a democratic façade is maintained, elections have often been only a contest to determine which group of upper-class partisans will control the country.
>
> Into that situation we are asked to put Peace Corps volunteers. Community Development is essentially a revolutionary process, consisting of helping these outsiders to get in. Our job is to give them an awareness of where the tools are to enable them to assert their political power. The only reason that groups take a part in the political, social and economic life of their country is because they are noticed and taken account of.[13]

The parallel between the situation among the poor in Latin America and in the United States is obvious, but it is seldom made real to the American student or teacher. International relations and world affairs are not taught that way. During visits to colleges and universities situated near the rural and urban poor, I heard often from faculty members about the difficulties there were in finding places for practice teaching; there weren't enough schools to go around, too many student-teachers. I would then find that quite often the Spanish-American, Negro, or white poor in nearby areas were almost completely neglected by the colleges of education, either because they did not consider the poorer schools suitable for learning to teach, or because the students were not interested in preparing themselves to teach that sector of the population. It seemed not to have occurred to them that tutoring the children of the poor, after school, or working with them in recreation or the arts in the evenings or on weekends, or showing them how to make

[13] Quoted by Andrew Kopkind; "Peace Corps' Daring New Look," *New Republic*, February 5, 1966; p. 17.

playgrounds out of vacant lots, or helping their parents to form educational committees, is a form of teaching and learning which is more important in some ways than learning to work in the classroom.

What the Peace Corps Volunteer, the VISTA worker, the inner city tutor, and the member of the National Teacher Corps have learned is that teaching and community development are part of the same profession and that as soon as you begin to become involved in the lives of the children in the slum school, you would have to be fairly obtuse not to see the connection between the problems of the child and his total situation in society. "They have lost their belief that they can accomplish anything for themselves . . . Our job is to give them an awareness of where the tools are to enable them to assert their political power." It is because the Peace Corps has tried, through its educational programs, to bring its Volunteers directly in touch with the reality of the foreign culture, that these programs are of such significance in the reform of teacher education. By breaking down the distinction between something called "world society" and the society of the United States, by giving a living demonstration through the training and service abroad of the connection between the problems, cultures, and societies of the world, the Peace Corps is providing a genuine international education.

One of the most interesting of the experiments of the Peace Corps in training its volunteers[14] is an example with many lessons in it for reform in the American system of teacher education. Although it was designed to prepare volunteers to teach in Nigeria, the experimental program could be put into effect, with or without the Peace Corps, with or without Nigeria. The program was arranged under contract from the Peace Corps by Educational Services, Inc., the organization started by Professor Jerrold Zacharias and others to invent new curricula in the sciences, and which has since taken up a wide range of experimental work in the social sciences and the humanities.

The contracting system should also be considered as an important contribution by the Peace Corps to the field of educational experiment. As they have begun to use it recently, that system allows for a much greater range of experiment outside the academy

[14] A full account of the experiment is contained in the Proceedings of the Conference on World Education, 1966; Roger Landrum, Director of the project, described how it was run and answered questions about details.

than most colleges and universities are capable of allowing, owing to the nature of the commitments colleges and universities are bound to make in the appointments to the faculty for the training programs. The Peace Corps style calls for faculty membership, not in terms of degrees held and academic position, but in terms of usefulness and relevance to the project. By contracting with Educational Services, Inc., and arranging with its officers to allow a free hand to the Director, Roger Landrum, in the appointments to the faculty and the design of the program, the Peace Corps gained use of the backlog of experience and research in curriculum of ESI and, at the same time, kept the situation open for full experiment in applying new methods and curriculum content to the training program.

Mr. Landrum, who had served as a Peace Corps teacher in Nigeria, followed by service in the Peace Corps administration in Washington, was given responsibility for training ninety teachers in mathematics, science, and English for work in Nigerian secondary schools. He recruited a staff of returned Volunteers and Nigerian nationals for work in the language and culture, and called upon others from the universities as they were needed. In order to give the Volunteers direct experience in the problems of a culture other than their own, the program went to Roxbury, the Negro ghetto area of Boston, where the Volunteers found rooms in Negro homes in the area, held Environmental Seminars on the problems of the Roxbury community, did practice teaching in the Roxbury schools, studied the Nigerian language and culture, and immersed themselves in the issues and concerns of the Roxbury community while seeking ways in which an understanding of that community could be related to the issues, facts, and values of Nigerian society. The program ended with a week of seminars, discussions, and meetings of the whole group of ninety at Franconia College in New Hampshire.

The staff and the Volunteers had most of the responsibility for planning the program itself, under the direction of Mr. Landrum, with an emphasis on the fact that once the Volunteers were in service in Nigeria, they would be responsible for adapting themselves to new conditions there which, although unlike those of Roxbury, would be easier to understand once the habit of responsible adaptation had been established by the Roxbury experience.

The success of the Roxbury program as far as the aims of the

Peace Corps are concerned will be measured by how well the Volunteers function in their work in Nigeria. Considered as theory and practice in the education of teachers, the success of the three-month program can be measured by how well the students learned to teach and to serve the school and community to which they eventually go as teachers, the degree to which they became committed to teaching as a fulfillment of their own talents and as a profession, the amount of knowledge they acquired in the language and culture of a foreign country, all this to be judged in comparison with an equivalent amount of time and energy devoted to the conventional three months of courses on a college campus.

Leaving aside the two years of teaching experience which the Volunteers will have had before their cycle of Peace Corps service is complete (that too should be counted as part of their educational preparation for teaching in the United States) it seems to me that the three months spent in Roxbury is a vastly superior teacher education program than any of the conventional patterns presently in operation for the education of teachers.

INTERNATIONAL EDUCATION AT HOME

This suggests the application of the idea by colleges of education across the country who, under modified circumstances, could place fifty to one hundred student-teachers for one semester of their Senior year in Watts in Los Angeles, Hough in Cleveland, Harlem in New York, the central city in Newark, or smaller groups in the Spanish-American communities of the Southwest. Instruction would involve the help of foreign students, returned Peace Corps Volunteers, exchange Peace Corps students and teachers from foreign countries, under the supervision of faculty members from the college of education.

It also suggests seminars on college campuses led by selected foreign students and teachers, especially recruited for that purpose, in which the study of foreign cultures in relation to their educational systems would involve field work in neighboring communities and schools where social, personal, and educational problems are most pressing. Or, returning to a basic idea in the Peace Corps Task Force report, the foreign cultures already existing within the United States and neighboring countries—French Canada, Spanish-speaking America, Puerto Rico, Mexico, the Virgin Islands, Indian communities, Negro communities—should be considered as cultural resources for the education of teachers in world affairs, not simply as deprived areas in which poor people live.

One promising area of development in the exchange of student-teachers interested in world affairs lies in direct collaboration with the British. British problems in education and community development have reached a state of some degree of crisis in dealing with the race problem in the urban areas of England, where the influx of colored immigrants from the Commonwealth has raised the level of tension between the white population and the new arrivals sometimes to the breaking point. In this situation, there would be considerable advantage to both the Americans and the British in organizing cooperative programs by which young British volunteers, both black and white, who are being prepared to become teachers or community workers in Great Britain, could join with their American counterparts in educational and community programs sponsored by American colleges of education in our major cities.

Over the past year, more than a thousand British university students have been brought to this country under the sponsorship of the National Student Association for a summer of work and travel designed to acquaint them with America. If suitable arrangements could be made to shift the emphasis of this program to the areas of social development and social conflict in the educational system of the American inner cities, teams of British and American students could engage in teaching and community projects designed to find ways of coping with both the British and the American problems.

THE QUALITIES OF CULTURAL LEARNING

Some of these ideas are already at work in the programs of VISTA, the National Teacher Corps, and the various kinds of educational patterns developed through the poverty program. But they have never been connected by the colleges of education to a concern with world affairs, or to the idea of recruiting into the teaching profession the young activists who are already concerned with social issues and world problems, and who find few ways in which these concerns can be turned to social use within the profession itself. In comments on the use of the Roxbury model as a basis for further experiment, Michael Rossman says the following:

> Programs in which young teachers are given freedom to evolve their own teaching relations, when they are left free to explore, involve much more time-and-energy per student, and are much more effective. Thrust

under a standard load of courses, students can't put these to work, let alone explore further. But a teacher in a Roxbury-style program would have half-time classes, roughly, which would in turn permit him to take on a group of students with whom he could explore relationships at some depth.

More and more, young teachers complain about not being able to enter their students' lives in a broad enough fashion. Ideally, the hybrid role of teacher-community worker, would enable a teacher to know the families of his students, and to work with them: thus, to work with the child in and on his entire environment.

This in turn would enormously broaden the spectrum of possible ways the teacher could involve his students in learning situations suited to them. The sensitivity of both components of his role would be or could be increased.

The Roxbury model has a different kind of academic component, and with good reason: the usual academic experience tends to impede engagement, constrict the sense of the possible, and prevent the development of autonomous skills. A variation of the Roxbury model might be used to change the nature of the academic experience directly, rather than by outside example.[15]

Another way of looking at the extension of the Roxbury example into other forms is to ask where the teachers and the students for such programs would come from, or to ask the broader question, what are the sources for new teachers among young people already interested in social issues and world affairs, and what are the resources for teaching them in the unconventional situations which are suggested?

We have some clue to the numbers when we consider the number of those already engaged in comparable projects, and add them to those who have indicated that they want to be.

In the potential for recruitment of students, we can count approximately 250,000 who have already been serving as Volunteers in tutorial programs and community work around the country; to these we can add a good proportion of the 44,000 Peace Corps applicants each year, only 7000 of whom can be selected, along with the 7000 Volunteers who return each year from abroad; in addition we can count the 13,000 applicants for the National Teacher Corps, only 1200 of whom are in the program; the 15,000 applicants for VISTA, of which 5000 are in service; 20,000 now

15 Memorandum to Harold Taylor, study files. Among other assignments, Mr. Rossman studied the Roxbury program in some detail, and spent the final week with the staff and students at Franconia College. His detailed reports of his findings are among the records of the present study.

working as teachers in Head Start; 5000 members of Students for a Democratic Society; perhaps 10,000 members of the National Student Association campus branches interested in educational reform, social problems, and world issues; 10,000 students associated with religious organizations—the equivalent of the American Friends Service Committee and the youth groups of the denominations. This would provide, as of now, at a rough estimate, 375,000 young people who, in one way or another, already have the kind of interest for work in the human services which would indicate the need for programs of the kind described. The point is that except for the Peace Corps, VISTA, and various parts of the poverty program, all of them *outside* the colleges of education, or as in the case of the National Teacher Corps, brought in from outside, there are scarcely any arrangements now being offered to some of the country's most interesting and talented students which can give them a sense of personal commitment and provide them with the kind of education they are seeking and which they genuinely need.

It is obvious that the Peace Corps alone cannot produce all the teachers with foreign experience which the country must have to staff its schools in the future. What it can do is to provide the machinery and the prototypes for a vastly enlarged program of teacher education, through the involvement of its returned Volunteers in the American teaching system. Once in it in sufficient numbers, they will recruit their own Peace Corps successors, those who will volunteer for Peace Corps service with the intention of teaching when they return. This will demand initiatives by the colleges and universities to invent programs in graduate education built upon the talents and experience which the Volunteers bring with them when they return, rather than dealing in a grudging way with the matter of granting academic and certification credit to those who wish to teach.[16]

SCIENCE AND INTERNATIONALISM

Just as the Peace Corps can be converted into a college for teachers, so can the National Science Foundation, among other institutions. In fact, the Foundation has already become one, with a great many more implications for the reform of the teacher

[16] See Chapter 4 on *The Certification Question.*

education system than is commonly recognized. The Foundation spends nearly one half billion dollars a year on behalf of science, most of it in the colleges and universities, a great deal of it for the education of teachers of science. Because of a serious misunderstanding of the nature of science by nonscientists among American educators, science is classified, for educational purposes, as a separate academic discipline, contrasted in both form and content with the humanities and the arts. It suffers by being so classified.

The spirit of science, which is another thing altogether, is humanistic, universal, international. It belongs with the arts and the humanities as a moral and intellectual force, asserting the claims for the use of the intellect in resolving human questions, in inculcating the habit of truth and the desire for truth-seeking. In this it is the ally and friend of the arts, perhaps the greatest ally and friend they have, since it teaches a fundamental respect for the mind and for the fruits of intellectual inquiry without which no society can grow from an anonymous collection of mass men into a genuine civilization.

This point of view is reflected in the work of the National Science Foundation, where $12 million is allocated to the social sciences—anthropology, sociology, social psychology, history, and philosophy. As the Foundation Report of 1966 puts it, "The social sciences seek to explore the nature of man and to understand individual and group behavior. Because the social sciences are less well developed than the natural sciences, potential for new ideas, new techniques, and new paths of inquiry is very great."[17]

But more than this, there is no sharp line to be drawn between the environmental and biological sciences and the social sciences, properly conceived, since all three are parts of the study of man in his environment. What is to be found, for example, through work in cultural geography is directly related to what can be found in the complementary fields of environmental biology, physiological processes and psychobiology. It is the separation of the disciplines which does the damage. The separation is only necessary in order to mark areas in the organization of knowledge into manageable parts, not to separate the total inquiry into forms of intellectual discipline. While we continue to need to know specific and special things about physiological structure and processes, about the oceans,

[17] *Report for the Fiscal Year Ended June 30, 1966,* The National Science Foundation, U. S. Government Printing Office, Washington, D.C., p. 7.

the deserts and the sky, the concern of the educator must lie in a total understanding of the interrelationships between all of them as these relationships center themselves in human consciousness and affect human growth and awareness of the larger world.

Therefore, when we talk about educating teachers, we should be concerned not merely with the fact that they are teachers of science, but that they are learning to teach one of the greatest bodies of knowledge which the human mind has ever been able to put together, and that the purpose in teaching it is to enlarge the understanding of students as to the nature of the world, not just to give them enough information to progress into other science courses. The National Science Foundation Report notes that scientific and engineering progress has created problems which the natural sciences cannot solve by themselves, and goes on to say "Solutions to the problem of poverty . . . lie in a combination of scientific and social developments. These cannot be produced on order . . . As social scientists search for a deeper understanding of the interactions between man and his environment, they strive for increasing precision in their data. They, like other scientists, have two basic ways of approaching their material—they may observe an existing situation, or they may set up a model experimental situation. Studies of existing situations help show how man actually behaves under conditions that the scientists cannot control. Model situations permit social scientists to vary conditions, and find out how individuals and groups react to the variations. Both types of study are necessary and both have produced results of interest and significance."[18]

If ever there were a description of the way in which sound educational research should be carried out, it lies in this brief passage. The best work which has been done in the field of education as an instrument of cultural and social change has been the result of applying these two phases of the work of social science to the problems of poverty—by examining what exists, by setting up various models, through educational inventions and experiments, to see what can be done through new hypotheses and programs. An extension of this basic approach to the whole field of education would consider the school and the college as experimental models for the development of new forms of human growth and intellectual ad-

[18] Ibid., p. 10.

vance. The curriculum, the community life, the social organization, the lines of authority, the emotional content, the entire ecology of the school and college in society would then become the central focus for serious research and experiment in creating new kinds of development in the education of teachers in an awareness of their world.

An example of what I mean is to be found in the work of Urie Bronfenbrenner of Cornell University, who has been studying, under a Science Foundation grant, child-rearing practices in different cultures and "their effects on two aspects of the child's value-system: (1) The extent to which he aligns himself with the values of peers versus those of adults; and (2) the extent to which these value orientations are maintained or modified in response to social pressures from either adults or peers. Comparative studies have been conducted among preadolescents in the United States, England, Switzerland, the USSR and West Germany."[19]

The significance of this kind of research for the field of international education is obvious, and a wide range of suggestions for further research in these and other areas of world culture flows from the work of Bronfenbrenner and others who, should they become engaged in the education of teachers, would add significantly both to the curriculum of internationalism in education courses and to the methods by which the education students are taught.

Other studies supported by the Foundation—the problems of food-gathering in primitive societies, biology and the medical sciences, the effectiveness of language in communication—have serious implications for the development of new curricula in the elementary school, where the new knowledge provided by the biological and social scientist can be put to work in teaching children about the ways in which basic human needs are satisfied through a variety of local methods around the world with which the children can compare the methods of their own society. The lyrical title of one international project sponsored by the Foundation, "International Years of the Quiet Sun," suggests other projects equally appropriate to the aims of the Foundation, including International Years of the Quiet or Unquiet Child.

In the field of teacher education itself, the work of the Foundation in science teaching could very well serve as a model for educators as to how progress might best be made in raising the level of teach-

19 Ibid., p. 11.

ing talent in general. The goals of science education, as stated by the Foundation, include the improvement of the public's understanding of science, the improvement of subject-matter competence at every level of the educational system, and increasing the scientific knowledge and experience of high school students and college undergraduates. Most educators are familiar with the fact that the new developments in science curricula have come from the amalgamation of the talents of university scientists and those of experienced science teachers, in order to inject new knowledge from contemporary science more directly into the materials offered to the public schools and their teachers.

This approach, with its obvious virtues, has only just begun, in the most tentative of forms, in the field of world affairs and teacher education, partly because funds have not been available on the same scale as funds for the natural sciences, but mainly because the initiatives have not been taken either by university scholars or by the educators. I recommend the language of the Report to describe the coordinated way in which the teacher's education in world affairs should be tackled.

"Faculty-centered activities," says the Report, "are directed toward three major groups: college science teachers whose initial preparation was once adequate, but whose teaching effectiveness has been eroded by years of classroom work unrelieved by adequate refresher training; those who were never adequately prepared for their present duties; and those whose preparation for their major duties is adequate, but who are assigned to collateral teaching in subspecialities in which they are not fully qualified."[20]

That pretty well sums up the problems of raising the level of teaching in the other sectors of the curriculum, including the world affairs sector, except that in the latter case the evidence is that rarely has the initial preparation been adequate, and teaching about world affairs has almost always been collateral as well as subspecial.

The methods by which the Foundation has approached its problem of teacher education have been to organize institutes, both full-time and summer projects for teachers, financed with grants, conferences, research projects, and pilot models in undergraduate colleges. In 1966, 43,400 secondary school teachers of science and mathematics were given study opportunities in 851 Foundation-supported proj-

[20] Ibid., p. 97.

ects, or about 20 percent of all the science and mathematics teachers through grades 7–12 in the country. In addition, nearly $38 million was spent for precollege teacher education activities for more than 48,000 participants, including four special projects to improve the education of the teachers of teachers, of which one was designed to help a State Department of education in the development of in-service work for elementary school teachers.

To accomplish serious results in the field of world affairs we are going to have to attack the teaching problem with a degree of intensity and intelligence and an amount of money equal to that now dispensed on education in science. In this, the National Science Foundation has a large role to play in the future. What it does will depend, in large part, on the amount of initiative educators take in asking for its money, and in making proposals for ways in which the Foundation can support international education. It is worth noting that even the Foundation college-teacher projects in science —an area fully recognized by teacher educators as a crucial one for teacher improvement—were awarded on the basis of only 207 proposals, from colleges, when more than one thousand colleges are specifically eligible to apply.

Since science, like music and dance, has its own universal language, in many ways international cooperation among natural scientists and artists is easier to arrange than cooperation in the social sciences. The latter must always take account of the politically explosive nature of the materials with which they deal. My proposal is that the forms of cooperation already open to the natural sciences, armed with their own particular advantages, should be extended more and more widely into the international community.

For example, should a college of education concern itself with the teaching of elementary school science on an international scale, it should be able to count on a sympathetic hearing from the National Science Foundation for funds which would enable it to establish an international center of research and education on its own campus, with field work abroad. Student-teachers from foreign countries, supported by AID or Fulbright-Hays travel grants, or young teachers with a year or two of experience in teaching science, would come to work at such a center in curriculum development, teaching methods and materials, but also in examining cultural and social factors in education through seminars in world affairs, international problems, and the development of internationalism as an educational and political concept.

The Elementary Science Advisory Center at the University of Colorado in Boulder, established under the leadership of Professor David Hawkins in collaboration with Educational Services Incorporated and the U. S. Office of Education, is a most congenial setting for an international project of this kind. Professor Hawkins, as a philosopher of science with a deep interest in education and the development of science teaching, brings to the work of the Center a broad point of view in international culture, and represents the kind of university scholar whose own work in philosophy brings him in touch with contemporary developments in many other fields. Through the focus of effort on creating new science curricula for the world's children, it would be perfectly natural for that rare combination of university research, undergraduate teaching, educational research, and teacher education to come together in a form of internationalism based on common interests among persons of different cultures.

AN IDEA FOR THE USE OF EXISTING RESOURCES

I present one basic proposition upon which a sizable amount of educational strategy can be built in developing international programs for teachers. The proposition is this:

Wherever there is in existence an organization, private or public, with the slightest interest in international affairs and education, or the slightest possibility of becoming interested, efforts should be made to turn the use of its resources in the direction of the education of teachers. Rather than deploring the fact that too little time, money, and attention are available for educating teachers and citizens to understand the nature of the contemporary world, rather than turning constantly to foundations, Government agencies and organizations which already have the name International attached to their titles, departments, and functions, we should be inciting the whole array of American cultural institutions to turn their attention to what should be presented to them as the major need in the whole of world society—the education of teachers.

If we broaden the definition of teaching and teacher to include all those, in whatever capacity they serve, who are capable of exerting cultural, moral, and intellectual influence we extend our range of international interest all the way from poets to engineers, doctors to dancers, scientists to philosophers, teachers to students. We gain a new frame of reference for the work of teacher education by the simple device of extending the definition of teaching to include the exercise of cultural influence, and the definition of world affairs to include the interrelationship of the world's people and their ideas. We deliberately take advantage of the ambiguity in the term education itself, a term widely used to describe whatever is carried on to develop new attitudes on the part of present individuals in society toward certain goals of the society—as in the education of the public in understanding foreign policy, educating children to become good citizens. An international film festival can then be perceived as an educational instrument for internationalism. It brings together ideas, experiences, realities, and people possessed of a full variety of differences, expressing the variety of the world and its values, yet revealing the essential unity of mankind in the imaginative representation of elements in the universals of human experience. The unifying effect is gained through an aesthetic experience, shared on a world scale.

An international congress in sociology, in biology, geophysics, theater, water supply, public health, engineering, is a means of educating members of the world community, including teachers, to understand each other once they assemble themselves around common interests. The fact that these common interests do exist is the greatest single factor that we have in the continuing struggle to bring the world together and to build new institutional and cultural forms in an international order.

The range of organizations with international potential for teacher education moves all the way from the obvious ones of UNESCO, WHO, the International Association of Universities, and the newly forming groups of scholars in the World Academy of Art and Science, or in Universities and the Quest for Peace; to the Camp Fire Girls (who have made the beginning of an international program), the Home Economics Association (whose member institutions provide upward of 400 home economics graduates a year for services overseas in the Peace Corps), and World University Service (which for years had had a serious influence in internationalizing the thinking and attitude of American college students). We simply ask the question, How can programs in the education of teachers be made a functional part of the work of organizations which already have budgets, a staff and a general intention of serving as an "educational" organization?

The answers in each case may differ, but the intention remains constant. The United Nations Association, through its student branches with their leaders, could organize summer travel-study projects for student-teachers who could spend two months in Africa with their African counterparts on an English-teaching workshop project; United Nations Association summer institutes could be established similar to the Workshop of Nations in San Francisco for foreign and American students of education. The Rotary Club could extend its international fellowship program to include teaching fellowships for college Juniors and Seniors. The American Association of University Women could organize a project for women college students interested in teaching, to travel abroad and study specific topics in the education and status of women. State Education Associations could arrange teachers' workshops in foreign countries for Association members as part of the preparation of reports and discussions at their annual meetings. The Society for Medical Technologists could organize study-tours for investigation of problems in public health in developing countries in which teachers from American medical schools could be helpful. In other words, wherever there is an organization, use it for the international education of teachers and of students preparing to be teachers.[21]

THE ROLE OF COLLEGES FOR EDUCATION

All of this points to an entirely new role for colleges and departments of education. The colleges of education must now take their own initiatives without waiting for all-university committees and collective faculty bodies to deal with the key issues. The colleges of education must make their own alliances abroad, as a few have already done, invent their own programs, recruit their own scholars and students, their own foreign experts, artists, scientists interested in curriculum, sociologists and anthropologists interested in education, and prepare themselves to teach a much more varied student body of social activists, young poets, composers, internationalists, political scientists, and students interested in foreign service.

If they are to retain the title Colleges of Education, they must

[21] Appendix B contains references to various kinds of programs which could be devised or extended in this way.

make good on the claim implicit in that title, and take the leadership in educational reform in the universities and schools, by joining forces with the educational and social reformers among the students who have begun their reforms through protest and social action and have now turned, hundreds of them, to the development of educational programs of their own. This would immediately make the colleges of education the allies of the students I have described, nearly 375,000 of them, and allies of teachers and intellectuals in this country and abroad who are seriously concerned to reform education, teaching, and society, but have few places to go in order to fulfill their concerns. If the colleges of education arrange their programs imaginatively, the best students will beat a path to their door.

There is no area in the entire field of education which is more open and interesting than the field of world affairs, if only because, in a college for teachers of the kind I have described, it offers the student the rangier and tangier experience of getting out to the world, of traveling, of seeing with his own eyes, of having responsibilities of his own to prepare himself for service, abroad or at home. In this, both the colleges of education and the students have official sanction from the United States Government and Congress, in the International Education Act, which specifically calls for the improvement of undergraduate and graduate education in its international dimension. Although the legislation contains no specific provisions for the education of teachers, it is obvious that the provisions for work in the graduate and undergraduate field must be applied to teacher preparation, otherwise the rest of the legislation makes no sense.

Suppose, in the worst situation, the appropriations from Congress of the funds necessary for carrying out the International Education Act are not granted. If they are not, initiatives from the colleges of education are even more essential. Even with the appropriations, the new Center for Educational Cooperation and the entire U. S. Office of Education are powerless to act unless there is a surge of energy and enthusiasm from the teacher education institutions to take on the tasks implicit in the legislation. The philosophy of education represented by the International Education Act, and the President's message which introduced it, is far in advance of the present stage of planning by the educators. It is time to close the gap.

3

International Experience Abroad and at Home

I think in terms of the wider consequences of a particular event, no longer only of its effects upon me or upon a scattering of people close to me. A world issue has meaning in space and time.

Po Chong Mar
Student at the World College Pilot Project, 1963

If it were possible for every American student preparing himself to become a teacher to spend one to two years abroad in teaching, study, community service, preferably in Asian, Latin American, or African countries, we would, in a short term of years, have a situation in the American schools and colleges in which the curriculum and the intellectual life of the student were enlightened and broadened by an international dimension. As U Thant put it, the time may be close at hand, perhaps by 1970, when people everywhere "will consider that one or two years of work for the cause of development either in a far-away country or in a depressed area of his own community, is a normal part of one's education."[1] The opportunity for teachers in America to undertake this kind of service abroad or in the "foreign" cultures at home is far greater than that of any other country in the world, and far greater than American educators have as yet realized.

We obviously cannot send the entire American student-teaching population abroad each year. But we can plan in a realistic way over the next few years to place 25,000 to 50,000 students each year in teacher-community-service posts abroad and at home. It

[1] U Thant, "University Service," published by Division of National Voluntary Service Programs, Peace Corps, Washington, D.C.

should become natural to think of service, teaching, and study abroad as a regular part of the teacher's preparation for his profession. One of the major reasons it has not become natural to think this way sooner, aside from the recency of a broad national interest in world affairs, is the meager financial support we have been giving to teachers and their education in the past. Our magazines and newspapers are full of accounts of the million Americans who travel abroad each year, the 1.5 million Americans living in 130 countries, the comparative ease and modest expense in such travel, but we have never applied the idea of spending money to enhance the possibilities of travel and study for teachers, either inside or outside the United States. Even now, apart from teacher education itself, 59,-000 students and 17,550 teachers were abroad in the summer of 1967.

There are colleges, including the public colleges of California and, more recently, of New York State, which are beginning to take note that study and experience in foreign countries can be arranged for only a little more in expense than an equivalent year in the United States. Yet the ideas for such study have not been applied to the education of teachers. The Junior Year Abroad, for example, which started as a year for liberal arts students who could afford it, has never been used as an instrument in teacher education. Study-travel projects, for college administrators, arranged in cooperation with AID, by the American Association of Colleges for Teacher Education, have been the first small beginning in the use of foreign travel to acquaint the administrators of teacher education institutions with problems of world education. It is not too much to hope that a large percentage of student-teachers, from 25,000 to 50,000, through a variety of possible programs, from eight weeks to a year in duration, can have such experience, and that the rest of the 175,000 new teachers each year can have comparable experience within the boundaries of the United States.

THREE LEVELS OF INTENSITY

In purely educational terms, within the system of teacher education there is a descending scale of vividness and intensity of experience for those learning to teach and to understand the reality of cultures other than their own. The first degree of intensity can only be reached by direct participation in the life of another culture, by residence in it for at least a year, by teaching and by carrying out common tasks with members of its communities, learning the language by speaking it in the foreign community, and, as a teacher, working directly with other teachers and the parents of children in the schools. The figures I have used as the potential number of student-teachers or teachers who could spend part of their education abroad are from 25,000 to 50,000 each year. They are based on analysis of existing programs, including the fact that 35,000 students are already abroad under Junior Year Abroad arrangements, that many pioneer projects are already under way through Operation Crossroads Africa, the Experiment in International Living,[2] World University Service, International Voluntary Service, the Council of Student Travel, church groups, community service organizations, and educational organizations, with charter flights, summer work-camps and intergovernmental cooperation.

The experience of Operation Crossroads Africa, World University Service, the Experiment in International Living, and the colleges has shown that often short, intensive summer travel-study and work projects have a dramatic effect in creating new attitudes and a new awareness of world problems on the part of the student and teacher. The short-term experience is often enough to start a chain of consequences lasting an educational lifetime. In those cases where colleges have made this kind of experience in foreign cultures or American subcultures a regular part of their educational programs (at the University of Michigan College of Education and Antioch College, for example) the effect on the curriculum has been direct and dramatic.

This kind of field work can also be added to the high school, as has been demonstrated, for example, by the Hudson High School of Hudson, Ohio, which has experimented with two-week travel-study projects in the United States by bus, and during the present year hopes to experiment with a semester-abroad-in-the-United States for its Senior class. With the introduction of short periods or semesters of non-resident field work, as at Beloit College or Justin Morrill College[3] at Michigan State University and the growing number of between-semester field projects in the liberal arts colleges, a new opportunity is opened up for the enlargement of experience for the

[2] The possibility of the use of the Experiment in International Living approach on a broad scale in cooperation with the colleges is discussed on pp. 182–84, Chapter 3.
[3] See Description of Justin Morrill College, pp. 178–82.

teacher. It remains to make these opportunities directly and regularly available as a normal part of the teacher's education.

FOREIGN STUDENTS AS TEACHERS

The second level of educational effectiveness below that of immersion in a foreign culture is direct contact with members of those cultures, in situations in which Americans and foreign students or teachers can learn from each other. This can be arranged on a much larger scale than at present through summer institutes in the United States resembling the Peace Corps training projects, either at home or abroad, to which foreign students and teachers could be invited as the main body of instructors. There could be concentration on one country, for example the Philippines, whose experience with the Peace Corps would make the recruitment of the instructional staff relatively simple through present connections with the Peace Corps; or Nigeria, or Ethiopia, which have similar connections.

For the education of teachers and students in America, one of the most important sources of new talent lies in the new Exchange Peace Corps project, or Volunteers to America, which, although recommended by President Johnson for the inclusion of 5000 foreign Volunteers in the American schools and communities, was eliminated from proposed Peace Corps legislation in 1967 in favor of a pilot project for 200 volunteers during this year and next under the supervision of the Bureau of Educational and Cultural Affairs of the State Department. Sixty-four men and women from twelve countries in Africa, Asia, and Latin America, many of whom have already served in community projects at home, are now in this country and have had training in Brattleboro, Vermont, in Boston, and in Los Angeles before assignments to elementary and secondary schools and communities across the country who have asked for them and who will pay a share of the costs of their services. Some of the Volunteers are working in VISTA-style programs with their American counterparts, others are teaching elementary and high school classes, and will not only add their knowledge and talents to the American educational system, but will use the experience acquired in this country when they return home.

Aside from anything else, the Volunteers to America program illustrates the way in which existing Government programs can combine resources in funds and personnel to support new projects in international education. In this case, the Fulbright-Hays Act of 1961 supplies the funds for training, travel in the United States, and administrative costs; the foreign governments supply the travel to the United States and return, the schools and agencies receiving help from the Volunteers supply the rest. But the most important thing about the new program is that it has started an official Government project which links the American educational system directly to those of other countries.

We have had visiting teachers before now, through cultural and educational exchanges sponsored by the Government and private agencies, but we have never had a national program, similar to our own National Teacher Corps and Peace Corps, which explicitly declares the need and significance of the contribution which foreign students, teachers, and community workers can make to the improvement of American education and social welfare. Members of this project, if it can be expanded in size to a scale at least approximating that of the President's request for 5000 visitors, can make a serious difference in the quality of American teaching and learning in the public schools. American student volunteers could be recruited, for example, in teams with foreign students already in this country, for special summer institutes in world affairs, where issues in international politics and culture could be studied in depth by multinational teams. New literature for the curriculum, films, video tapes, texts, translations of novels and plays, and presentations in the arts of foreign cultures could be prepared by the visitors and ourselves. The whole problem of world poverty and social change could be examined in the context of field work by the visitors and their American co-workers in the inner cities and rural slums of the United States, with consequent benefit to the visitors and to the American social system.

Any college interested in doing it could, even with a very small budget, start its own undergraduate area studies program in the African, Asian, European, or Latin American field by recruiting interesting and well-informed foreign students who are already in this country, and paying them enough to allow them time to work with American and other students on developing courses of their own. Talented foreign students already here are usually in touch with others like themselves back home and can recommend students who might be recruited through scholarships and fellowships to join in special teaching and exchange projects where the main goal was to develop internationally minded teachers through the work they all did together.

Another way of finding the most talented potential teachers from abroad to join in this kind of work is to ask members of the education faculty who are abroad on AID missions to consult the Cultural Affairs officers and Peace Corps supervisors in the country they are serving for the names of the key people who would be able to help in selective recruitment or to work through the International Volunteer Service, or the Experiment in International Living, whose students very often know other students in the country they have been visiting.

I would like to see much greater use made of the general idea that students can and should be recruited, from abroad as well as from the United States, to join in teaching projects of this sort, and I would like to see these students have a chance to try out some of their new materials in American schools, directly with the children and their teachers. Once the American and the foreign students begin to work together in this way, the ground is laid for return visits by the Americans to the countries from which their partners in the projects come. With very little more expense than a year of undergraduate or graduate work in this country, an American student, once having begun to know more about a given country through his association with some of its students, could spend a year of his preparation as a teacher in a project abroad which was the counterpart of the one which got him interested in the foreign country in the first place.

If we consider the matter of cultural power possessed by the United States, and the use of the United States as world center for teacher education, it is clear that in the 100,000 students and scholars from abroad who are here each year, nearly a quarter of all those who go to the rest of the world combined, we have a very great resource for the development of a living concept of international education. The present number is only a fraction of the total number of foreign students, in education and every other field, who would come to the United States if given a chance and the small amount of money needed to make it possible. By percentages of foreign students to the rest of the American student body, we have comparatively fewer in numbers than do many other countries.

That is to say, 1.5 percent of the students in colleges and universities in the United States are from foreign countries, which puts us eighth on the list of leaders in the field, far behind Austria (20.4%), the United Kingdom (11.4%), France (10%), Canada (6.3%). In some U.S. colleges and universities there are no foreign students at all, in many there are so few that their presence makes little difference to the texture of the institutional life, and in most cases where they are present in larger numbers, very little is done to give them a chance to teach what they know, either about their own country or about subjects they have previously studied. On one campus where there were nearly five hundred foreign students, I discovered that they had formed national or regional groupings, particularly the Arabs, the Africans, and the Asians, that they held their own national meetings, and that the experience of the American campus, with its invitations to talk to the local Rotary Club or the Kiwanis or the Association of University Women, and its invitations to dinner in local homes, tended to make them more self-consciously and sometimes aggressively nationalist than they were when they first arrived.

A cultural policy adequate to the present situation would call for acceptance of the idea that foreign students and teachers in the United States are a major resource for the development of a wider understanding of world affairs on the part of Americans, and that every effort should be made to involve them in teaching here, especially in relation to the education of American teachers. The visitors are also crucial to an understanding of American aims, attitudes, and ideas in the part of the world from which they come and to which they will return.

At present, the attitude of the American schools and colleges toward foreign students has been to consider them as a category of "foreign students," people who are not American and who have a particular set of problems in adjustment to American education and American society. There is no doubt that they do have special problems because they are inexperienced in dealing with unfamiliar situations in a society about which they know comparatively little. But the services in counseling and the general management of their lives, on and off the campus, are only one part of the practical aspect of their education, and are aimed at induction into the culture rather than at the full development of their intellectual and personal resources.

It is also true that not all of them have the kind of personal and intellectual resources which could be made available for the education of their fellow students, or that their interest in coming to the United States extends beyond a wish to receive particular kinds of training in a given field—engineering, agriculture, natural science, technology, etc. The point is that in developing a national policy of internationalism and the use of public and private funds to achieve international ends in relation to a broad and enlightened foreign policy, the recruitment of student-teachers, educators of teachers, and others who are involved in the educational systems of their own countries, is a far more important item on our educational agenda than most of the others on which we are now concentrating.

This is not only a matter of supplying the funds, from foundations, federal agencies, Congress, and existing university budgets for bringing more teachers and student-teachers into the American education system (a minimum of 25,000 additional students from fifty to sixty countries would be a suitable beginning), but of seeking out students already here and giving the opportunity to those most qualified to teach and learn in partnership with Americans, inside and outside the institutions of education.[4]

THE NON-WESTERN COURSES

At the third level of intensity and effectiveness are the regular courses in non-Western cultures and foreign languages taught by American professors who have studied abroad, or have gained competence in the field through study at home in the various graduate programs provided; for example, through the International Program of the State Department of Education in New York. These courses can become part of the general education requirements for all teachers, as at Western Michigan University where the faculty has agreed that the courses now offered in Western civilization should be supplemented by courses in the cultures of the East. The reservations expressed in Chapter 1 about this approach to internationalism should be repeated here. The non-Western courses are better than nothing at all, but the further away we get from direct experience with the foreign culture and its representatives the less likely it is that the student will gain a genuine sense of the reality of the

[4] Appendix C contains descriptions of the Ogontz Plan and Nations Incorporated, two seminal projects in the involvement of foreign students in teaching in the American public schools.

culture he is studying. For example, if courses in non-Western culture are to be added to the general education requirements for teachers, it would be much sounder pedagogy to invent them from original materials in collaboration with visiting teachers and students from abroad than to offer them, as is contemplated at Western Michigan, to 5000 students, through lectures by American academic experts, televised and taped for re-use, and texts drawn from standard sources. If television is to be used, would it not be much wiser to encourage American students and teachers abroad to make original films, and foreign students and teachers to make such films through their joint resources on the American campuses, than to rely on the lecture system staffed by experts, and fitted into the mechanical system of the regular general education programs? Would it not be possible to staff the entire course with foreign graduate students who were themselves preparing to become teachers, under the supervision of foreign-educated American faculty members?

The use of films and television tapes of all kinds for the study of foreign cultures is still a relatively undeveloped area in teacher education, although progress has been made in experiments like those carried out at Stanford and at Antioch College, where student-teachers have a chance to see immediately what their own teaching is like through the use of television taping of classes, with playback and discussion while the experience with the class is still fresh in the mind of the student-teacher. There are of course documentary films of foreign cultures, and some superb foreign films which, like Apu's magnificent series on Indian life, can become a central part of the curriculum in undergraduate and graduate education. But the unexplored territory where work is now just beginning lies in the use of film-making by students to extend the idea of the photographic essay into the preparation of scripts, made by students together, calling upon children, parents, other students, young people in the neighborhood, storekeepers, policemen, teachers, to act their parts in real-life situations.

STUDENT FILM-MAKING

Many purposes can be served at once in projects of this kind. The student film-makers gain the experience of having to construct a plan for the script and scenario which calls for a far deeper understanding of the social and personal situations they are to document than, for example, an assignment to write a paper on adolescent psychology or the problems of poverty. The film assignment calls upon the imaginative resources of the makers to decide what pictures to take of what, who the people are who would best express the ideas on which the film is to be based, what is the central point of the film itself, what is the setting in which the participants are to be placed.

Although the purpose is not necessarily to make a work of art, but rather to photograph an idea, a situation, or a reality, the components of a work of art exist when the film-maker is asked to undertake the presentation of a given subject. On the side of the participants, or "actors" in the film, there is an unusual opportunity for expression, or for the preparation of what one would say in a given scene in order to present accurately what life is like in the situation being photographed. We have had enough experience in children's theater to know that when children are asked to make up their own plays and to act in them, they gain a degree of insight into the arts which is seldom available to them simply by watching other people perform in plays designed for them. In the case of student films which document social and cultural situations, research is necessary as a central component of the film-making, along with critical review of the results by other members of the class who are also studying the problems and issues treated by the film.

It is not hard to think of a very strong program of student filmmaking on issues and problems in American culture, society, and education as part of their education as teachers. Students could make films on the Indians, the Spanish-Americans, the Afro-American, the Puerto Rican, the Chinese-American, or the American small town, or on whatever topic whose treatment would illuminate their experience of the culture, and could build up a library of film materials for use in their own college of education classes. In connection with foreign study, students who had had enough experience in the use of the movie camera, at even a primitive level, could include as part of their research and teaching experience abroad the preparation of documentary material in film strips and moving picture form, for use in the college of education back home. Or in courses like the one proposed at Western Michigan University, the student who had returned with his films from abroad could, with help from foreign students, discuss the content of his film essay with the students of the country in which the film was made.

In the absence of an opportunity to go abroad oneself, such films and discussion would serve some of the purposes already described, including that of sharpening the sense of immediacy of the American nontraveling student who must rely on books, lectures, seminars, and art objects to gain a knowledge of the foreign culture. In this form, the use of closed-circuit television begins to make much more sense than its use simply for transmitting a lecture by an academic expert. It becomes a live medium for the transmission of direct experience and, since it transmits the ideas of students, is less likely to keep a formal relation of the kind kept by an academic lecture, between the student and the material. The student's questions will flow more easily, since he is not questioning the information and knowledge of a professor, but the ideas and presentation of other students about whose work he can be perfectly candid.

The experimental work carried on by Professor T. H. McKinney, Director of the Field Study program at Justin Morrill College, Michigan State University, has broken some new ground in this form of student film and television production. A great deal of what he has been doing can be applied directly to the international education of teachers. For example, Professor McKinney, as a regular part of his work in teaching, arranged taped interviews and sections of speeches by visitors to the Michigan State campus, including Martin Luther King, Sargent Shriver, Hubert Humphrey, James Farmer, Paul Douglas, and Eli Ginzberg, which he then used directly with his classes in social science. The interviews, which were usually done with one or two other faculty members in the discussion, were the beginning point of class discussions which are led by the students themselves, since that is the way they were designed; students were encouraged to conduct their own interviews with other faculty members, visitors, and each other, for use in their own discussions.

In a more formal application of the idea, Professor McKinney assigned to a group of 46 students in one of his courses, ten hours of video tapes, a producer-director to handle the technical problems, and a studio for four hours each week. The students were divided into three groups, each of which spent five weeks in the preparation of television presentations and mimeographed materials related to topics drawn from the texts in the course, with the results shown to the class as a whole during the last four weeks. Among the other educational advantages Professor McKinney achieved were the experience and knowledge the students acquired in interviewing, in preparing materials for themselves, and leading discussions, along with the opportunity it afforded for him to supervise the learning and teaching, that is to say the education, of students in seven different groups, with the aid of two faculty colleagues.

The possibilities for the extension of this experimental work into the field of world affairs and foreign study are interesting and obvious; they involve the use of foreign visitors, foreign students, local faculty members with foreign experience and training, the preparation of symposia, documentaries, and filmstrips based on materials the student-teachers can collect abroad, as a specific part of their work in preparation to teach their fellow students when they return.

WORLD CENTERS AT HOME AND REGIONAL
CENTERS ABROAD

One of the most intriguing ideas which keeps rising spontaneously in a variety of places is the idea of regional world centers for the development of educated talent to administer to the social, technological, and human needs of every region of the world.[5] I have discussed some of these in Chapter 5 in connection with ideas suggested by the World Conference on Water, at which came the proposal from the United States to establish regional water centers with the help of American money and scientific resources. The idea of regional world centers also emerges in several of the reports issued by Education and World Affairs on the role of American professional schools in international education, particularly in the report on Medicine and Public Health.[6] In that document, the proposal is made for establishing regional "staff colleges" around the world, where "research, planning and seminar-type training activities would bring together professionals in medicine, public health, engineering, agriculture, education and public administration. Students and faculty in these diverse professions might design mutually cooperative plans and programs for the utilization of what will remain into the

[5] See *The Idea of a World University*, by Michael Zweig, edited by Harold Taylor, Southern Illinois University Press, 1967. The Appendix contains a listing of institutions and proposals for institutions which approximate or might become world centers of education.

[6] *Committee on the Professional School and World Affairs; Report of the Task Force on Medicine and Public Health*, Education and World Affairs, 522 Fifth Avenue, New York, 1967.

next century inadequate human and material resources to deal with the needs of the world."

The Report cites the National Institute of Health Administration and Education near New Delhi as a useful model, and suggests links to the United Nations, or a voluntary world federation of professional schools. It also cites the example of the School of Public Health of the University of North Carolina, which has contracted with the Peace Corps for training Volunteers to serve the rural areas of Malawi. The Volunteers will work in teams of two Americans and one Malawian in testing and treatment for tuberculosis. The North Carolina School of Public Health receives the benefit of field experience for their students in broad community health problems, the faculty of the School receives invaluable experience in research and practice by dealing with the organizational and administrative problems of public health in a foreign setting, new contributions to the field of research in tuberculosis will undoubtedly be made by work in a physical and psychosocial environment different from the American, and "documented experience has been gained in teaching (and learning about the use of) intelligent but nonprofessional health workers to perform specific functions, under strict professional supervision, which were formerly considered to be professional in nature."[7] The implication in this approach for the entire field of education is obvious.

Under the title of "A Healing Diplomacy,"[8] Dr. William D. Lotspeich, formerly of the University of Rochester Medical School, and executive secretary of The American Friends Service Committee, proposes a similar plan. Dr. Lotspeich says, "I visualize a regional cooperative center for graduate training in the medical sciences. In sub-Sahara Africa, for instance, there are six or so medical schools that could cooperate in this venture. The Center might be located in one of the participating schools with a good nucleus of African staff and facilities that could be easily expanded. This staff would be supplemented by a mobile pool of scientists from other countries." The scientists would come for periods ranging from one month to a year, depending on availability; students would be drawn from medical students in the participating schools, and would include a year to two years of study and research in their regular programs,

[7] Ibid., p. 83.
[8] "A Healing Diplomacy," by Dr. William D. Lotspeich; *Saturday Review*, July 1, 1967, pp. 45–46.

returning to their work as teachers of medical science, public health, or the practice of medicine to posts awaiting them at home.

If we were to broaden the concept of the healing arts to include education, community development, social planning, and research, early childhood, family needs, and home economics, we would then designate in it a central place to education, knowing that without the continuing spread of practical and theoretical knowledge of how to cope with the total problem of creating a congenial environment for the world's people, from birth to old age, we are not going to be able to make use of those scientific and technological discoveries which the Western world possesses in such profusion. Unless the cultural development of each of the world's countries keeps pace with its technical and economic programs, the peoples of the world will be unable to make use, for themselves, of the tools available to them for human betterment.

As Dr. Lotspeich points out in reference to Africa, the major causes of sickness and death in that region are infectious and parasitic diseases and malnutrition, "all readily controlled by well-known public health and therapeutic measures now standard practice in the highly developed countries. Magnificent as are the efforts of agencies such as WHO, UNICEF, and FAO, these do not represent a long-term solution to the chronic problems of health and over-population that plague the under-developed world. These countries must create their own institutions to train the medical and para-medical personnel who can then plan and sustain their own apparatus of public health."[9] Exactly the same doctrine applies to all educational problems.

THE BRAIN DRAIN

By reference to the idea of the international Brain Drain, we in the United States are continually made conscious of the fact, seen most vividly in the case of medicine, that in the process of educating foreign students, too often we later strip the countries whose students come to us of some of the most important talent they need for the solution of their own development problems. As the Education and World Affairs Task Force on Professional Education in Medicine and Public Health points out, "The richest nation in the world, it

9 Ibid., p. 46.

(the United States) has depended on foreign medical schools for the education of 49,300 of its 302,600 practicing physicians (as of December 31, 1966) and is licensing foreign graduates at the rate of 1500 per year."[10]

The following sentences from the Task Force Report could be cited with equal relevance as applicable to Schools of Education, if the words *Schools of Education* were substituted for *medical schools.*

"The international content of the curriculum in most U.S. medical schools is very limited indeed, and most physicians in this country have little concept of health problems in the rest of the world. This situation will not be improved by mere curriculum manipulation, but only by *involvement* of faculty and students in much larger numbers in programs abroad and in work in this country with students and physicians whom they have also seen in their own setting."[11]

The solution does not lie in forbidding foreign students from finding ways in which their own talents can best be used, in the United States or abroad. It lies in working cooperatively with foreign governments and international agencies to provide the educational help they need in the countries and regions where it is needed, and in creating the conditions in the home countries which make it possible to use to the full the talents of those who have been educated abroad. It is possible to find only partial solutions to this problem by educating foreign students in this country, or even through bilateral exchanges.

Through our AID programs in educational assistance we have done, and are doing, some very useful work in institution-building abroad. But in the next ten years, if a philosophy of internationalism as proclaimed in the International Education Act is to be basic to our foreign policy, that assistance must be given more and more through international and regional projects in which American initiative and funds can and should be central but which are aimed at pooling our resources with others in multinational ways, in order to transfer the initiatives away from ourselves and into the hands of those who are able to take them because we and others have helped them to gain experience in doing so. Otherwise the integrity of our political

[10] Chapter on "The Medical School and World Affairs," Report of the Task Force on Medicine and Public Health; *The Professional School and World Affairs;* Education and World Affairs, New York, 1967, p. 50.
[11] Ibid., p. 51.

and social intent will continue to be questioned on the grounds that it has to do more with gaining political allies in the world power structure than with helping the world to solve its own problems.

Or, to put it more positively, our major effort must be to build into the institutional structure of the world community a truly international point of view of the kind generated by such projects as the International Geophysical Year, the Pugwash Conferences, the Water Conference, UNICEF, and the work of the U.N. agencies. Bilateral projects through AID and other public and private agencies have short-term advantages. For one thing, they skip the interminable negotiations and political complexities of organizing any project at all through a multiplicity of Governments. But the long-run and basic disadvantage is that they fail to blend the variety of national interests, our own included, into the new forms of internationalism the world must have if it is to create the conditions of a stable world order. Fortunately, we are in a situation in which it *is* possible to take the initiative in beginning any number of useful international projects, provided we set about it by calling upon the cooperation of colleagues in education and public service abroad in carrying out projects which are clearly in their interest.

THE INTERNATIONAL SECRETARIAT FOR VOLUNTEER SERVICE (ISVS)

The most striking example of the development of this kind of international idea into new institutional form, and one which has direct relevance to the possibility of establishing regional world centers for teacher education in the human services, is in the International Secretariat for Volunteer Service (ISVS) with offices in Manila, The Hague, and Washington, D.C.[12] The Secretariat is sponsored by forty-nine governments involved in one or another kind of volunteer service in development projects of Peace Corps style either at home or abroad, and is an outcome of the International Conference on Human Skills held in Puerto Rico in October of 1962 to deal with the problem of developing trained manpower for work in technical assistance programs around the world.

[12] A series of documents and publications describing the Secretariat is available at the International Secretariat for Volunteer Services, 1000 Sixteenth Street, N.W., Washington, D.C. 20036.

My interest in ISVS lies not only in its contribution to the international technical assistance movement, but in the promise it gives of finding some new ways to bring the members of the new world generation of youth in touch with each other. It can provide, in realistic terms, a series of practical situations in which international relations are established on the most solid of all foundations—the experience of persons from a variety of national, cultural, and political origins in working together on common tasks of human service to which they are committed. Out of that can come the organization of a body of precedent and a body of literature on the theory and practice of international cooperation. By literature, I mean not only research materials in the social and natural sciences, but poems, novels, short stories, and plays written about new persons in new situations which have never been written about before, since so many of them have lived unnoticed lives in cultures largely illiterate.

Since 1963, ISVS has served as the center of organization, information, research, and planning for the member countries, during which time Australia, Austria, Belgium, Canada, Denmark, France, Germany, Israel, Japan, the Netherlands, New Zealand, Norway, the Philippines, Sweden, Switzerland, the United Kingdom, and the United States have either started or expanded programs for volunteers in service abroad, with most of them administered by private agencies with experience in the field. In 1962 there were many private voluntary organizations sponsoring volunteers in technical assistance, with less than 5000 volunteers who had any kind of Government backing. In 1967, over fifty governments were supporting more than 100,000 volunteers in programs of national development in their own countries and general assistance overseas.

There are now, including the United States Peace Corps, over 19,000 volunteers from eighteen countries serving abroad in 95 states and territories of Africa, Asia, and Latin America, and it is clear that the idea will continue to spread and its programs to expand into other countries. In addition, there are projects similar to VISTA in which volunteers are working in their own countries; over 17,000 young people are involved in domestic volunteer projects in 18 countries of North and South America, Asia, and Africa. A third category of service consists of programs of basic education and training, similar to our Job Corps, for unemployable youth who learn while doing useful projects in public works. In Ethiopia a year of service in a rural development program as teacher or social worker is required for the University degree. Elsewhere, as in Israel and Iran, the program is linked to national service, with the civilian components in education combined with the development of skills necessary for the armed forces.

A WORLD ORGANIZATION

As an international institution, ISVS is a natural beginning point for a world organization in the education of teachers in world affairs. It already has a highly significant reason for existing and a high cause to serve in providing the organization and research center for the recruitment and education of a new and untapped sector of talent in the world's youth—those who wish to serve the cause of human betterment everywhere in the world. It exists for the strongest of reasons—that it is deeply needed, and the needs it serves will continue to grow. It has practical solutions to offer, both to the way in which youth can be trained to serve and to the way in which their service can best be used. It brings together at its regional World Assemblies, in its daily work and in its staff, a cross section of people from around the world who are engaged in the human services and whose ideas about education, social change, and economic development are grounded in experience and enriched by contact with the world's other cultures. It furnishes both personal and institutional links between the educators, teachers, government officials, technologists, intellectuals, and social planners of forty-three countries.

From this base, and continuing with its present task, ISVS could, if its member countries agreed, extend its work into the development of world regional centers for the education and training of volunteers from a number of countries to serve abroad as teams of teachers and community developers in whatever capacity they were needed. Regional education and research centers could be established in Asia, Africa, Latin America, the United States, and elsewhere, staffed by selected teachers who had already had experience in community development and teaching in previous programs, along with university faculty members, U.N. personnel, and others specifically interested in world education and community development.

The centers would be attended by volunteers from a number of countries who would be trained as teachers, medical technologists, or in whatever field their assignments indicated. This would mean the beginning of a new kind of curriculum and program for teachers with many implications for the future involvement of national educational systems with each other. If the regional center were in Nairobi, for example, half the volunteers could be recruited from Kenyan universities, secondary schools, and technical institutes and the other half from Israel, the United States, England, Peru, Iran, Thailand, Vietnam, and France, with service as teachers in Kenya to follow, the relationship between the Kenyan educational system and those of the countries represented at the center could very easily be made direct. A Kenyan student-teacher could return with a volunteer to his home country for volunteer service there in teaching, as part of his continuing education to become a teacher in Kenya.

There could also be two- and three-month summer camps in international education, where volunteers returning from their foreign service could work together, with half their time teaching youth of the country where the camp is located, the other half in studying problems in world affairs, through seminars, discussions, and research which drew upon their experience in the volunteer service. As the report of the Government of Kenya Plan, 1964–70, points out, in developing countries "the government is aware that the great energies of youth, if constructively channelled, could become a vital force in the development of the country. Large numbers of young men who are keen to contribute to the task of nation-building find themselves unemployed, unable to contribute and frustrated by their idleness." In Zambia, thousands of young people are unemployed "because they have received only sufficient education to make them dissatisfied with the subsistence economy of the rural areas but have been given no training in the skills which will enable them to become cash crop farmers. Great numbers have migrated to the towns where they live on the charity of their friends and relations. Many of them played their part in the political struggle of the last few years and now look to the new government in the hope that their past efforts will be rewarded. Zambia's new Government faces a 'crisis of expectation'."[13]

[13] Quoted by Y. Benron, *Camp Oriented Volunteer Training*, Secretariat Experience Exchange Report, International Secretariat for Volunteer Service, Washington, D.C.

THE IDEA OF A WORLD COLLEGE

These are exactly the problems inherent in the social changes now happening in the developed countries to an extent equal to those in the undeveloped. Practical experience in dealing with them in Africa, Asia, or Latin America by graduate students, teachers, and a multinational group of U.N. and university experts, would provide a rich educational program for those involved in it, especially if it were combined with research and educational planning of the kind which the International Secretariat has already been carrying on. The United States could very well serve to experiment with some pilot projects designed in this way in this country, with invitations to volunteers from countries with membership in ISVS to join them for a summer term, possibly with field work in Detroit, San Francisco, or in Appalachia.

As the curriculum developed through such centers and pilot projects, and the number of direct relationships between governments, educational systems, teachers and students increased, the curriculum itself would broaden and deepen in its international and cultural dimension by the personal contributions made from the students and teachers involved. This was one of the most successful results of the pilot project in a World College carried out during the summer of 1963 on a campus in Long Island with a student body drawn from twenty-two United Nations countries, an international faculty, and a curriculum devoted to the development of student and faculty research projects on problems in world affairs.[14]

Each student worked independently and in groups with students from the other countries on topics ranging from the formation of a world youth movement (in which a Communist student from Romania who later went to serve in the Romanian U.N. delegation worked with a student leader from Malaysia) to the effects of international trade on the politics of Indonesia. Each student and faculty member wrote an autobiographical account of the content and character of his own education and what he considered to be its strengths and weaknesses, as the basis for further research on problems in the construction of an international curriculum, and as a basis for the actual discussions of education and world affairs which made up the

[14] A brief account of the World College experiment is contained in *The Idea of a World University*, op. cit., pp. 169–83.

content of the seminars and symposia through which the College did its teaching.

In most instances there were no available texts which dealt with the problems in world affairs with which the curriculum was concerned, and the faculty members and students substituted for such texts written materials of their own which were mimeographed and distributed, as well as original documents from the United Nations, their own national Governments, international organizations, and elsewhere. For example, one of the major sections of study had to do with the control of nuclear weapons and the development of the test-ban treaty, which was in the process of negotiation at the time. The text of the treaty was used as the basis for analysis of the problem, along with materials from the Geneva disarmament conference introduced by Arthur Lall, who came as a faculty member to the College directly from his work as head of the Indian delegation to the Eighteen-Nation Disarmament Negotiations in Geneva.

Since many of the countries represented in Geneva were also represented in the College, students were able to identify with the positions taken by their own Governments as revealed in the documents, and to explain those positions in relation to political and cultural factors in their home country. At the same time they were freed to criticize the positions where they felt criticism was needed, since they were members of a college devoted to studying and finding solutions to world problems, rather than defending or attacking the correctness of national positions taken by Governments. The cumulative body of research papers from the twenty-two students and five faculty members form a basis of materials which, had the experiment continued to its next phase with an additional group of students, would have made the beginning of a new and original library to which subsequent students and faculty would contribute their own share of research and documents.

In other words, both the curriculum of the World College and the body of knowledge on which it was based emerged together from the content of knowledge and creative talent of the faculty and the students. It was completely international, in the sense that it used the ideas and point of view of every nation represented at the College as a means of coming to terms with the problems of world society. There was no confrontation between East and West; in a college as completely international as this one the East-West distinction was obliterated by the variety of nationalities and political points of view represented in the student body and faculty.

Had it been possible to combine with the serious intellectual and cultural activities of the experiment some practical work in teaching and community development in cooperation with American students and teachers, the World College students would have become the forerunners of the kind of regional world center I am suggesting could be organized by the International Secretariat for Volunteer Service. If the participating governments were asked to choose students for such a center who had given evidence of capacity for leadership among students in their home countries, and were expected to enter their country's service in teaching and in related fields on their return, this would guarantee the existence of a common set of interests and concerns among them. To study world problems together would be for all of them an immediate way to learn to understand the size and character of those problems and to learn to look at them from a truly international point of view. It would furnish some of the links we need to put this generation of youth in touch with itself.

The curriculum of the regional center could extend itself into the arts, and could be designed to prepare volunteers not only to help with the variety of technical assistance and public health missions typical of the work of volunteers, but to teach the dances, painting, sculpture, plays, poetry, music, and literature of their own culture. Here the use of tape recorders and films, and on a larger scale, radio and television, eventually with the benefit of broadcasts from world communication satellites, would make a significant difference in the ability of the members of one culture to understand and enjoy the arts of another.

The social and educational problems of the United States and the West are world-wide. They consist of poverty, rural and urban, the under-education of large sectors of the population, the uneven character of the social progress of one sector and one region as against other sectors and regions of the society, the necessity of assessing and meeting the needs of the new generation of youth. These are what determine the common interest which we who are educators and teachers in the West have with those in other countries. It is time to concentrate on these areas of common interest rather than continuing to divide ourselves up into categories as historians, mathematicians, elementary school teachers, postdoctoral scholars. The new areas of subject matter which can link the world together are not only the conventional ones recognized by scholars and teachers everywhere, but the new combination of knowledge of all kinds which creates itself as it is used, and which in the largest sense may be called education. Education in this sense means teaching people to make use of the resources of science, technology, the arts, and the intellect for the collective and personal good of the human race.

THE INTERNATIONAL BACCALAUREATE

One of the forces at work to develop a new kind of international school in the United States and abroad lies in the unnoticed sector of family life among the international community of scientists, scholars, administrators, businessmen, diplomats, and other professionals. When invited to accept posts abroad with organizations like UNESCO, WHO, the United Nations Secretariat, the European Organization for Nuclear Research, or commercial and financial firms, or the American Government, those with families have a natural and serious concern for the education of their children, and in some cases make stipulations about good educational facilities, school curricula and good teachers a condition of their acceptance of overseas assignments. Out of these needs have grown a number of international schools, aside from the American Overseas Schools, in Great Britain, Chile, Denmark, West Germany, Ghana, India, Iran, Lebanon, Switzerland, the United States, and other countries, with the two largest schools in Geneva (1500 students) and in New York, where the United Nations School now has more than 600 children from sixty-eight countries.

For schools of this kind, a set of new educational problems immediately arises; on the one hand to meet the educational requirements of a sound education with a truly international flavor, applicable to all young persons in the modern world, and at the same time to present an education which will prepare most of the students for admission to an institution of higher education in their home country. That means preparation for meeting the demands of national university entrance requirements, without sacrificing the breadth and depth of the international curriculum in the schools themselves, and without concentrating excessively on the academic specialities of any one kind of examination or national system.

The International Schools Examination Syndicate was organized in Geneva in 1964, with funds from the Twentieth Century Fund and the Ford Foundation and the support of UNESCO, to see what could be done by way of constructing examinations which could be applied to a number of national university systems simultaneously, based on an international syllabus of the subjects required by most countries. At a conference held in Sèvres, France, in February of 1967, attended by educational administrators and members of examination boards from ten countries, a general structure of international examinations and syllabi was approved, and plans were made for a six-year experiment from 1970 to 1976 with a group of 500 students each year drawn from groups in various international schools in Europe, Latin America, and the United States. Following two years of preceding discussion and research, there was general agreement at the Sèvres conference that the aims of an international curriculum for the last two years of secondary school should include:

(a) The general development of the powers of the mind rather than the acquisition and temporary retention of an encyclopaedic range of information;

(b) The development of those skills which are necessary to enable the student to profit from a university course;

(c) Sufficient experience in chosen limited fields to enable the student to start specialized work at the university;

(d) The development of at least a limited acquaintance with the contemporary world and an international outlook.[15]

As will be evident, the aims are stated in minimal terms, in view of the particular élite clientele the international schools are designed to serve, but they do furnish a beginning to what may develop into a larger conception of what international education can be.

There are obviously some very serious problems in making a curriculum and a set of examinations which can satisfy even these aims, without restricting them by the entrance examinations required in the European universities. There are also some equally obvious problems in the recruitment of teachers who have the facility in foreign languages and the depth of scholarship to be able to deal with an international curriculum at the level of seriousness required by the experiment. The title, International Schools Examination Syndicate,

---

[15] The International Baccalaureate, International Schools Examination Syndicate; 37 Route de la Copite, 1223 Cologny, Geneva, Switzerland, p. 8.

is somewhat misleading as a description of the work of the educators involved, since the development of examinations is merely the motivating impulse behind a far larger educational experiment—that of developing a new kind of education in the liberal arts and sciences which is truly international. In view of the difficulties inherent in the task, and the conservatism prevalent among educators in general and European educators in particular, it is a tribute to the determination and imagination of the educators in the Syndicate that they have been able to produce outlines of syllabi and a structure for examining which satisfies the requirements and interests of ten national systems of education. To meet the problem of teacher recruitment and teacher education, the Syndicate is developing a series of Teacher's Guides, to be written by present teachers in international schools which, together with bibliographies and library grants, will help the schools and the other teachers to teach the new courses.

But more than anything else, the Syndicate project will provide one of the most interesting laboratories yet in existence for research and experiment into the content of contemporary knowledge relevant and necessary for the modern educated person and, at the same time, to investigate the concept of education itself in its application to the lives of late adolescents born and raised in a variety of cultural, social, and economic circumstance. Not all the children of foreign nationals living abroad have had an elementary school education at home which would satisfy the requirements of admission to a European, American, or British high school, or one which would make it possible for them to keep up the pace in a curriculum concentrating on university preparation. This moves the educator into the question of the comprehensive high school on a world scale, and for the Syndicate project provides the opportunity for research and inquiry into the question as to who is educable, and in what terms.

Should a fully international school concentrate only on the preparation of high school students to go on to university? What can be done to rescue intelligent children with inadequate elementary school education from the oblivion to which they might be condemned by lack of further education suited to their talents? What can be done, or should be done, to enrich the purely academic curriculum of the international preparatory school with allied and complementary forms of education in the creative arts, community development, preparation for the human services? What is the relation of independent study, laboratory and field work, and student-initiated projects to the conventional academic methods of texts and bibliography, lectures, recitation, etc.? What use can and should be made of new materials drawn from films, television tapes, records, and other technical devices? By what means can the students in a fully international setting learn to understand each others' culture, politics, and social ideas? How can an international school best serve as a center for the education of internationally minded teachers?

Although at the present time the educators in the experiment have their hands full simply in developing the new courses and the examinations to go with them, they are conscious of the possibilities of what might result from the present beginning, and have noted some topics for research related to the examinations themselves. These include questions about various kinds of testing other than written examinations; assessment of the relevance of the kind of education usually offered in the last two years of high school to the concepts, skills, and information actually used by the students after they go to the university; comparative study of the content of education in the last two years of high school in European and American schools.

It would be possible, for example, to try out the new international curricula in a variety of American and European schools, as well as elsewhere around the world, and to find out whether or not a unified approach to the study of the sciences, philosophy, mathematics, and other fields could make it possible for teachers everywhere in the world to agree on certain common elements in the content of education both for those who are not likely to go on to the universities and those who are. The Syndicate intends to organize a central research unit in one university, and to develop particular projects in collaboration with other universities and schools.[16]

It is possible that through cooperative research and teacher education programs in the United States, with a research center located at the United Nations School in New York (this School is a member of the experimental group in the 1970–76 project) the work in Geneva and in other countries with interested teachers and students could stimulate new international curricula in the arts and sciences

[16] International examinations and syllabi are being prepared in Philosophy, History, Classics, Foreign Languages, Geography, Economics, Physics, Biology, and Mathematics.

in a variety of schools and colleges of education in the United States.[17]

OVERSEAS SCHOOLS

Coupled with these kinds of internationally sponsored schools and curricula is the possibility not only of using American universities' foreign study centers abroad as a base for international teacher education projects, but of collaboration with the American overseas schools where internships, practice teaching, and curriculum-making can be carried out, in ways comparable to those in effect at the American School in Guatemala which cooperates with the Memphis City School system and the State Board of Education of Tennessee.

The best pattern for beginning such projects by individual colleges in the future is the one in which a modest experiment has been started by the State University in Plattsburgh, New York, which has sent two student-teachers to the American School in Tunisia, along with a faculty member from the Glens Falls High School who has supervised the work of the students during the year, as well as serving with the School itself. Even in American or International schools abroad which are relatively undeveloped, arrangements could be made by which a college of education or university could send a member of its faculty interested in comparative education and foreign cultures, with several students, for a year of internship, practice teaching, and research.

The supervising faculty member would be responsible for placing the students in a given school or in a nearby area, and for supervising the research, language training, or other activities in which the students could become involved. These could include study of education, community development, family life, child-rearing, value systems, or teaching problems. At the same time the student, as an assistant teacher, would make a contribution to the school and to the community. Under the best circumstances, the student-teacher would consider himself to be based at the school while he explored

[17] Appendix C contains a description of a UNESCO project in Education for International Understanding involving three hundred schools in forty-three countries, and a description of a research project in admissions procedures for the universities of the world, a matter of serious importance for the extension of national systems of education into an interlocking world system.

the community, the social structure, the history, and educational problems of the country in which he was located.

What has already been said about the way in which the Peace Corps Volunteer can relate his Peace Corps work to his preparation as a teacher would be applicable to student-teachers sent from a given institution in the United States to work in one of the American-sponsored overseas schools. There are 132 such schools in 80 countries, enrolling 28,000 American children as well as 22,000 others from 100 countries, and their combined resources can contribute in some very important ways to the international dimension of teacher education in the United States. Among the stated purposes in the support given to the schools through the Office of Overseas Schools of the Bureau of Administration in the State Department is to increase mutual understanding between the people of the United States and people of other countries by maintaining demonstration centers for American educational philosophy and methods.

This is a very difficult thing to do in many of the schools where there are shortages of funds and staff, and often a lack of clarity as to what American educational philosophy amounts to, aside from the idea of using the schools to prepare children for admission to institutions of higher education. President Johnson's February 2, 1966, message to Congress in proposing the International Education Act helped to establish one element in what might be called an official international philosophy for American education when he said, "International education cannot be the work of one country. It is the responsibility and promise of all nations. It calls for free exchange and full collaboration. We expect to receive as much as we give, to learn as well as to teach." In referring to the Overseas Schools, the President added that they are a rich resource for helping to carry out the provisions of the Act and for providing "close contact with students and teachers of the host country."

Among the resources which the American Overseas Schools afford for the education of teachers and the extension of international education in general are the following:

> Nearly 1500 foreign teachers and professionals from fifty-six different countries are employed in the American-sponsored schools abroad.
> Local citizens serve with Americans in more than half of the schools' governing boards.

Students in most of the schools can take regular courses of study in the local language and culture.

In nearly all schools, non-American students take English-language instruction.

In a number of the larger schools, special materials have been developed in language and area studies—course outlines, tapes, filmstrips, films, etc.

There are open opportunities for exchange of students, faculty and school board members.

Many of the local educators in the host countries visit the schools to learn how they operate, and there is a broad range of projects in which local educators could cooperate in the development of joint international curricula and research.

Many of the local teachers take inservice courses in extension work with American institutions.

Hundreds of American teachers and supervisors are serving overseas in the schools, on short- or long-term contracts.[18]

The Office of Overseas Schools of the U. S. State Department is concerned to improve the quality of teaching and education in these schools, and is open to cooperation with colleges of education in the development of new projects in teacher education abroad. The schools could, under the right circumstances and with the proper financial support, become genuine international centers for research and teacher education and could extend their present limited forms of binational internationalism into a world dimension. They could, for example, carry further the implications of the new international syllabi developed by the International Schools Examination Syndicate in Geneva, and the UNESCO Associated Schools project in Education for International Understanding and Co-operation, aside from starting new projects of their own.

Although I have visited only a few of the overseas schools, and can write from only a limited experience of their direct operations, that experience and the testimony of others leads me to say that the internationalism of the schools is seldom carried very far, and the character of the schools is essentially American, a suburban white middle-class school transposed into a foreign setting, with nationals from the host country entering what amounts to an American curriculum with all its parochialism, strengths and weaknesses. The governing board with their American members, the American

[18] See "American Sponsored Overseas Schools—A Rich Resource for International Education," by Paul T. Leubke, International Educational and Cultural Exchange, U. S. Advisory Commission on International and Cultural Affairs, Washington, D.C., Summer issue, 1966.

faculty, and the American parents, combine to create a cultural surrogate which is in many ways antithetical to a spirit of internationalism, with pressures, noticeable even in so international a setting as the International School in Geneva, for a curriculum and instructional approach as much like an American school as possible; that is to say, with only a slight trace of international flavor.

Like the schools developed for the children of military and business personnel abroad, the parents, faculty, and students form an enclave which is part of an American colony and, as far as the influence of the foreign culture is concerned, the school might just as well be in Scarsdale.

Yet the potential is there, as the above listing of resources would indicate, and it remains for educators in this country to create the imaginative projects through which the schools can make full use of their privileged situation. One beginning has been made by the American Association of Colleges for Teacher Education in cooperation with the Department of State in pairing seven teacher education institutions with seven selected schools in all parts of the world, with help in the recruitment of staff, visits to the schools by educational experts, teacher exchange, and curriculum development. These activities have been mainly for the purpose of strengthening the existing schools rather than stretching the scope of their work in world affairs. There is also a project in existence for pairing selected overseas schools with selected American school systems; foreign teachers are brought to this country for experience and training, and American teachers work abroad in social studies and foreign languages.

Aside from the usual things which can be done by way of exchange of teachers and materials and the use of local educational resources and community life for field study and curriculum development, there are some variations on the theme of undergraduate and graduate teacher education work abroad which should be considered. Among these are the possibility of regular junior year abroad programs for American undergraduate student-teachers to serve as tutors, teachers' aides, and assistant teachers, while carrying on study and research in the language, culture, and school system of the host country. The presence of a succession of lively young college students, interested in foreign cultures and in teaching, whose purpose in going abroad is to learn more about the world, would have a marked effect on the quality of the education offered. If the concept were agreed upon that each school is a center for the development of international education and a true demonstration of the philosophy of American education in action, we would have exactly what we need to extend the work of preparing American teachers in world affairs, in addition to improving the education of the children and teachers overseas.

There is a very good set of possibilities for doing this with new M.A. programs, sponsored by colleges of education, in which three months of preparation would be spent in the United States, followed by a year of research, study and practice teaching abroad, and return to the home campus for a final semester with individually planned work based on the year's experience. The M.A. candidate, or, in some cases, in a comparable plan, the Doctoral candidate, could use the materials he had gathered in the foreign country as the content of a new course or courses he would teach on his return to the United States, or as the basis for a research study in fulfillment of his doctoral requirements. Programs of this kind would not only be valuable to the college of education and to the overseas school, but would add a new range to the career possibilities for students with the B.A. degree for whom a year abroad would be a way of opening up new areas of interest in the teaching profession, possibly with a view to educational administration abroad, while developing a new and satisfying alternative to some of the dead material in present graduate programs.

In order to free the American schools abroad from some of the restrictions on their international growth, it should not be too hard to make arrangements through American college admissions officers to work with the Overseas Schools to encourage new work by their students in the foreign cultures they are living in. This would simply mean revising the academic requirements which already do so much to prevent curricular experiment in the American high schools. The fact that a student applying for admission to college was educated abroad should be considered a point in favor of that student's admission to an American university, not a defect in his record because he does not present a conventional American set of credits. It should be a requirement for admission that the American student educated abroad must show a knowledge of the culture and language of the country in which he has resided, unless he can show cause why this could not be arranged. At the moment I cannot think of any reason why it could not.

AMERICAN INITIATIVES

If this kind of effort to internationalize American educational enclaves abroad is to succeed, or if the idea of American support for international education centers in other countries is to go forward, most of the initiatives will have to come from the American colleges and universities, especially from those where teachers are being educated. The other countries do not have the money, the facilities, or in some cases, the interest, although most of them are glad to cooperate with those who do.

But in the long run, the development of international interests on the part of American teachers and educators and of a desire to take international initiatives will have to take place on the American campuses, since a relatively few in the near future will be receiving their education as teachers through residence or travel in a foreign country. Whatever is done will have to be done through the local American institution. This calls for a strategy which gives students the responsibility and freedom to conduct a large part of their education by their own efforts, and assumes that the best way to learn to teach is by actually teaching.

The strategy moves from there to the idea that if you want teachers with a large and generous attitude to the world, prepared to understand it, act in it, and teach about it, you must give them a chance to experience the world at first hand, or as close to first hand as it is humanly possible to arrange. You must then accept the fact that the curriculum comes out of the students and teachers working together, not the other way around. Teachers do not come out of the curriculum. What comes out of the curriculum is people who have taken courses, not people prepared to give them.

I therefore return to the idea that the college for students who will be teachers is a staging ground for expeditions, a planning center for an education which can take place all over the world, whether or not the teacher ever intends to teach something called world affairs, world history, or international relations. How far into the world the student can get depends on the local circumstances—his own initiative, his previous education, his temperament, but above all, the attitudes and ideas of the institution he is attending. If he has the misfortune to be in a college which simply grinds out graduates through courses, he may never know that there is anything else than what he sees around him and learns from his courses. On the other hand, if a college turns its attention to how the student can move into the world in order to use it for learning purposes, then he is twice blessed, since he is taught what he needs to know on his campus by what is given to him by his teachers, and he can learn to use it in his life as he practices teaching, that is to say, goes to Ethiopia, or to the Philippines, or to Watts, to practice what he can do to help children and others to learn what they need to learn.

The problem then becomes one of making use of the world outside the college for educational purposes, of using the reality of society and the people in it to stimulate serious intellectual activity, while teaching the student to collect his own knowledge and to find ways of using it in the content and style of his eventual work as a teacher. I have known students who dropped out of college to work in a Head Start project who learned more about education and social science in three months than they had learned in the previous two to three years of their college curriculum. I have known other students enrolled in the Friends World Institute, the successor to the World College pilot project already described, who in two years of study and travel had learned more about international relations and world problems than most graduate students.

It may therefore be useful to turn to some of the examples of college programs which have followed a strategy of internationalism, and have woven into the fabric of the college curriculum the strands which link the student to a wider world.

THE FRIENDS WORLD INSTITUTE

The Friends World Institute, soon to become formally a College, is the outcome of planning and action by a group of members of the Religious Society of Friends who in 1961 formed a Committee on a Friends World College, on Long Island, New York. The members of the group had found that most American colleges to which their children might go were lacking in a point of view about the unity of world society and the need for infusing the curriculum with a sense of the common humanity of the world's people. They set about to build such an institution, nonsectarian and open in its philosophy of education, by which students could spend each of their four college years on a different continent at centers established in Latin

America, Africa, Asia, and Europe with the collaboration of local citizens and educators, and could, with the aid of internationally minded teachers, develop a curriculum of world studies in the humanities, the arts, and the social sciences.

Having obtained property for a central campus in Long Island, and having arranged an inclusive tuition fee which compares favorably with that at most private colleges, the Institute or College has now been in operation for three years, has 100 students, with two groups of them in Africa, one in Mexico, one in Europe, the remainder at work in the first phase of the four-year cycle in residence at the Long Island campus. It would be premature to estimate the quality of the education the World College students have achieved in these first three years of their work together, although the evidence until now is that their intellectual and personal development and their understanding of world society is greatly in advance of those whose education has gone along conventional lines. The startling fact is that in a little more than nine years, beginning with a small group of concerned American citizens, a new educational form of great significance for the future of international education and teaching has been created simply on the faith that it could exist and on the determination that it should begin.[19]

JUSTIN MORRILL COLLEGE

Justin Morrill College at Michigan State University is a different kind of example. Its existence contradicts one part of a generalization I have been making throughout these pages—that initiative for new kinds of education is not coming from the collective university faculty bodies—but it confirms another part, that when initiative does come, it comes from a few people who get up their own ideas, not from the official policy committees. The College was "suggested, investigated, debated, approved, planned and opened" in less than a year, in 1965. It is established as an inner college, eventually to be 1200 in size, using the residence halls of the University, with a curriculum in the liberal arts and sciences which allows its faculty members, who are regular members of the University faculty, to teach courses in their own area of interest and which encourages students to carry on independent study. My reason for citing the

[19] *Bulletin of the Friends World Institute, 1967–68,* East Norwich, New York, 11732, 23 pp.

College here is that it provides an example of some ways in which the large universities and the state colleges can organize their programs to give an international dimension to the curriculum, to release new ideas from the faculty, to give more freedom and personal responsibility to the students, and to do it all within the framework of a large institution. It remains to make more specific the relationship between a college of this kind and the preparation of teachers.

The students at Justin Morrill College are based there for work in the arts and humanities, the social and natural sciences, for foreign language study, foreign study *or* independent field study in the United States, and a Senior Seminar, with the rest of their work, including enrollment in a major field, in the University at large. The College is intended to be an experimental institution, in the sense that it will continue to revise and experiment with the courses and the elements in the program from year to year as more experience is gained, and intends to involve the students in the planning and revising. For those students who wish to follow the prescriptions, the Michigan teaching certificate is available with the B.A. degree.

The international flavor of the College is introduced

(a) by the requirement of a full year of intensive foreign language study,

(b) by the international content of courses in the humanities and social science taught by faculty members with international interests, a good many of whom have had foreign experience,

(c) by the inclusion of foreign students in the residence arrangements,

(d) by the inclusion of all-college lectures by foreign scholars in the curriculum and by their membership in the regular faculty, and

(e) by an optional requirement for a term of field study in the United States or in a foreign country.

Out of the total of 535 students enrolled in the College in 1967, 220 or 42 percent will have had at least one term abroad by the end of the College's first two years of operation. An effort is made to place students who go abroad in homes and community projects through which they can come to know the foreign culture at first hand, with the possibility of a more extended foreign experience later in the college years. In this way, both the motivation and the educational justification for the intensive language study of the first year becomes clear to the student, and the possibility of genuine use of the language and the term overseas is vastly increased by the formal inclusion of both in the curriculum.

In addition, the flexibility in the system makes it possible for a student interested in teaching to plan for the kind of independent study, study and teaching abroad, and elective courses in foreign area studies which would give him the range he needs for his education to enter the teaching profession with a knowledge of world affairs. The foreign study is divided into French Speaking programs in France, Morocco, Switzerland, Belgium, and French Canada; a Spanish Speaking program in Spain, Colombia, and Peru; and Russian Speaking in a Soviet Seminar Tour and a Leningrad-based project which includes six weeks of classes at the University of Leningrad followed by three weeks at a binational camp. The cost to the student ranges from four to five hundred dollars for the places closest by, to $1000 to $1400 for the more distant, with loans and scholarships available to the students. Most of the arrangements for study and community projects are made in cooperation with the Experiment in International Living.

It is quite possible that once the College gains more experience with the ways in which foreign projects can be made an integral part of the education of prospective teachers, liaison with the Michigan State College of Education, with the many area studies centers on the Michigan State campus, and with the dozens of faculty members on that campus who have various kinds of assignments overseas, could result in a much greater variety and intensity of work in international education than is now being carried out. The framework is there. That is the main thing, and that is what makes the Justin Morrill idea so adaptable to other institutions, including the Colleges of Education.

For example, within the present pattern at Justin Morrill, a careful selection of foreign students combined with returned Peace Corps Volunteers could add tutors, seminar leaders, and instructors to the staff of the College, to begin experiments in student-organized seminars and projects, which could then be developed off the campus in the field study term into community development projects in teaching and organizing in the industrial cities of Michigan and the midwest.

Similarly, foreign students and their American counterparts could do comparative studies of the educational problems of American and foreign cities, small towns and villages, by organizing two-year projects which would alternate study at Justin Morrill with field work in the United States and abroad. Since there are already 900 foreign students from 89 countries at Michigan State University, the possibility of recruitment of foreign students to help with the Justin Morrill teaching and project-planning is clear, particularly since at this point the teaching talents of the foreign students, as far as the Michigan undergraduates are concerned, remains relatively unexplored.

So does the possibility of using the variety of international projects in which Michigan State is engaged to support research and study by graduate as well as undergraduate students of education. I have been speculating, without knowing the difficulties involved, on what it would be like if each Michigan State Faculty member abroad made himself responsible for at least three to five graduate or undergraduate students for placement and supervision in a learning situation either in connection with whatever might be the project which took the faculty member overseas, or in some aspect of educational or community development in the area of his assignment. Other speculations entail the possibility that students themselves could be asked to devise projects which could be included in the general framework of Michigan State AID missions, and could be tied directly to the College of Education, to the area studies centers on the East Lansing campus, and could send a mature graduate student with five undergraduates to one of the places where Michigan State holds AID contracts. Whether Justin Morrill College is the right center for developing such ideas is another question. But at least, for 1200 undergraduates at the College, there will be room, and perhaps even time, for speculation about what else can be done in linking the world to the campus, and in creating a genuine international community in the College itself.

The College has already begun experimental work in the use of student-teachers for courses in sociology, through undergraduate discussion leaders and a member of the faculty who serves as Senior Scholar, or roving supervisor for the student discussion groups. The point of view expressed by the faculty members who have planned this program is to develop the unused teaching talent of the students and to call upon their intellectual resourcefulness to find out for themselves the things they need to know. It would remain only to bring into their work in equal terms the Exchange Peace Corps and foreign students who wish to join them in work having to do with international affairs and foreign cultures.

THE EXPERIMENT IN INTERNATIONAL LIVING

Justin Morrill College operates as a base for planning how to use the Michigan State campus, the communities and schools nearby, and foreign countries as resources for the education of their students. Its example suggests another set of uses for international organizations whose business is not necessarily to educate teachers, but whose structural arrangements are such that they could be helpful to that end. I am thinking particularly of the Experiment in International Living, which was started thirty-five years ago by a small band of dedicated citizens who wished to apply the simple principle of bringing people from different countries into each others' homes and communities as a means of creating a better understanding between their countries.

The Experiment has now become a para-educational institution with a spread of connections around the world and a body of experience in conducting education which goes far beyond that to be found on most college campuses. In one sense, the Experiment serves as a service organization to make placements for individuals and groups in one part of the world or another, or to provide, through contracts, parts of educational programs carried on by other institutions and organizations. In another sense, it serves as a source of ideas and energies which flow from a philosophy of education on which the Experiment is based, and, like the Peace Corps with whom it has had affiliations from the time the Peace Corps began, has a very important educational function without having established its own formal institutions. The exception is the case of the Experiment's School for International Training which alternates, over a fifteen-month period, study at the School in Brattleboro, Vermont, with placement in international organizations in various parts of the world.

Such is the skill and organizational talent within the Experiment that it would be quite feasible for any college of education interested in a program for teachers in international education to turn over a group of students for a year to eighteen months and trust the

Experiment to turn them back again in a condition suitable for teaching with an international point of view in the American school system. What still seems unusual to most educators of teachers in the use of a varied set of experiences for preparing students to teach, is a comparatively simple affair to the staff of the Experiment.

They propose no grand theory of education; they simply go ahead with the most direct way of making it possible for people to learn and to teach themselves whatever it is they need to know. Since 1961 they have trained 1265 Peace Corps Volunteers for service in 16 countries in skills ranging from rural public health, primary education, urban development, school construction, to credit unions and cooperatives. Since 1932, the Experiment has placed 22,991 persons in homes and communities around the world, 17,781 in this country, for a total of 45,059 persons. In one year, 1965–66, the Experiment dealt with 52 different groups from 24 different countries on every continent, 468 persons in all, who came to the United States to learn at first hand about their counterparts, in engineering, the Girl Scouts, teaching, political science, student leadership, medicine, and other fields.

It will be obvious that the body of knowledge collected by the Experiment on the question of what to do to satisfy the interests and educational needs of teachers in world affairs would go much beyond the resources of most large universities and could be of very great importance, as it has proved to be in the case of Justin Morrill College, and of institutions without large international program staffs of their own. When asked point blank if the goal of 25,000 teachers and student-teachers abroad each year would be a reasonable increase above the 18,000 American students now studying in 68 foreign countries, Dr. Gordon Boyce, President of the Experiment, immediately replied in the affirmative, and mentioned several centers where numbers could be greatly increased, including the University of Algiers, one hour and twenty minutes by air from Paris, for the study of French and Arabic, with an international student population ranging from Arabs, to French, to Bulgarians and Chinese.

A plan by which several colleges of education in a given region of the United States combined forces with the Experiment to make a program of American and foreign study for periods of six months to a year would make available a whole variety of new plans, programs, and student placements beyond any yet contemplated, even by the Experiment.

ANTIOCH COLLEGE

Antioch College is another institution which has shown by its experiments in combining academic study with direct experience in society that the education of teachers can be extended to an international dimension within the regular educational plan of a liberal arts college. The College is essentially a college for students, with full participation by the students in making educational policy and administering the policies made. Although it is not known as a teachers college, a fairly large proportion of the undergraduates become teachers, approximately 225 of the 1800 students, and at least half of the teacher candidates have had experience abroad by the time they graduate. They meet the teacher certification requirements of Ohio through their work with teachers from the regular Antioch faculty, in courses which do not suffer from the usual student criticisms of education courses, since in this case the content of the courses have relevance to the student's own experience in teaching and education. In fact, one of the main courses in psychology for Antioch undergraduates is an education course which meets the Ohio requirements, and is elected by more students interested in psychology than any other course in the College.

Of the 1800 students enrolled, approximately 900 are in residence on the campus in Yellow Springs at any one time. The rest are working in a variety of ways in occupations ranging from the factory to government service to teaching, with more than 250 abroad for a year to fifteen months in study programs and jobs arranged through six regional centers in Mexico, France, Germany, Italy, Japan, and Lebanon, and through arrangements made with foreign universities in twenty other countries. Through its affiliation with the Peace Corps in training volunteers from its student body for service in the urban and rural areas of Colombia as teachers and community workers, the College has expanded the range of its instruction and field work to include practical experience in the rural and urban sections of Ohio, with the help of returned Peace Corps Volunteers and young teachers and community workers recruited from Colombia.

However, it is in the Antioch-Putney Graduate School of Education that the more advanced experiments in this style of teacher education have been made. More than half of the 120 students at the school are returned Peace Corps Volunteers; they are given a full chance to use their previous foreign experience and knowledge in constructing M.A. study programs for themselves, rather than submitting to the usual set of graduate school requirements. In a period of one year, the students serve as teaching interns in inner city schools in Philadelphia, Baltimore, Washington, D.C., or Green County, Ohio, with two months of independent study, field work, travel, and observation, based either in Yellow Springs or in Putney, Vermont, at the beginning and end of the internship. The variety and richness of student experience of the year, from field trips to the United Nations to two weeks of study in the poverty areas of Southern Appalachia, from intensive study of Camus or James to research on the Kashmir problem or the power structure of a Vermont community, is greater than I have seen in any program of graduate education.

Yet by concentrating on the central matter of the relation of these experiences, in and out of teaching, to the development of the student as a teacher, the variety is of a kind which remains constantly relevant to the intellectual and personal growth of those who are learning to be teachers. By including so many returned Peace Corps Volunteers in the program, an international flavor and point of view are guaranteed, and, were funds to be provided, the international dimension could be further increased both by recruiting foreign students into the program and by arranging for the teaching internships to take place in schools in foreign countries.

The example of Antioch College is especially important in suggesting possibilities for the reform of teacher education, since it underscores the fact that once a progressive attitude toward education and teaching is built into the institutional habits and administrative structures of a college, it becomes possible to use an enormous range of outside agencies, institutions, and organizations to advance the education of the teacher. In few other colleges have I found such an amount of educational energy combined with practical intelligence in finding ways to use the world outside the campus to foster the intellectual growth of students, nor more ideas which could be easily adapted to the education of teachers in world affairs. If colleges of education were to adopt plans similar to those in effect at this liberal arts college, the possibilities for the enrichment of teacher education in all its dimensions—the international included—would be increased by a factor of at least 100 percent.[20]

WORLD URBAN TEACHING CENTERS IN THE UNITED STATES

Finally, I would like to describe a way in which college and universities in American cities can create a new kind of center for world education. The idea begins with the fact the world's political, economic, social, and cultural power is centered in its cities, that each city, including the American, is a microcosm of world problems—poverty, under-education, housing, disease, social inequality, racial antagonisms—and that whatever basic forces there are for internationalism, educational reform, and cosmopolitanism exist in the cities, where the world's major intellectual, artistic, and political community is gathered.

In varying degrees, Calcutta, Djakarta, Nairobi, New York, Chicago, Peking, Rio de Janeiro, Singapore have been overwhelmed by immigration from the rural areas, and the population expansion has crowded the unprepared urban areas of the world with social and political difficulties of unprecedented force. The solution to these difficulties is not only crucial to the welfare of those living in the present cities, but crucial to the achievement of at least some degree of world stability and world peace. The frustrations of the urban population, especially among the students and the poor, their rapidly increasing need and expectations for which the means of fulfillment do not yet exist, breed hostility, aggression, distortion of perception and political anarchy. In their power of destruction and potential unmanageability, the crowded cities create everywhere the kind of internal crises which can disrupt the life of whole nations and spread the elements of disaster far beyond the city limits into the politics of the world.

Belatedly, the American universities in the cities are beginning to come to terms with these matters for which in former years they have taken little responsibility. Centers for urban studies have now been established in some of the major universities, and colleges of education within them have turned their attention more directly to

[20] A fuller description of the Antioch program is contained in *The World and the American Teacher,* pp. 183–86.

the reforms necessary in the structure and content of urban education. A way now presents itself for bringing together an international
community of teachers and students to work at the educational problems of urban life, using the American cities as laboratories for the
development of new plans and programs of use to the entire world
community.

As a beginning, with the use of existing funds for foreign students
and teachers, international teaching centers could be organized
within colleges of education in major American cities and could
make links with urban study centers already operating in the universities. Young people here from abroad under the Volunteers to
America project (Exchange Peace Corps) and others recruited under an expansion of the present plan, plus others who have come to
the United States for work in education, could join together in international teams for research and action on the social, economic,
and educational problems of the city. The research and study would
be of a practical kind, and would include experiments in the development of indigenous leadership within the educationally underdeveloped areas of the city, the development of textbooks and
curricula which could be used in various countries for a variety of
age groups, research in the mental and physical health aspects of
urban education, including nutrition, medical technology, housing,
school construction, social work.

Limited experiments in this direction have already taken place
through the inclusion of a small group of foreign students in the
National Teacher Corps, VISTA, and, as noted, the Exchange Peace
Corps. Although the number involved is too small to produce con-
clusive evidence as to results, it is clear already from this experience
that (a) for the foreign students, direct involvement with American
community problems, in the city and outside it, is a deep-going experience in the reality and content of American culture, (b) for the
Americans who have worked with the visitors, the effect is to achieve
a comradeship with and an understanding of persons whose own
national background is completely different from their own, and (c)
that the idea of the common interest of all countries in helping to
teach those who need teaching most introduces a world concept into
the thinking of those who are in these projects together. Aside from
this it has been found that the American ghetto children with whom
the foreign students have worked are able to relate more easily to

the visitors, and to learn more from them, than they can in the case of many American student teachers.

We know enough about the tutorial movement among American college students teaching in the slums to say that it has brought them in touch with the housing, employment, educational, and racial problems of life in the inner city, and has extended their practical knowledge of anthropology, sociology, social psychology, and political science. The opportunity for foreign students to work in teams with Americans would not only serve to enrich their total educational curriculum in this way, but to help them to understand the application of the social and behavioral sciences to living problems in the context of their own culture. This form of operational research and community action is unfamiliar to most foreign students, whose studenthood is assumed to confer upon them freedom from responsibility for the uneducated and underprivileged. To become part of a studied effort to solve the educational problems of the urban society would be of specific benefit both to the visitor and to his host community in the United States.

Additional confirmation that a plan of this kind is workable comes from discussions with members of the college of education faculty at San Francisco State College, where direct links both to the community life of San Francisco and to foreign countries have been made over the years in connection with AID projects in Liberia and elsewhere.[21] It is possible, for example, that by collaboration with Chico State College, located in a rural area of California, San Francisco State could start an international program of this kind in which students and teachers from abroad could work not only on urban issues but on problems of education in agriculture, public health, rural development, and elementary education in connection with Department of Agriculture programs already under way.

Additional resources for a world teaching center can be found within the Experimental College at San Francisco State, where the students have developed courses and projects of their own, with students teaching other students, often in collaboration with members of the community, usually dealing with issues in contemporary American culture and in world affairs. Collaboration between American students in the Experimental College and foreign students who

21 A longer account of the work at San Francisco State College is to be found in *The World and the American Teacher*, pp. 190–98.

joined them in teaching and in community projects could become part of the work of an international center.

There are many other colleges and universities across the country whose latent interests, existing programs, and future possibilities make the development of this kind of world teaching center a direct extension of ideas already being applied to meet the needs of American communities. It remains to consider the American community as an integral part of the world community, and to take steps to ensure that in every way possible, the one can help the other.

4

The Certification Question

I believe that all reforms which rest simply upon the enactment of law, or the threatening of certain penalties, or upon changes in mechanical or outward arrangements, are transitory and futile.

JOHN DEWEY
Reconstruction in Philosophy

I had hoped in writing about the education of teachers to avoid the question of their certification, since it is almost impossible to write about the subject without becoming involved in technicalities of a kind which can destroy all of one's interest in education as a living thing. But I found that it could not be avoided. There is too much at stake, and too many people in the educational system who consider it to be the central point at which the standards for all education are sustained and improved. To me, the certification of teachers is a bookkeeping problem and should be treated that way, while the teachers and their students of teaching then become free to concentrate on teaching and learning in the schools and colleges.

I have held the oversimplified view that the philosophy, history, psychology, principles, methods, or foundations of education, whatever they may be called, if they have to do with education, can by that reason be among the most useful, fascinating, and intellectually stimulating areas of study in the whole university curriculum. I also hold the ordinary view that the test of the worth of a teacher lies in his demonstrated ability to teach from a store of knowledge and experience which he has made fully his own, not from the number of courses he has taken in a certification program. The test lies in what and how well his students learn.

Now that I have studied the certification question in far greater detail, I hold the same oversimplified views, although more strongly than before. Having visited a full array of classes in education, the main problem in certification seems to me to be inherent in the emptiness, irrelevance, and redundancy of so many of the education courses, not primarily in the rigidity of the requirements, and I believe that it is up to the colleges of education to use the responsibility which is already theirs to modify and enrich the content of the work they ask their students to do. They and the State Departments of Education must see to it that the requirements are minimal in number, maximal in relevance to the practice of teaching, and are administered with a degree of flexibility not common at present among the certifiers.

I would also like to see everyone in education spend a great deal less time discussing certification requirements and all the rules about them, to free themselves for more time to work out what they should be doing to make education interesting and engrossing to those undergoing it. As of now, certification involves hundreds of people whose talents could find better use than in holding endless discussions, conferences, and management sessions about standard-setting, coordination, units of credit, and the rest of it, in the interlocking agencies of the State legislatures, the State Boards of Education, the national and regional accrediting bodies, the National Council for the Accreditation of Teacher Education, the National Association of State Directors of Teacher Education and Certification, the National Commission on Teacher Education and Professional Standards, among a good many others.

There is something about certification and licensure which, once it becomes ingrained in the consciousness of those who think in its terms, has the effect of narrowing the range of educational discussion into a set of details essentially unrelated to education itself. Like all modes of regulation, it comes at the subject it regulates in an essentially negative mood—it demands observance rather than inciting action. It can therefore be used equally well as an alibi by the acquiescent or a club by the stern, a challenge by the rebel or a defense of the status quo.

The fallacy in taking the whole apparatus of licensure so seriously is that education itself is already too formally conceived. What we need is not more rules and administration but more excitement and display of intellectual energy. The less concentration there is on the eternal ordering of requirements, both inside and outside the schools and colleges, the more attention can be given to the process and content of education itself. Otherwise education very soon becomes a series of structures designed to hold prearranged content. Like the teacher-proof curriculum, it produces the student-proof certificate.

The most definitive analysis of the system by which teachers are granted certificates is by James Conant in *The Education of American Teachers*,[1] where the subject occupied the major portion of the book and commanded most of Mr. Conant's attention. In his judgment, the State Departments, with their close connections to the professional education associations and the professional educators, exercise so tight a grip on certification requirements and therefore on the pattern of teacher education that Mr. Conant not only considered this to be the central problem in the education of teachers, but urged the removal of the responsibility for certification from the State Departments to the individual colleges and universities where teachers are prepared.[2]

The effect of Mr. Conant's criticisms and recommendations, along with previous and subsequent discussions of the impact of accrediting agencies, State Requirements, and the whole problem of bureaucracy in teacher education, has been to assign a heavy responsibility for the obstruction of new programs of teacher education to the inhibiting effect of the requirements themselves and the agencies which insist on them. The popular way of saying it is to complain that Albert Einstein would not be allowed to teach physics in the high school or even in the third grade; he would not have met the requirements or taken the proper courses. Each of us can submit his own horror stories. They are many and they are true. But the point is that there are specific ways in which the regulations can be changed, and are being changed, and that is what we should be talking about.

Another effect of Mr. Conant's book, and of the seriousness with

[1] *The Education of American Teachers,* by James B. Conant, McGraw-Hill, New York, 1963. 275 pp.

[2] According to the replies of the State Departments of Education in 1964 and 1967 in responding to a National Education Association research question, the responsibility was already in the hands of the colleges, since forty states report the use of some kind of approved-program approach by which the State Departments accept for certification as teachers those recommended by the college in programs previously agreed upon by the college and the State Department.

which it has been taken in public discussion of the education of teachers, has been to concentrate attention on requirements in general and on the structure of the curriculum—number of credit hours, sequence of studies, minimum standards, major and minor fields—rather than on its content; on the need for release of teacher education from the restrictions of the bureaucracy, rather than on the way in which the bureaucracies and agencies of education can work for improvement in the quality and breadth of education in general. I would like to see what the bureaucracies can do with their resources. No matter what else can be said about them as a massive establishment, the agencies of Federal, State, and local Governments, along with the educational associations and private organizations, are composed of people working at educational problems, some of which are regulatory, others administrative and responsive to policies set elsewhere. The growth in size of the bureaucracy is a necessary outcome of the massive spread of popular education, and this being the case, ways must be found to use its size and strength on behalf of wise and enlightened policies. That is the issue.

WHERE THE PROBLEM IS

The requirements for teacher certification are administered by State Departments of Education. But that is a comparatively simple matter. The crucial point is that the requirements themselves are developed and formulated mostly by deans, departmental chairmen, and professors of education in the colleges of education and universities, and that the requirements are heavily influenced by a variety of educational organizations, each with its own pressures for courses and credits in given disciplines—chemistry, health education, English, mathematics, and others. The State Department is often in the role of referee rather than combatant; in many cases it needs protection rather than attack.

If the present requirements are standing in the way of educational programs which could develop in teachers an awareness of the world in its larger dimensions, then something should be done about them and some changes should be made. Conversely, if changes in the requirements would make a positive difference in encouraging new work of an international kind, then they should be made for that reason.

In order to find out what the inhibitions and initiatives of the certifying officers and departments amounted to, I talked to a number of the officers, attended some of their meetings, read the literature, and wrote to each state officer to ask three questions. The first of these was a question about whether the state departments gave credit toward the teaching certificate for practice teaching and service in the Peace Corps, VISTA, Head Start, and tutorial teaching in the ghettos. It seemed to me that this would be a good place to test the bureaucratic rigidities, since the Peace Corps and VISTA workers are volunteers in teaching, many of them have taught two years, are fairly carefully selected, have had good supervision and training, and have usually had a wide variety of experience with parents, teachers, and community problems, whereas the regular candidates for the certificate have seldom volunteered for anything, have taught for shorter periods, and usually lack the richness of teaching experience of the Peace Corps-VISTA-Head Start group. If state requirements made no allowance for special cases of this new breed of teacher, then they would certainly be fairly backward about all the others.

A SURVEY OF STATE REQUIREMENTS

The letter of inquiry follows:

(1) Have you made any changes in the teacher certification requirements to allow credit for service in the Peace Corps, VISTA, tutorial programs and other forms of practical teaching experience? The reason I ask is that I am recommending that teachers be educated by direct experience with social issues and problems, both in the U.S. and abroad. Many who agree with me about the importance of this kind of experience tell me that it is an impractical idea since the state certification requirements would prevent the award of credit for anything but the regular academic and professional courses. What would be your own response to this kind of problem?

(2) In his *The Education of American Teachers,* Mr. Conant criticized the state certification provisions as a major obstacle in the reform of teacher education. Do you feel that the requirements in your State prevent experiments and new developments which otherwise would be happening in the colleges and universities?

(3) Do you see any special trends in teacher education in your State? In the direction of more interest in foreign affairs and world issues, for example? Has your department interested itself in any projects to increase the international emphasis?

The replies ranged from a simple No, written in the margin by the side of question 1 and 2, with the notation "We do not control the teacher training program in our State Colleges," to some serious and thoughtful letters from State Directors who discussed the problem, enclosed further information, and presented their own views.

According to the replies, the only state which unequivocally accepts Peace Corps experience in teaching abroad as a qualification for receiving a certificate to teach in the United States is California, where, in 1965, the legislature passed legislation to make this mandatory. If the candidate for teaching has a baccalaureate degree with an academic major and has served eighteen months in the Peace Corps with at least 50 percent of his time spent in teaching, he may be certified without further work in education courses or professional training. There is also a waiver of student-teaching requirements for administrative, supervision, and counseling certificates if the candidates have had certain kinds of field experience as part of an approved program of an "experimental, exploratory, or pilot program of preparation."

The most frequent response from the officers to the question about field experience was that although no specific changes had been made in certification requirements to accommodate returned Peace Corps Volunteers, VISTA workers, or others, the Certification officers believed that present arrangements for temporary certificates, and the ability of the universities and colleges of education to grant credit for what they considered to be appropriate teaching and professional experience, give qualified persons the opportunity to become teachers without too much trouble. Except in a few isolated cases, I found no unwillingness among the State Officers to consider the problem seriously or to look for ways in which practical experience in the field could be given credit. Since the academic faculty in control of college programs are usually resistant to the notion that direct cultural and social experience, i.e., anything outside formal classroom instruction, has educational value, a great deal of the apparatus of certification reflects that point of view.[3]

[3] There are eleven states which grant temporary certificates to returned Peace Corps Volunteers under certain circumstances, ten states allow Peace Corps teaching experience as a substitute for the student teaching part of the professional requirements, five states have a policy of review in individual cases, four states give partial credit toward either the renewal of the certificate or toward a permanent certificate. New Mexico reports the beginning of adjustments in its provisions in cooperation with the University of New Mexico. Colorado State College in Greeley, Colorado, with the State Department's approval

A typical and fair reply on this point from one of the moderate conservatives among the State officers reads as follows:

> We have not made any changes in the certification rules in the State to allow credit for service in the Peace Corps, VISTA and other programs of this type. Certainly we are not disinterested in teachers having experience with social issues and problems, both in the United States and abroad. We do feel, however, that this type of experience does not make up for the specific kind of preparation the teacher should have to teach children in the public school setting in this country, and that if this type of experience is to be substituted as part of the teacher's educational program, some basis should be worked out for identifying what kind and how much of such preparation can be accepted with gain, and without loss, to the teacher education program generally.

A 1964 survey by the New York State Education Department found that twenty-eight states grant "some sort of credit for overseas experience. Such experience must in general be related to the individual's teaching field. In some cases, this credit is only for renewal of teaching certificates; in others, overseas experience may be used in lieu of student teaching or other professional experience."[4]

The most common way of dealing with Peace Corps returnees and other special cases of people who have had teaching or field experience abroad or in this country is to have the candidate enroll in an accredited teacher-training program. Once in the program, the candidate's experience in VISTA or elsewhere can be evaluated by the faculty or administration, and allowance toward certification requirements can be made on an individual basis. Most of the replies emphasized the fact that the individual institutions could do most of what they wanted to do under the present regulations, provided the teacher education programs were carefully conceived and backed by the appropriate faculty and administration approval at the college or university. If the college authorities were backward in granting credits to students and teachers with foreign experience, this might be regretted by the State Department officers, but they felt powerless to do anything but accept the recommendations made by the colleges. An Eastern-state Certification Officer writes,

---

and encouragement, enrolls returned Peace Corps Volunteers who have degrees and foreign teaching experience in a summer of professional study followed by a one-year internship at half pay under supervision. At the end of the three-semester program, if all goes well, students are recommended for certification.

[4] *American Education in a Revolutionary World: the Role of the States,* The University of the State of New York, The State Department of Education, Albany, 1964, p. 15.

". . . we approve teacher education programs that deviate markedly from the minimum certification regulations. These programs are designed by creative teacher educators. We encourage this."

The problem of how foreign experience can properly be evaluated came up again and again in the replies. When you have the students with you in a classroom or you watch them teach children in a local school, you can see what they are actually doing. Although some certification officers expressed doubt about field experience of all kinds, most felt that a reasonable evaluation should be worked out by the teacher education institutions themselves. As one officer reported ". . . the State Department of Education is not an operational agency comparable to a college and the evaluation of individual experiences poses problems difficult to handle in the mass numbers that must be handled by a very limited staff."

A typical and vigorous statement, placing the responsibility squarely on the colleges and universities, came from one officer who said, "The belief that state certification requirements are the main obstacle to educational progress is so deep-seated that any attempt to show the fallacy of this reasoning gives the appearance of defending 'lichen-covered requirements' . . . If we have certification requirements which are not desirable, the leaders in (our) colleges and universities are at fault. Certification requirements (here) are determined by an Advisory Council which has been in existence since 1940. If our regulations are too exacting, the blame can be placed on college representatives who dominate the membership. The State Department of Education has three votes on a Council composed of 43 members."

SOME SPECIAL ARRANGEMENTS

The most enterprising State Department of Education as far as the returning Peace Corps Volunteers are concerned is New York State, which has sent an official from the Department to the main Peace Corps training centers to see what the work there is like and whether all or part of it can be used to meet New York State professional requirements. The Department has also organized state-wide conferences each year since 1966 for the recruitment of returnees, and allows credit for evidence of "solid teaching experience" in this country or abroad in place of the regular student-teaching programs.

Other colleges of education, working with their State Departments of Certification, have organized special programs for returned volunteers, usually involving an internship during which the candidate can earn a salary while in preparation, with professional courses as needed. There are 23 such programs around the country, as of early 1967. In addition, 17 school systems, mainly in the east, in cooperation with State Departments of Education, have shown a special interest in recruiting returned Peace Corps Volunteers for teaching service precisely because of their foreign experience. One of them, a program at the Cardozo School in Washington, D.C., was organized especially to recruit and prepare the returnees for service in the school.

GENERAL CONCLUSIONS

On the basis of the findings the general conclusions to be drawn are:

1. While there has been no inclination among the States to grant blanket credit toward teacher certification for practical experience in teaching in foreign schools by Peace Corps Volunteers or others, there has been a general acceptance of the validity of requests for such recognition.

2. Through either the "approved program" by which within certain limits the individual institutions can take responsibility for certifying that teachers have met State requirements, or through flexible administration of present requirements by the State officers, in most States, Peace Corps returnees and others with foreign teaching experience can receive academic recognition for their work abroad.

3. The State officers and most professional educators assume that some actual experience of teaching in the American schools and some knowledge of the history and philosophy of American education is a necessary prerequisite for certification no matter what other kinds of experience a teacher-candidate may have had.

4. There has not yet been any general tendency for certification agencies to take initiatives in changing the requirements in order to encourage new work in the international sector.

5. The certification officers do not believe that state requirements are blocking educational progress, but that the colleges and universities do their own blocking by the way they deal with their own requirements.

THE NEGATIVE INFLUENCE

After reviewing the situation on the campuses and talking with faculty members and students in the colleges of education and the arts and science divisions, it is clear that in their minds there *is* a problem about certification, and that a large proportion of university people, both students and faculty, consider state requirements to be both excessive and inhibiting. On the one hand, the certification officers say that their regulations represent the views of educators and that if changes are needed, they can be made through the regular process of developing new programs in the colleges. "To some of us," says one certification officer, "it seems that 'the Education Department won't allow it' is a convenient excuse."

On the other hand, students and faculty members, especially those from the arts and science divisions, believe that the combination of the rules made by State legislatures, the accrediting and certification associations and the State Departments of Education present a major inhibition to the development of new forms of international education as well as other kinds of preparation for teachers. What seems to me to be closest to the truth is that when serious efforts are made by men of independent mind and informed judgment in the universities and in the colleges and departments of education to carry out programs of whose value they are deeply convinced, the State requirements, whatever they may be, do not prevent the programs from being put into effect.

The main problem is to develop institutional backing within the universities for new ideas, to develop initiatives among the educators themselves which can then form the basis for changes in requirements where changes are needed. Even in the State of California, where the state legislature has taken an excessive role in regulating teacher education, the variation among individual institutions in the quality and character of their programs is still the most important factor in determining what happens to students. A semester in international education, spent in foreign experience and accredited by a given college or university, is acceptable under the state requirements. As one member of an education faculty in a Midwestern university put it, "I can certify students of mine, from the Peace Corps or from Mississippi, if they have had practical teaching experience outside the regular system. If they satisfy the requirements of my courses, and if I honestly think that their practical experience is the equivalent of the requirements set by the State, the State approves."

The real difficulty lies in the reluctance of the educators, working within the system of the universities and colleges of education, to allow change and innovation to become a regular part of their educational planning. That is why educators of more liberal persuasion have found more satisfaction in working with VISTA, Head Start, and National Teacher Corps projects than in the usual structure of the universities and colleges. For the same reason, the innovations developed by volunteer students in tutoring children in the inner cities are much more satisfying to the students than the programs in which they would enroll were they to take the regular certification courses.

As far as the international dimension is concerned, the overriding need in every situation is for faculty members who have a full degree of knowledge of foreign countries and a high degree of motivation for doing something with what they know in the education of teachers. Whenever there are faculty members with appropriate qualifications, or wherever there are programs in operation to develop such faculty members, things begin to move. This is also true of students, particularly those who have had even as short an experience abroad as a summer with the Experiment in International Living or with the Friends Service Committee, and of course a longer experience of the International Voluntary Service or the Peace Corps. When, in fortunate situations, such students come together on the same campus with faculty members with international interests and experience, new ideas for curricular change are generated almost immediately.

THE EDUCATION COURSES

To find out at first hand what the student must do to fulfill the requirements in the professional side of his work, I visited a cross section of education classes around the country, and did a survey of the textbooks most commonly used in a variety of these courses.

What follows is not meant as a definitive answer to all questions about education courses, but it does represent part of the answer to quite a few questions.

First of all, I was struck by the variety in the amount of requirements, as well as by the actual amount of them. The assumption seemed to be that whatever is not required will go undone, and that no one in teaching ever docs anything because he wants to and needs to. The general pattern of curriculum calls for 50 to 65 semester hours in general education, usually in the first two years; 10 to 25 hours in a major academic field, 15 to 30 hours in education courses, and 6 to 14 in practice teaching. The variations in quality of teaching in the education courses was staggering, and ranged from methods courses, related to direct experience of students with children in school and the community which were vibrant and full of interesting educational ideas and practical content, to courses which were quite obviously a waste of time for everyone concerned. I must report that the latter kind predominated.

I do not wish to join in the general denunciation of education and methods courses, except to say that in most of those visited and in most of the texts reviewed I found little intellectual nourishment and little practical help in becoming a good teacher. The heart of the matter lies in giving the student who intends to become a teacher a direct experience in teaching children very early in his preparation, preferably in high school, and certainly not later than the Freshman year in college, in order that the study of the methods and content of education as a discipline and a body of knowledge can give him something to which he can respond from his own experience. He needs to study education, but as he studies he needs to practice it. Otherwise, it is simply like teaching a boy to play basketball by showing him charts of plays.

The education courses as a whole were, as is so commonly reported by critics, intellectually sterile and largely irrelevant to the needs of students and to their preparation as informed teachers and educators. In one class, the 150 students and I (most of the students were Juniors) spent the fifty minutes in desultory discussion, led by the professor, of one half-page of mimeographed description, the entire reading assignment for the day, of present teacher shortages. The intention of the professor seemed only to be to reassure the members of the class that jobs would be waiting for them after they graduated, depending on whether they expected to teach mathematics in high school or the general program in elementary school. That is literally all that was learned that day.

In another class, for thirty elementary school candidates, I spent fifteen minutes listening to the professor tell us how to teach first-graders to fold a letter and to indent the first paragraph. In another, for a mixed group of one hundred students, the professor raced through a description of existentialism, scholasticism, and pragmatism, one after the other, in fifty minutes, with references to two or three philosophers representative of each as he went, pausing at intervals to allow the note-takers to catch up with him.

On the other hand, one of the most interesting and stimulating classes of all those visited in the liberal arts *or* education, was in methods of education, with forty students of various ages, each of whom had been conducting field work on the problem of the high school drop-out. The class, of two hours in length, listened to a twenty-minute taped interview with a drop-out, conducted by a student who, with two other students, was responsible for presenting a three-quarter hour symposium on the subject of the drop-out, using the case materials collected.

The rest of the class time consisted of reports and discussion by the class of their own experience, and critical evaluation of the methods for rescuing drop-outs which each had found in progress in the schools and cases studied. The teacher of the class remained in the background of the circle of students, occasionally raised her own questions, made sure that certain points were developed, counting on the momentum generated by the students themselves to carry the ideas and theories into a sufficient degree of clarity.

The tragedy is that in a field as rich in intellectual content and aesthetic experience as the field of education, so little is done to infuse the lives of the students with ideas and modes of knowledge drawn from history, philosophy, anthropology, sociology, literature, and the creative arts. To be involved in one or another kind of education, formal or informal, is the universal experience of man, and the study of education is the study of every question of importance in the field of philosophy and history which man has ever asked, from the question of how should a life be lived to the question of how things came to be as they are. To study a school is to study the entire culture of man in one of its particular manifestations. To prepare oneself to become a teacher is to undertake a process of personal development and cultural growth which includes the added dimension of learning how to transpose what one knows into a form which can make it available to others.

Yet when the general education courses offer surveys and brief descriptions of elements of knowledge from the academic disciplines, when history is taught and education is taught by the use of lectures and texts which seem to be one long series of topic sentences and subheadings about things which possess no intrinsic interest or importance, one can see why so many teachers entering the service of the schools carry with them no serious intellectual interests of their own and so often have learned nothing more than a technique for the use of similar materials and texts adapted to the age group of the children they are teaching.

In the course of visiting the classes and reviewing the texts, I came to a clearer understanding of what are the operating mechanisms in keeping the system of teacher education at its present level of achievement. It is not only the interlocking forces of custom and habit which join together the State Departments of Education, the colleges of education, the accreditating and certification agencies, and the practices of the schools. What dominates the profession and its practices is a false conception of what knowledge is, and how it can be organized and communicated. The conception is based on a confusion between knowledge and information. It is assumed that the known facts about a given subject must be organized systematically in linear form, and communicated in the same form by the written or spoken word.

Once that idea is accepted, the rest of the system—from textbooks to audiovisual aids, to semester hours of this and that, to practice teaching and methods courses—logically follows. What the system does is to eliminate the teacher as "an intermediary inventive mind." Although I can align myself with Mr. Conant in his wish to make the practice of teaching the center of the student's professional work, and to make colleges and universities fully responsible for certifying that their graduates can actually teach, I do not think that the kind of practice the students are now getting is very likely to do much more than encourage the deadly idea that becoming educated is the same thing as collecting an organized body of information.

Let me give an example. In one of the education texts, a reputable one, I found a series of readings which had to do with the theory of learning. One of the readings was introduced by the following note:

This description of the learning process is taken from a study by a national committee of the relation between learning and instructional process. After suggesting a definition of learning, the authors outline the structure of the learning process in a simplified schematic diagram, discuss its interpretations, and indicate the key processive concepts which they believe to be useful in understanding the characteristics of change in learning.

Most of what I mean is included in this unhappy pair of sentences. Why on earth would anybody, a student or a nonstudent, want to read a description of the learning process by a national committee? What good could come from looking at a simplified schematic diagram? Or "key processive concepts"?

All the trappings of the academy are here, the flat banal style of academic language, the didactic tone, the habit of summarizing the topic to be dealt with, the reference to academic authority. I will spare the reader the excerpt of committee prose which follows the introductory note, and describe it simply as a set of statements which answered no questions which students would be likely to ask about how the mind works or how learning takes place, and could serve no useful purpose in helping the student to learn about teaching or about learning.

Most of what is taught to undergraduate students, in and out of education courses, is organized according to this style of pedagogy. This is what I mean when I say that all the parts of the system, from lecturer to text to examination to grade to award of credit, are coherent.

Another side of the same pedagogy turns up in the constant use of anthologies and readings for courses in introduction to education which, as far as the title of the course is concerned, opens up a full opportunity to include anything at all which seems important to the teacher. I mean by this that an introduction to education could be one of the very best and most valuable courses in the whole of higher learning if only it were taught with a degree of understanding and knowledge appropriate to its title. It could include the study in depth of children in the neighborhood, it could include tutoring children and college students, novels and plays, a study of child-rearing and education in French Canada, Mexico, Poland, or Bali.

Yet the anthologies and introductory texts are arranged in the conventional sets of topics familiar to all colleges of education, without reference to readings in foreign literature or culture, as if there were only one content to the whole of education. If anthologies with a variety of topics and writers are to be used at all, they should be used as reference books, to be read over a period of a week or so, and to be consulted for figures, topics, and information. In several of the anthologies I came across articles of my own, and was astonished to find that even these seemed not very interesting to me, and, I would imagine, not very interesting to the students, since they had been written in other contexts and for other purposes. It seemed to me that it would be much better if the teachers of student-teachers wrote their own articles and asked their students to do the same.

In any case, short pieces, classified under topics and administered to students week by week, cannot provide the nourishment they need or the impetus to further thought. The whole procedure does not allow the student to put together a body of knowledge and a set of experiences which can give him an intellectual life and a style of his own. It does not call upon the best that is in him, but only on those peripheral human abilities which have to do with following a given outline, pattern, chart, or guide to a stated and prescribed body of information.

THE EDUCATION TEXTS

"Are you ready for the most interesting, the most satisfying, the most thrilling of your educational experiences thus far?" trills the opening sentence of a text on student teaching in the secondary school.

Another text begins, "'This semester I'm doing my student teaching,' What does the foregoing statement mean to you? Have you thought through the term 'student-teacher'? What abilities, skills, and understanding should you possess?" On the next page, a student is reported as saying, "Well, this is it. This is the time when I go out and see if all the things they taught me in the past three years are true. What is it like out there?" Later, the text warns about possible problems the teacher will face. "One of the major weaknesses among student teachers is that they have spent four years in a University where they were subject to a great deal of front-of-the-class lecturing. Many student-teachers assume this same technique when they begin teaching." Why then have the writers of this text and the other educators not stopped weakening their students by front-of-the-class lecturing?

A third text, in wide use, after describing what schools are like, produces the usual check list of teachers' attributes for the student to consider, and among the items raises the questions:

> "Is your hair neatly arranged, free from dandruff, frequently washed?"

> "Are your nails carefully manicured and your skin free from blemishes?"

> "Do you have an upright posture and a free-swinging walk?"

Other texts, with their own lists, ask the student-teacher to decide whether he has the appropriate personality for the classroom, and to rate himself and other teachers on such questions as personality, sparkle, drive, vitality, warmth, radiation. Another defines the teacher as one who "stimulates and directs learning activities." Another provides the information that "The modern library usually is housed in an attractive, well-constructed building, and it is so organized that readers can meet their needs effectively and with as little lost motion as possible."

As I read the texts I could recognize the tone of voice and the feel of the classrooms in the education courses I had visited—the treatment of college students as if they too were elementary and high school children, to be spoken to and encouraged, with sparkle, warmth, friendliness, and well-combed hair. I could also see, in the conflicting internal evidence of the texts, like the one which warned students about carrying over a front-of-the-class lecturing style, the other which warned the student that he was about to be thrilled by meeting real children, and the student who declared that he was about to go out to see if what he had been told all these years was true, that even the practical implications of what was being said in the college classrooms were not examined to see if what was being said had anything to do with reality.

When I turned to the classes and to the texts in the philosophy of education and in the introduction to education, I found different but comparable materials. In one of the latter classes and its text I found the following topics, all included within fifteen pages which the students had been asked to read:

The Advance of Science and Technology
Impact of Industrialization
Growth of Nationalism

Consequences of Imperialism
Effects of Militarism
Uses of Propaganda
Tragedy of the "Great War"
Failure of the League of Nations
Rise of Dictatorships and Totalitarian States
World War II and the United Nations
The Threat of Russian Communism
Challenge to Education

I leave to the reader the task of working out how much space in the text was devoted to each of these huge topics.

In the text in the philosophy of education I found the same absurd summary outlines which I had found in the lectures of the education professors. In a chapter of nineteen pages, there were short statements on free will, the nature of man, the meaning of metaphysics, and a description of the philosophy of education from Plato to Aquinas. Later in the book, we were told, "Impatient with scholastic thought, Sir Francis Bacon urged men to discard the idols of thought and begin anew by careful empirical observation of data and the treatment of these data by an inductive method. Hobbes, a materialist, believed mind to be motion in the head . . ."

Without completing the full circuit of basic education courses as they are commonly taught, this may be enough to indicate what I found. There were some good courses and good teachers. There were occasional good texts in the history, philosophy, psychology, and sociology of education, although not very many of them were in general use, mainly, I gathered, because the teachers of the education courses did not think the students were ready for works of as serious a kind as these. In any case, the idea of using a basic text around which an entire course can be built seems to me to be false pedagogy from the start.

I am therefore compelled to submit the testimony that most of the courses I visited were of the kind I have described, and that I was struck over and over again by the fact that under the present system the colleges and departments of education do control a sizable block of time of the students intending to become teachers, for periods ranging from twenty to thirty semester hours of instruction, along with additional time for whatever practice teaching may be considered appropriate. Yet at no point, except for a few instances where comparative education courses were offered as electives, was there any indication that the study of education itself had within it some extraordinarily important areas for the study of foreign cultures and world affairs.

SOME SUGGESTED REFORMS

If the development of the professional courses in education had all along been the work of diverse minds, trained in a variety of fields and skilled in the arts of teaching, able and willing to bring the fruits of scholarship into the lives and working interests of students and teachers, we would already have the rich blend of professional, vocational, and liberal studies our educational system so desperately needs. What makes a study liberal is not its detachment from something else called vocational or professional, or from the cultural context in which it will be used. It becomes a liberal study by reason of the way in which it enriches one's understanding of man, nature, and society.

Academic study detached from aesthetic, personal, or cultural relevance to the life of the student and teacher is not liberal education, it is vocational. It gives him a stone when he asks for bread. Vocational training detached from intellectual interests and cultural concerns is not preparation for teaching, it is technical training for doing something other than teaching—for performing the duties of a paid employee. In a broader conception of teaching, the college student who listens in class to a record of Dylan Thomas reading his poems is learning to hear, to feel, to understand the words and the truth the poet has to tell, not learning how to use the gramophone to teach poetry. The student who spends time in class with children who tell stories, draw, paint, and sing is not being technically trained to teach, but is learning to understand children and the arts through being in the presence of children. Is one liberal and the other vocational? They are both valuable kinds of experience in practical learning. What they are depends completely on the way they are done, and the way the teacher who is inducting the student into the world of teaching can make the experience of working with children a liberating art, and can make study in the liberal arts a liberating experience.

The most natural thing to do in developing education courses which can bring the full variety of the world into the consciousness of the student would be to use the approach of the anthropologist, which in essence is the approach of comparative education. If we analyze the curriculum of education courses from this point of view, internationalism, or the study of cultural values and ideas in a world setting, is at present badly served. There are only seven centers of research and teaching in comparative education in the United States where serious work in comparative education is now going on, and even in the case of those centers, with one to four faculty members each, the influence they exert on the main body of education students is minimal.

There are approximately 700 faculty members who teach comparative education in all schools and departments of education in the United States. Most of them teach only part-time, in one course in the field, with their main work in the foundations courses and the conventional curriculum. The history of the comparative education movement within the educating community has been relatively short, having begun to take shape in the late 1940s, with an emphasis on the philosophy and history of education in various countries. Since then, the movement has broadened its interests and increased the scope of its research, but not at a rate comparable to the speed of advance in centers for area studies and for international economic and social development, in spite of the fact that in many ways these are supporting and complementary disciplines to the study of education.

The hope for the future of this kind of advance lies in persuading into the field students and scholars who have not as yet realized what an amount of vitality can be injected into the study of education when you study the way it works in several different countries. One road to persuasion is to send graduate students into foreign countries as part of their M.A. and Ph.D. programs and ask them to prepare themselves to teach new courses in education which use what they have learned abroad when they come back home.

Suppose a college set out to build some new courses in education in this way. Suppose three cultures were chosen for the work of an introductory course—Nigeria, Indonesia, and the United States. It would be perfectly natural to send three or four graduate students to Nigeria and to Indonesia with a specific assignment to study the educational system of that country by working in it —with Nigerian and Indonesian teachers, university scholars, and community leaders—and for them then to return home for further work in developing a teaching program in education. Selected Nigerian and Indonesian students, some already in this country, others recruited on scholarships, could be brought together with American graduate students in education who knew something about these countries from texts available in the United States.

Together, under the supervision of a faculty member in comparative education who knew the Nigerian, Indonesian, and American fields, these students could carry out the basic research necessary for putting together an introductory course for freshmen and sophomores who intended to become teachers. Practice teaching by the graduate students could be done in freshman seminars which the graduate students could conduct, under faculty supervision. Original materials about Nigeria and Indonesia could be brought into the graduate seminar and into the work with freshmen by asking for collaboration from the Indonesian and Nigerian governments, and by asking the Nigerian and Indonesian students to prepare special essays, articles, reviews, etc., in English as part of their graduate work toward a degree in education.

The main thrust of the colleges of education should be in the direction of making this kind of new courses. In other words, the purpose of the graduate study of education would be to develop new courses for high schools and colleges with new content drawn from the materials of foreign cultures. Then the idea of the student going abroad for a semester or a year makes much more sense than it usually does, since the purpose in the foreign study now becomes quite specific and the research and educational experience abroad is directly related to what the graduate student has done before going and will do when he returns. The colleges would then find that they were recruiting many more first-rate students into the teaching profession, simply because the entire program of foreign study and travel, educational research, practice teaching in college and in the school, becomes a much more interesting and lively affair than most of what is now going on.

American students would work with students from other countries on problems which interested them all; summer travel-study projects would naturally spring up for teams of American and foreign students to do research and collect information for the courses to be developed on the American campuses. It would also be a simple matter to arrange for students who are usually encapsulated in their own requirements in the academic majors of political science, sociology, economics, and other fields to join with the education students in developing research teams to study the politics of education, the economics of educational development, and many other matters, and also joining forces with the foreign students in developing travel-study projects and research of their own.

I would like to see us mix up the education students with a whole variety of other kinds of students, American and non-American. Mixing and desegregating in this way, inside and outside the field of education, has an enlivening effect, not only on the students involved in work on common problems, but on the faculty members who teach them. The main thing is to get the initiatives going, and to think of the block of time represented by the requirement of twenty to thirty credits of education courses as a beautiful opportunity to extend the whole meaning of education into its world dimension. There is no reason why these requirements have to be chopped into three-credit courses. Why not award ten credits for a full semester in which the student works at nothing but the educational problems of two or three different cultures, one of which is his own, and sets aside the other courses in the liberal arts and sciences curriculum so that he can give his undivided attention to being a practice-educator and genuine student in the field of education?

THE EDUCATION CURRICULUM

It seems to me, as I have said elsewhere, that rather than relying on the rest of the university faculty to provide courses in world affairs, foreign cultures, and international issues, and trusting to the luck of the elective system and the counseling services to decide whether or not students actually work in them, the college of education should develop its own curriculum, with the help of members of the university faculty and selected students and scholars from abroad, right in the middle of its own courses. Otherwise, it is unlikely that the intellectual vitality which can be developed through the introduction of ideas from outside the usual pattern of American educational thinking, or the content of knowledge which could enrich the student's understanding of foreign cultures and world affairs, will ever become available within the present structure.

My colleagues among the professional educators, many of whom make similar criticisms of the pattern of professional courses, have insisted that the main obstacle to any advance in the direction I have been urging lies in the fact that colleges and departments of education are staffed mainly by persons who have taken higher degrees in education to prepare themselves to teach the departmental courses already offered in their present form, and that there is thus a self-perpetuating mechanism in all the required education courses. More than this, in the assignment of given faculty members to teach courses required for certification, too often a person trained, for example in curriculum development, will be asked to teach a beginning course in educational psychology or introduction to education, and will simply follow the syllabus and the text which it is customary to use in such cases. The superficiality of the text then becomes a characteristic of the course.

The answer to that problem is the same answer which must be given, and used, to the problem of improving teaching throughout the entire educational system—new appointments of persons with a serious interest in educational change and the improvement of student learning, new forms of collaboration with scholars in the universities, foreign students and scholars from abroad, research seminars for faculty members already teaching in the colleges of education, all of them based on a clear-cut decision by those in authority to alter the content and form of the present courses in education. Someone is going to have to make the moves.

We have the evidence of the brilliant work of those psychologists, political scientists, sociologists, and historians, men like Nevitt Sanford, James Coleman, Merle Curti, David Riesman, and Frederick Rudolph, who, once they become involved in the study of education, bring to the field the knowledge and insight of their own kind of intellectual experience and show what can be done in breaking the bonds which hold tight the study of education within the province of its own practitioners. I have found that a great deal of the time, the social scientists with a concern for social change and a high level of research intelligence have not become involved in educational questions in general and international education in particular, simply because of prior interests in other matters. But I have also found that when they do become involved, as is the case with James Coleman and his editing and co-authorship of *Education and Political Development*,[5] the study of education immediately jumps to a new range of significance in its political

[5] James S. Coleman, *Education and Political Development*, Princeton, N.J., Princeton University Press, 1965.

and social content. We have yet to see very much of this talent applied to international education *per se*, although the *Education and Political Development* book, containing first-rate essays by political scientists, shows the way in which a very important contribution to education can be made. So does the work of Seymour Martin Lipset in his empirical studies of international politics, culture, and student movements. But again, the major initiative in getting the contribution made will have to come from the educators. It cannot wait for the political scientists or anyone else.

If, as I am constantly assured, the System is such that the moves will not be made within the faculty membership of the educational establishment, that they will not be made by the State Departments of Education through changes in their requirements, or through progressive or radical proposals from the certification and accrediting agencies, then they can only come from three sources: (1) students, both graduate and undergraduate, who demand broader and better work in their preparation as teachers—including those who intend to serve abroad in the Peace Corps or in other volunteer services at home; (2) individual faculty members who have had experience abroad and who simply undertake the reform of their own courses by new methods and new content; (3) deans of colleges of education and chairmen of departments who have a clear idea of the direction in which they want their institution to go, and who make new appointments to match; these can be joint appointments with other departments, of anthropologists, foreign scholars, experts, and graduate students, but preferably appointments by the college of education of those who have had overseas experience, are familiar with other educational systems, are interested in educational reform and the education of teachers, and can simply remake the education courses under their present titles.

To such teachers will come many of those students who want to teach but do not want to lull themselves into a stupor while learning to do it, others who seek some way of using their talents in foreign service, and others who, not knowing what it is they want, are just meeting their certification requirements. There is absolutely no doubt that at present the education courses are driving away most except the latter group. Neither is there any doubt that the whole area of education courses is one of the most fertile places for new growth in international education that exists anywhere in the system. A rich reward waits for any man who cultivates that area. He will not only have the undying gratitude of generations of students. He will have the reward of answering the academic critics of teacher education, not by meeting their terms of surrender to the ubiquitous all-university committees, but by converting the wasteland of undergraduate education in the universities to an oasis where good teaching and good teachers grow.

WHAT STATE DEPARTMENTS OF EDUCATION CAN DO

As far as the organized bureaucracy is concerned, there is evidence of an open possibility for new international work sponsored by the State Departments of Education, wherever there is leadership from the Department and cooperation from the colleges, teachers, and schools. Fifteen states have worked out at least the beginning stages of international programs in the public schools. As a minimum, some of the states have been revising the state-wide curriculum and including revisions in the way world affairs are taught; others have brought in foreign consultants to the staff of the Department of Education.

The most comprehensive effort by a State Department to increase the international component in the education of teachers is to be found in New York.[6] Although obviously New York has certain advantages not shared by others, by reason of its geographical location and cultural setting, most of the items on the New York agenda could be transferred to other states, at least for discussion and intended action.

In their set of Proposals made in 1961 for the "Expansion and Improvement of Education in New York State" the Board of Regents of the State said flatly, "The proper dimensions of general education in our schools and colleges are global in nature . . ."[7]

Since the State Commissioner and his colleagues of the State Department of Education share this view and took the Regents' statement seriously, in 1963 an Office of Foreign Area Studies at State Department Headquarters in Albany was organized to take

[6] A survey of the work of State Departments of Education in promoting studies in foreign cultures as of 1964 is contained in *American Education in a Revolutionary World: the Role of the States*, The University of the State of New York, The State Department of Education, Albany, 1964, pp. 1–14.

[7] *Investments in the Future: the Regents' Proposals for the Expansion and Improvement of Education in New York State*, 1961, The University of the State of New York, Albany, 1960, p. 28.

state-wide action in creating the global dimension. The Office has a New Delhi Educational Resources Center, where Americans are working with Indian educators to develop new curricular materials for use in the New York State public schools; it has a foreign Area Material Center in New York City, and a Center for International Programs and Services.

After the new office was started in the State Department, The University of the State of New York installed an International Center in Planting Fields, Long Island, New York, to do work in world affairs in the fifty-eight colleges and universities in the state system. Since fourteen of the fifty-eight institutions are State Colleges with a major interest in teacher education, and most of the other institutions in the University system produce a fair proportion of candidates for teaching, the State Department of Education and the University will obviously have many ways of collaborating in the future.

In many cases, the Departments of Education do not think it their business to start up programs of the sort New York has organized, and in general the assumption is made or implied that the State Department is an administrative and regulatory agency whose business happens to be with education.[8] This makes it even more important that the educators in the colleges and universities act to bring about changes in requirements, curriculum, programs, and the whole apparatus of licensure. Otherwise there may be no motion forward in international education at all, or it may be motion backwards, should the State Legislatures decide that they do not want international points of view officially installed in the educational system. The problem arises in its most extreme form when, in a given state, there is no initiative taken by the faculty, the teachers in the schools, the students in the colleges, *or* the people in the State Departments of Education.

A different kind of problem arises when, as is frequently the case, there is not much connection between the community organizations, World Affairs Councils, United Nations Associations, Foreign Policy Association branches, and the work of the schools, universities, and the State Departments. In the Department offices, usually placed in one building or set of buildings as part of the State Civil Service, and quite often geographically removed from the main centers

[8] New York State Department of Education, Albany, 1963, pp. 1–14.

where the universities and colleges of education operate, the members of the Departments see more of each other than anyone else. When the staff members travel to the schools and campuses, they usually see administrative officers on administrative and business matters rather than about anything to do with the teaching or with the curriculum in world affairs or other areas.

If we can find some ways to distract the attention of the bureaucracy from its unavoidable concern with rules and regulations and can turn that attention to substantive issues in education and the world, at the very least there will be more openness to change, and at the very most an intelligently planned program to create a world dimension in the educational system.

The general need is for members of the State Departments of Education to break out of the routines of the Department and of the colleges of education, and to travel to universities and schools outside their state and outside the country. One of the best ways of bringing the State Department of Education more closely in touch with the ongoing educational issues and problems in the education of teachers would be to arrange for sabbaticals for key people in the certification and accreditation sections to spend time overseas visiting Peace Corps teachers and others involved in education and community development abroad; or, if this is not possible, at least to spend a semester on a campus where some very good work in world education is under way. Projects could be organized on American campuses with foreign students who are articulate on the subject of their own education and its social and cultural setting, and with persons in the faculty who would agree to work on a team research project having to do with developing new programs in the State Department of Education, with or without change in certification requirements.

It would be of great use to the State Department of Education to have for a semester or a half-year well-qualified faculty members who would join the State Department staff to study the problems from that side of things and to organize some research on curriculum and other matters. If two or three faculty members at a time joined the staff on a temporary basis, this would be even better, since one person has only a minor amount of impact, everything else being equal, to do the sort of loosening up and looking around made possible in a group of interested persons going to work together with the staff of the Department of Education.

Another useful idea would be for one or two key staff people from various State Departments to spend three or four weeks working with counterparts in the New York State Department, or the Pennsylvania, Connecticut, Indiana, or Hawaii programs, comparing notes, carrying out informal research by collecting information and visiting recommended schools and colleges where new international programs are in effect.

In extension of the idea of making many more direct relationships between State Department staffs and the inside of the educational system, a great deal could be done by arranging for graduate students of education to serve as interns in Departments of Education to carry out research and study of the problems which the Departments are administering. The students could bring to the Departments the fresh outlook of those who have been in the middle of the system and have been looking at the bureaucracy from the outside. Some of these interns should be foreign students and foreign educators, whose purpose would be to look freshly at what we are doing and to join in the plans for what to do next.

Key people of the State Department staffs should go abroad for six to eight weeks on study trips to foreign countries where they could work on questions having to do with the way cooperative programs can be arranged for curriculum development (the New York State Center in New Delhi is a good case in point) and would visit the foreign schools and teacher education colleges to see what they are doing and how they are doing it in relation to the administrative problems of their Governmental services. It would be a good idea for such persons to travel with graduate students and faculty members interested in educational matters, since the Department traveler would then have the privilege of thinking about what he was seeing with the additional perspective of those from outside his own administrative orbit. The idea of volunteering for the Peace Corps would also be made a great deal more attractive to teachers if they could be granted a two-year leave of absence from a present teaching post in order to go abroad. At present very few public schools grant such leaves.

CONFERENCES FOR STATE DEPARTMENTS OF EDUCATION

Over the past year I have been part of two conferences organized for their staffs by State Departments of Education, one in Educational Reform, the other in The Role of the Humanities in the

Schools. Representatives from the colleges and universities were present as speakers and panel discussants, with a large representation of State Department staff. When I asked elsewhere whether or not there were many such conferences on substantive issues as well as on State Department problems, I learned that very seldom did Department members meet together with university or public school faculty members for discussion of substantive issues in the reform of the curriculum, the problems of world education, or even on the question of new forms of collaboration with university scholars in foreign cultures. A lack of budget for the purpose was usually given as the reason.

At the conferences I attended, some interesting questions in educational policy came up, and it was obvious that the participants from the State Departments were not at all familiar with what is happening on the campuses where there are young intellectuals among the students who have serious criticism to make of current educational policies, and where there are critics in the university faculties who have been writing and talking seriously about education in the humanities, the arts, and the social sciences. All the State Department relationships seemed to be with those who are teaching or administering education courses, and who are insulated from the ferment of educational discussion going on in the activist groups of students and faculty. The main questions at the humanities conference, I discovered to my alarm, were about how units of credit might be given for new humanities courses in the high schools, how these additional hours could be fitted into the present schedules, how computers might be used for rescheduling units of time (an important matter, but only after some priorities of time allocation have been decided), and how, if at all, courses in the humanities could be organized before the publishing companies had produced the necessary course outlines and textbooks.

Teachers and State Department officers alike seemed to feel helpless before the idea that new materials and activities in the arts and humanities can and should come from the efforts of teachers themselves, and that to postpone action until the textbook, electronics, and audiovisual industries came to the rescue was in effect a confession of trained incapacity among teachers of the arts. Faced with this kind of reality in the situation of the State Departments and their personnel, most university critics of teacher education simply write them off, or content themselves with denunciation, or cite evidence that the whole system is hopeless. But how could it be assumed to be otherwise if no effort is made by the scholars and critics from outside the State Departments to reach those on the inside, or if there is no program with a serious intellectual content through which the staff members of the State Departments can break out of their cultural isolation?

If the practitioner of education in the teacher education institutions or in the State Departments has no serious interest in issues and ideas, he does his work according to rules which he did not make and which he has no special concern to change. If, at the same time, there is no way in which he is confronted with serious issues, the resolution of which can determine what rules are actually desirable, he accepts whatever rules and attitudes are in effect. It does no good for publicists, journalists, Admirals, and others to denounce, deplore, and view with alarm. What is needed, aside from serious analysis of where the problems are, is a program of education and action. If education is needed among the educators, the point is to find out what kind is needed and to set to work to provide it.

ACCREDITATION AND ITS EFFECTS

Another way of looking at the formal requirements for becoming a teacher is to consider them as an expression of what the state authorities say they want on behalf of the children of their state. In the requirements for the accreditation of institutions which educate teachers, the states usually call for a broad "liberal arts training" and for basic work in social sciences, with the usual inclusion of American history, occasional inclusion of state history, and sporadic inclusion of world history or non-Western culture. Since the mental set of most of the requirement-makers and curriculum-developers is to think of college education as being divided into departments and courses, the idea that materials from the world's cultures should be an integral part of the entire curriculum and not merely a separate subject has not penetrated the system of requirements and regulations. Mississippi and Hawaii are the only states requiring world history for the preparation of social science teachers; Oregon requires either European *or* world history.

I have read carefully the statement *Standards and Guide for Accreditation of Teacher Education* prepared by the National

Council for the Accreditation of Teacher Education (NCATE) and used for the instruction of institutions which wish to receive national accreditation for their work in preparing teachers. The intention of the statement is to provide a "Guide to an institution in developing a report to the Council prior to a visit by a team of out-of-state and in-state evaluators," and "gives illustrations of possible ways of meeting standards." The sole purpose of NCATE, says the statement, is "to improve teacher education through accreditation."

If that is the sole purpose, the Standards and Guide should be able to produce something a lot more interesting, provocative, and imaginative than the present outline. It may be that the whole method by which such guides are produced is wrong. They start with committees of educators who prepare a draft of the kind of questions an institution should be able to answer if it is going to educate teachers properly. Then the draft is circulated to the educating profession for suggestions, revisions, and criticisms, until a consensus is reached. This finally becomes the statement of Standards and Guide.

But the Guide starts with the assumption that there is a basic and necessary pattern for the education of teachers, with three parts— general education, an academic major, and professional education, unspecified except as to the need for "laboratory" experience, including practice teaching. Any institution which took the present document as seriously as its proponents clearly expect them to would find itself making up a program sanctified by convention, not created by the imagination.

For example, the Guide asks about what arrangements have been made "for transporting college supervisors and student teachers to and from the laboratory schools and . . . for housing student teachers while away from the campus," but it does not ask the other kind of questions: What arrangements have been made to make sure that the student has direct experience in the way in which his society functions, how do you find out what other people are like, or what is it like to live in a culture other than your own?

When we look for the places from which educational leadership can come, it seems to me we have a right to expect that the agencies with the power to control the system will make special efforts to take the initiative, and to use their power on behalf of change. In the case of the National Council for Accreditation of Teacher Education, the approach is didactic, juridical, organizational, administrative, regulatory. The standards proposed by the Council have to do with a narrow set of professional qualifications for educators and a conventional set of characteristics for the curriculum. When these standards are analyzed, they turn out to be whether or not the faculty members who teach "professional" courses have taken the right number and sequence of professional courses in their own preparation to teach more of the same.

Would it not be useful to raise the question as to how well the students being graduated from a given institution can teach, what interest do they demonstrate in possessing an intellectual life of their own, what leadership have they shown in improving the quality of education, their own and that of the children they have been teaching? Otherwise one can only conclude that accreditation procedures are not designed to improve education but to imprison it within the status quo.

The American Association of Colleges for Teacher Education has completed the first year of a comprehensive study of the criteria for judging teacher education programs and institutions, to work out and recommend appropriate changes in present standards, to cite the areas where continuing research is needed and to make a plan for the continuing review of whatever standards are adopted by the accrediting agencies. A preliminary draft of a statement on proposed standards[9] has now been circulated to a cross section of the educating community, after a series of five regional conferences in 1967 and responses to an opinionaire on key issues from more than 1500 educators.

An analysis of the draft statement shows that the basic framework of academic and professional courses has been retained, and that preparation for teaching is still conceived as a process of taking courses within the subject matter of the arts and sciences, and of taking other courses in educational theory linked to "laboratory and clinical experience." That is to say, teaching and preparing to teach are conceived as classroom activities within educational institutions, and the element of direct experience in the world, the idea of cultural immersion and social involvement as a factor in the student's development have not yet found their way into the educational thinking.

On the other hand, the statement reveals some welcome shifts of emphasis within the present system, especially in the direction of

---

[9] *Standards and Evaluative Criteria for the Accreditation of Teacher Education.* A Draft of the Proposed New Standards, with Study Guide. The American Association of Colleges for Teacher Education. December 1967.

greater flexibility in judging the qualities of graduates, the use of continuing research to review present educational programs in the light of subsequent performance of the teacher, the inclusion of students in educational policy-making, greater encouragement for the development of ideas which break with standard practices. To those of us not directly involved in the day-to-day work of administering change within the teacher education movement, the process of change seems slow, cumbersome, and overwhelmingly circumscribed by professional and organizational interests.

Yet the circumscription is a fact, the organizational problems are real, and the question of how to speed up the process of change and to free the imagination of educators for a wider range of ideas and practices is itself a matter of study in the formation of new strategies, and a question which cannot be answered by frontal assaults on the bureaucratic structure. In fact, that structure seems strong enough to withstand almost any amount of attacks from outside.

What is called for is a deeper and more thoughtful strategy which turns the attention of educators toward the reality of the cultural and social conditions of their own society and the people in it, and calls upon them to find ways in which the entire apparatus of institutional life in the schools and universities can minister to the changing needs of a younger generation and a new society into which the generation has so recently been born. The levers of change certainly do exist inside the universities and schools, but the fulcrum lies outside the institutions, in the society at large, and it is there that the force must be applied at places indicated by the living reality of human need.

Stated in the broadest terms, our problem in America is to rouse up the initiatives of indigenous leadership, to give our people the impulse and the tools to educate themselves with the help of their teachers. Society is the ultimate teacher, possessed of new and enormous powers in its economic and social rewards and punishments, equipped with instruments of communication more powerful and far-reaching than those in the hands of school teachers. Whatever the regulatory organizations can do to release the energies of students and teachers to solve their own problems and to enhance the quality of their own lives will help to restore the balance in favor of the individual citizen and the individual teacher.

5

The Cultural Element in Foreign Policy

And, at last, after many devastations, overthrows, and even complete internal exhaustion of their powers, the nations are driven forward to the goal which Reason might have well impressed upon them, even without so much sad experience.

IMMANUEL KANT
The Idea of a Universal History

As I write about the relation of American education to world society, everything I am capable of thinking about the issues involved is assaulted by the reality of a series of world events which have followed each other in quick succession—the lies and furies of the Arab-Israeli war, the political confusion and organized violence in Nigeria, the Congo, Vietnam, in Communist China, in Hong Kong, in the American cities, the disintegration of rational discourse at the United Nations, the malignant race policies of the Rhodesian and South African Governments, the cursing and screaming of invective in threats against America and the West by the Castroites, the Chinese, the Arabs, and the Africans, the assassinations of Martin Luther King and Robert Kennedy—in short, the unleashing of new modes of violence and the decrease in the power of rational and enlightened authority everywhere. I would be foolish to believe that through the education of teachers, in world affairs or foreign cultures, a restoration of order and acceptable authority would be forthcoming, or that what we do in education in this country can have a controlling effect on the creation of a new world order more congenial to the true interests of mankind than the present one.

But it would be equally foolish to ignore the fact that *without* a profound and rapid change in the quality and outlook of American

education in its moral, social, and political dimension, there is little
hope that America will, in the future, be able to influence the course
of events in the direction of peace and international stability, or to
cope with the problems of poverty, racism, and violence which
wrack our own communities. There is no need to repeat the familiar
argument which links a high quality of education and the reality of
full educational opportunity for everyone to the moral and social
health of a democracy. I believe we can take as self-evident that
education of quality for all is what gives cohesion to a democratic
society, and provides, in Horace Mann's phrase, "the balance wheel
of the social machinery." But I do not think that enough Americans
understand that what we do with our educational system, how fully
it serves the American and world population in a generous, open,
and sensitive way, is what determines whether or not the rest of the
world can bring itself to believe in us, to trust our motives, and to
take seriously our claims to be building a fair and just society and a
peaceful world order. We cannot disguise the fact that as a country
we are very rich, that our resources are enormous, and that millions
of our citizens are poor, neglected, and uneducated. We cannot
exercise world influence in constructive ways until we can demonstrate our ability to educate and take care of our own people, and
to influence our own Congress, to take the necessary steps to use our
educational and economic resources wisely, for the benefit of the
widest possible sector of the national and international community.

At the moment the Congress is showing very little understanding
of either the needs of the country's expanding educational system
or the world's expanding educational needs and the part the United
States should be playing in meeting them. I think that this can be
traced in part to a weakness in the entire system of teacher education in this country, and one I have been discussing in one way or
another throughout the whole of this book—the lack of political
sensitivity and the absence of political activism in the colleges of
education and in the programs devised there.

There are complicated reasons involved in the success or failure
of enlightened social legislation in the Congress, more complicated
than usual in the case of foreign policy and foreign aid questions.
But ultimately the decision of a Senator or a Congressman to vote
for or against the idea of educational and economic aid to other
countries depends on the degree of conviction he holds that foreign
policy should be based primarily on positive efforts to use American

resources to improve world conditions or on other factors—mainly military and economic power exercised on behalf of a narrowly construed national self-interest. The degree of his conviction one way or another depends on any number of things, but in the final analysis on only two—the influence on his intelligence and moral sense of his education in world affairs and liberal democracy, and the influence of teachers and education on the attitudes of his electorate.

On the one hand, the educational system is responsible for the education of those who will become its leaders, in politics or any other field. On the other, it is responsible for educating everyone else to become interested in paying attention to what their leaders are doing and how the world is being run. The simple truth is that the teachers in the schools and colleges are the only ones who, in this society, are responsible for working full-time at the task of educating the citizenry to understand the nature of their world. The corollary proposition is that unless the teachers have an education which can enable them to reach some such understanding, they can do nothing but hand on to their pupils whatever is given to them through the myths, folklore and conventional wisdom of their society. It is with this in mind that I have been looking at the relation between the education of American teachers and American foreign policy, and it is for this reason that I have been unable to think of the education of teachers in the field of world affairs separately from their total education as serious intellectuals and as men and women of personal and social conscience.

SOME GENERAL CONSIDERATIONS

The foreign policy of a country is determined at a given moment by any number of things over which the country has no control, including the accidents of its own history and the condition and power position of the rest of the countries of the world. Short of a policy of territorial aggression, a country can do nothing about its geographical location, the existence and relative size of its natural resources, or even about the way in which its people have in the past created the particular cultural, moral, and social environment in which certain kinds of foreign policy decisions in the present are either possible or impossible. Foreign policy is conditioned by the size of resources in military power, nuclear and otherwise, the extent of industrialization and technology, and all the other familiar economic and social items in the calculus of power politics. But in the long run, to speak in terms of pure power, the entire capability of a given country to influence world events depends on its educational system, without which there would be no skilled manpower, talented managers, large-scale agricultural production, foreign service officers, engineers, linguists, economists, or statesmen—only politicians trying to manipulate a tribal system of ignorant and untrained people.

There are, accordingly, a series of foreign policies of various styles and content available to various nation-states, based on their capacity to exert certain kinds of power, positively or negatively. The Soviet Union could not do what it does without having taken over a manageable peasant population from the Tsars and putting it into a national system of industrial and agricultural production through an educational system which produced what the Soviet Government decided it had to have to achieve certain national and international purposes. There are other things the Government of the United States cannot do because it did not take over a population of peasants and has not had the control of the country's educational system. It is forced to do most of what it does at home by persuasion and social engineering. What it does abroad is subject to the same conditions.

In effect, what has happened has been an increase in the political power of world opinion, reflected, among other ways, in the shift of the role of the United Nations from a world organization designed to achieve collective security, to one which deals with any matter of international concern, according to the interests and concerns of its member states. J. W. Burton, in his *International Relations: a General Theory*, has argued the point at length and convincingly. "The goal," says Burton, "to which international cooperation is currently directed appears, on analysis, to be no longer a world government with enforcement potential against a member state on the analogy of provincial governments dealing with lawbreakers, but a universal international system in which communication, knowledge of consequences, feed-back, awareness of revisionist demands which a consensus views as legitimate, can lead to change and adjustment to change—a process not possible in conventional systems of alliances and collective security dominated by alliances . . ."[1]

The instruments of power available to the United States in exert-

[1] J. W. Burton, Jr., *International Relations: a General Theory*, Cambridge University Press, New York, 1965, p. 24.

ing influence in world affairs include all the military, economic, and political factors available to other countries, but on a vastly larger scale. The difficulty is that the relative strength of these and other factors has never been calculated with a sufficient degree of precision, and in recent years, American foreign policy has followed a plain pattern of assumption common to countries engaged in power politics, which places military and technological power at the first level of significance, with political and economic power serving as secondary and interlocking elements in the exercise of influence. We have learned, of course, as have the Russians, that you cannot do very much with nuclear military power except destroy yourself with it, and that seems now to have been clearly established in the lexicons of military strategy for all but the Chinese.

It is in the exercise of moral and cultural power—that is, the capacity to persuade and to influence world events by visible acts of humane principle under the sanction of international law and humane custom—that American efforts have been sharply reduced, while the rhetoric of moral principle goes on.

Yet American political theory and our stated international intent flow from a moral postulate—that the use of power must be in the interest of those for whom it is used—with military strength to protect the rights and interests of those who do not possess the means to act in their own defense. In the long run, the moral act, committed according to an unexceptionable and clear humanitarian aim, has the greatest power to influence world events, while there are self-defeating and narrow limits to the effect of military force in achieving political or social objectives. The same is true of economic power in the exercise of influence, as we and the Russians continue to learn from day to day in experience with bilateral aid programs.

A more adequate analysis of how a foreign policy exerts influence in world affairs would scale down the importance of the military, considering it useful only as an international deterrent to potential and actual aggression and as a means of stabilizing the world's military environment. The road to ultimate safety lies in general and complete disarmament. The way is then clear for a fresh conception of the interlocking use of economic, moral, and cultural power for the development of a world order. That conception would be based on the fact that as the quality and scope of democratic education increases within nation-states and throughout the world, it becomes increasingly difficult for any single power to take military action outside its own borders without strong negative response both inside and outside those borders.

Until very recently there has been almost no analysis of the concept of cultural power as 'a factor in American foreign affairs. The assumption has been made in public discussion and in the arguments before Congress that this is mainly a matter of building American prestige by exchanging art objects, performers, ideas, books, suitable intellectuals, and distinguished persons with other countries and thus, with the help of the U. S. Information Agency abroad and American culture at home, to please and impress the foreign public and foreign governments with American accomplishments. The entire budget for the State Department's educational programs was $51,201,000 for 1967, enough to include $34,363,000 for exchange of persons; 6724 foreign visitors, 2378 Americans, of whom 731 are foreign teachers and 305 are American. As far as teachers are concerned, we are working in the hundreds when we should be working and thinking in the thousands.

Yet the Congress decreased the 1967–68 budget by nearly $10 million, and for 1968–69 the budgets for all international education and cultural affairs have been slashed so badly that approximately one half of all existing programs have been eliminated at exactly the time they should have been doubled in size.

The pitifully low budget for exchanges in the performing arts is some indication of the low regard in which the work of our artists and intellectuals is held as far as the representation of American culture abroad is concerned. In this is reflected a general public attitude to the arts as something practiced by artists and enjoyed by their admirers but irrelevant to the national welfare or interest. It is assumed that foreign policy is one thing, culture is another, and that there is little relation between them. Foreign policy is a matter of politics, diplomats, public statements, and Government strategies having to do with wars, enemies, Communists, and friends; culture is what is done in concert halls and lecture rooms.

The failure is not simply a lack of public understanding of the place of the arts and ideas in the national life, but in the lack of a coherent body of thought or consistent set of practices in the United States to deal with the relation of this country to the cultures, educational systems, and peoples of the world. There is instead a welter of different institutions and agencies, from the business community to the Department of Agriculture, the American Friends Service

Committee to the moving picture industry, the Ford Foundation to General Motors, the universities to the Pentagon, the State Department to the Rotary Club, all of them with different programs, intentions, and degrees of success in communicating those intentions internationally.

In the case of activities outside the government, this is probably as it should be, since the spirit of volunteer action and the special interests of all kinds of people should be reflected in the variety of ways in which they can make direct connections with other persons and institutions in the total world community. But in the case of Government action, by the Congress or the Executive branch, the significance of the cultural element in national and international affairs cannot be left to the whim of individual Congressmen on appropriation committees, or to the accidents of administrative initiative and decisions in individual agencies. The biennial struggle for allocation of funds to the Foreign Aid bill, the identification of foreign policy issues with military concerns, the mixing-together of military and economic aid as if it were all to be used for the same purpose, and the cuts in the budgets of anything having to do with cultural and educational affairs abroad—all of this indicates the need for continuous and sustained effort on the part of Government officials and their intellectual allies in the universities to create strong and vigorous partnerships in the task of educating Congress and the country.

It is not too difficult to think that if a sufficient number of educators, universities, and university scholars took a serious interest in research, writing, and speaking out on the subject of cultural affairs in relation to foreign policy and foreign aid, a gradual shift would come about in the attitude of key Congressmen and Government planners as to what constitutes a wise and effective use of our cultural power in the achievement of enlightened foreign policy objectives.

A scholar who read the text of the hearings on budget appropriations in international, educational, and cultural affairs before Congress would be appalled to find that rather than the discussion of cultural, or even fiscal, policy, the hearings consist of a series of suspicious questions about whether or not an American scholar going abroad has or has not ever been critical of his Government, or whether there are foreign students in this country who have ever participated in demonstrations. Since the Congressmen who hold the hearings are responsible to the American people for decisions they make in cultural affairs, it would be most appropriate and immensely helpful if the academic profession, through its organizations and through its research and individual scholarship, followed the course of policy-making closely and made known to the Congressmen, the public, and to the university community the results of their enquiry. At the present time, few educators are even aware of how policy is made, aside from not knowing what happens at budget hearings.

At the moment, most of those at work in Government agencies who wish to expand and clarify the role of cultural affairs in our relations with other countries are doing what they can without much help from the universities, the intellectuals, or the serious critics of foreign policy. Few of the latter are drawn from the field of education and cultural affairs. They are almost entirely social scientists and historians whose intellectual and research interests are political and economic; their preoccupation with problems in these areas excludes consideration of the broader issues of cultural diffusion and world change. Knowledge of foreign policy is equated with knowledge of political, military, and economic strategy, and it is difficult for most people in Government agencies or in Congress or in the universities, unless already occupied with cultural issues and concerns, to associate them with the operation of a foreign policy.

THE POWER OF EDUCATION

On the other hand, since knowledge is power, and education is the means through which knowledge is generated and distributed, the educational system of a country is a form of power which exerts its influence both in determining what kind of foreign policy is possible for a given state and what kind of long-range goals are feasible for a society as a whole. I do not believe it is accurate, except in a rhetorical sense, to say with President Johnson that "our foreign policy will advance no faster than the curriculum of our classrooms." If we were to believe this literally, our foreign policy would be pre-World War II. What is more accurate to say is that the educational system is the major resource for developing attitudes and values which permeate the culture, and in the long run is what gives the society its national intellectual character and its moral and political point of view. The emotional content in the life of a country can be harnessed for political and military purposes by social engineers with talent. In large part that content is developed within the framework of the educational system by the teachers and what they teach and do not teach, by what is taught in history—pride of conquest, of ancestry, of power, victories, love of country, or love of humanity at large.

Yet the entire Educational and Cultural Affairs program of the State Department for 38 countries in Africa as far as teachers, professors, and students are concerned, involves 39 American professors to teach in African universities, nine American teachers to teach English in secondary schools, and 37 African secondary school teachers coming to the United States, plus 200 college students. This does not of course include additional programs of education carried on by AID and other agencies and foundations, but it does indicate the place of teachers and teacher education in the cultural policy of the United States in relation to one of the most important areas in the world, and one which is currently very much neglected by American aid for educational and social development. The total AID budget for teacher education abroad in 1967 amounted to $6,496,000 for thirteen projects in all of Africa. The scale of effort did not even begin to approach either the need or the possible effects large-scale effort might have.

PARTS OF THE WORLD SYSTEM

Looked at from a world perspective, it is possible to think of the educational systems of individual states as parts of an interlocking world system in which the power of education can, if properly used, be placed at the disposal of the world community. If education is considered as a factor in the international power structure, it can be consciously used either to further national self-interest or to help construct a viable international community. In the best of circumstances, it can do both. It can, for example, reconstruct the content of its national curriculum in a way designed to develop a sympathetic and accurate understanding of other cultures and ideologies, including those developed by the "enemy."

When observed and noted by the educated community and Governments abroad, this kind of curriculum will be taken as an act of good will, and in the broadest sense of the term, a positive political action. Another step is to invent ways in which teachers and scholars around the world can work together on common problems within their national educational systems—ranging from the problem of teaching science in the elementary schools to writing new kinds of world history in which each culture has a fair and honorable place.

The most extreme negative example of cultural values as an instrument of policy can be drawn from the present program of Communist China, which includes teaching the Chinese to hate Americans, on the assumption that this is beneficial to Chinese interests. A middle-range example can be drawn from current French policy, which, in the absence of her former economic and military power for use on a broad international scale, has concentrated on the exercise of political and cultural influence through a program of French nationalism and the Gaullist grandeur of France, involving, among other items, the financing of 45,000 French teachers in service abroad. The British, in a roughly comparable situation involving the loss of military and economic power formerly available for use on a world scale, must rely almost exclusively on political, economic, and cultural relations, particularly with the United States, in order to effect such influence as is now possible. The British are therefore turning more and more of their efforts toward the improvement of their educational system, both in making it more democratic, thus releasing more talent among wider sectors of the society, and in increasing the capability of its technological and scientific manpower.

One rapid way of making the point I wish to make is to ask what resources for the exercise of power and international influence are available to those countries whose economic, and therefore military, power is unavoidably kept to modest proportions, modest, that is, when compared to Soviet and American capability? In this instance, no matter what they would like to do in a military way, the British at Suez or the French in Indo-China, lack of military and economic resources makes such projects impossible. The creation of political and cultural ties then assumes the first level of significance.

In a different situation, in Indonesia, because the circumstances did not allow the United States to use military force to control the internal politics of that country, our policy did allow the uncompleted revolution of the Indonesians against outside control a chance to work itself out in its own terms. American cultural, political, and economic influence, exercised in an enlightened way through the preceding years mainly by the Ford Foundation and the American program of foreign aid, a fair proportion of which had to do with teacher education, was able to operate without the handicap of military intervention. The result was that after the change in political leadership, achieved not without violence and bloodshed, Indonesia created a new and viable political situation of very great consequence for the stability of the whole of Asia.

It is possible to argue, on the basis of the facts, that the subsequent change of Indonesian policy in international affairs in the direction of peaceful co-existence was in some part the result of the patient and clearly visible efforts of American educators and the American Government over a period of fifteen years, in putting American funds and personnel to work on behalf of the educational, social, and economic welfare of the Indonesians. Indonesia's present leaders were conscious during those years of the continuing contribution made to their country through the use of American cultural resources on their behalf; they knew at first hand that the educators and economic advisers were honestly working to achieve the goals of a self-sufficient Indonesian society. They also knew that the CIA had been helping the rebels against Sukarno in the 1950s when our declared policy was one of Indonesian self-determination. It was our good fortune that this piece of clandestine intervention was defeated by the Indonesian Government then in power before it could throw the whole of our foreign aid and educational program into disrepute.

In the wars and conflicts of these recent years, the strongest elements in creating the conflicts have had to do with nationalism, not with Communism, and it is to nationalism, combined with racism, that we need to look in the present and future for the most dangerous sources of war, conflict, and mass violence. The defense against extreme nationalism as a force in politics, war, and world affairs is, in the long run, the development of international, political, and educational instruments which can reach the root problems which produce the grievances and aggressions.

It is at this point that the United States, with its own particular form of nationalist fervor, is put to the test of international leadership. Unless our military power is used as a stabilizing force for a peaceful international order, it becomes simply another means of creating a greater intensity of nationalism everywhere else in the world. Unless our cultural policy is one which takes full account of the rich resources available within the United States for extending the advantages of education to a wider and wider sector of the world population, we will find ourselves using those resources to increase the spirit of nationalism, among ourselves and others.

EDUCATION AND COLONIALISM

It may be useful to point out in this connection that the history of educational imperialism subsequent to military conquest has had grisly effects on the culture and social developments of the countries thus colonized. Not only does it impose a false culture and a feudal social system on the country of occupation, but when the revolutions and revolts of liberation occur, and the societies are free to organize their own affairs, not only is the educational system inadequate to deal with problems of the society, but there is no cultural base from which a new educational and social system can grow. The United States is now providing in Vietnam a classic example of the contradictions between the use of military conquest for the achievement of political aims and the administration of educational and social welfare programs to rehabilitate the people and the society being destroyed.

The educational system left by the French in Vietnam was based on concepts of élitism and of social class which led directly to the kind of military dictatorship it has been our privilege to support in South Vietnam. The French left a curriculum and program of the most reactionary style of French pedagogy. It is perhaps too much to ask that a colonial system designed to subjugate and exploit a people should develop a democratic educational system which would enable the colony to determine its own cultural, political, and social future. However, in retrospect, that would have been the wisest course of action any colonial power could have taken, since it would not only have made possible a transition from a colonial relationship to one of cooperative liaison, but would have provided the fabric from which a new society and economy could be built, without the revolutions and wars of liberation which are now the common lot of the third world. Turning this to a positive precept, it is now clear that whatever else the United States does in connection with its foreign policy in Asia and Africa, the central thrust should be in social and economic development through education, which means the education of teachers.

The irony in our present situation in Vietnam is too obvious for extended comment. While AID and the Department of Health, Education and Welfare have limited programs for teacher education, we find our efforts and those of the Vietnamese frustrated in trying even to conduct classes for the millions of children, sixty in a class, with "unmotivated pupils, ill-prepared teachers, undelivered supplies, inadequate plants and insufficient finances." The irony becomes tragedy when we think what could be done were we to spend even three billion of our twenty-eight billion dollars a year on education and social development rather than on the military, or when we think of what the French could have done had they given Indo-China an educational system designed for the benefit of Southeast Asia rather than for its exploitation by the French.

Instead of a broad, large-scale, and effective Vietnam program of educational aid where it is most needed—in the education of teachers and in the supply of teachers and teacher aides—at a time so many young Americans are anxious to serve in that other kind of war, a total educational budget of $5,079,000 was allocated for the entire country from AID funds for fiscal year 1967. Of this, $1,780,-000 is for teacher education, with the rest for rural trade schools ($40,000), hamlet schools ($500,000), instructional materials ($700,-000), vocational education ($784,000), and leadership training (selected Vietnamese sent to the United States for professional and technical education) ($1,275,000). Two modest programs of the colleges of education of Ohio University and the University of Southern Illinois are continually inhibited in their efforts to give support and increase the supply of teachers and teaching materials by the internal politics and restrictions of American-Saigon policies. Again there is a failure in cultural policy. A great many of these restrictions have had to do with the freedom of Americans in Vietnam, or upon their return to the United States after service there, to express their own views about the war itself or to work in the ways in which some of the finest teachers in South Vietnam, the 170 Volunteers of the International Voluntary Service, are most capable of working.

American cultural policy, as administered by the military and civilian officials, with the latter now integrated with the military, has created the kind of tensions between the administrators and the civilian volunteers, who are widely recognized as among the most effective teachers and workers involved in reconstruction, resulting in the resignation in September 1967 of four major leaders in the volunteer movement. In the words of one of them, "As individuals

. . . we can not become part of the destruction of a people we love."[2]

"If we started building schools as passionately as we built air bases," says John Naisbitt, "and training teachers as thoroughly as we train pilots, we might bring something worthwhile to Vietnam. If we do not, our defeat will be as profound as that suffered by the French at Dien Bien Phu."[3]

While the Vietnamese suffer the consequences of severe educational shortages, the children of well-to-do Americans and military personnel in Saigon experience a similar shortage. According to a *New York Times* report of October 1, 1967, one hundred American students are attending a new school whose curriculum director is a man with experience in real estate and business who accepted the post because, as he put it, "I go where the money is." The report quotes one of the teachers as saying, "It's a kind of a funny place. The children are wealthy and no one ever talks about the war. The war doesn't exist in this school."[4]

That view is shared by at least one of the students, who is reported as saying, "For most kids, it gets sort of dull in Saigon. We drive around on our Hondas in the afternoon, we go down to the USO sometimes, or we just walk around."[5]

Is this an example of an American philosophy of education in action? Are there no projects in community aid, English teaching, public health, hospital work, social service in Saigon, which could put such fifteen-year-old Americans to work and teach them to understand a Vietnamese society in the throes of dissolution? Once more, the need is for an American policy backed by money and one which goes straight to the need for teachers, teachers who are themselves aware of the relation of social change and moral values to intellectual and educational growth.

Aside from the meager help being given to teachers and teaching in South Vietnam itself, there is little indication that anyone is think-

[2] *The New York Times*, September 19, 1967; pp. 1, 16.

[3] "America's Dien Bien Phu," by John Maisbitt, *Saturday Review*, July 15, 1967, p. 72. Mr. Naisbitt served as assistant to the former Commissioner of Education and Welfare, John Gardner, is now in private industry and visited Vietnam in the spring of 1967. His article reviews the educational situation in South Vietnam on the basis of that visit and available reports in the field.

[4] "Americans Study at Saigon School," Bernard Weinraub, *The New York Times*, October 1, 1967, p. 5.

[5] Ibid., p. 5.

ing seriously about how to develop the kind of student teachers and teacher educators needed to help in Vietnam with the rehabilitation and reconstruction of the educational and social system. We have ignored all this before, and even now when the drastic needs are staring us in the face, we are ignoring it still.

The extent to which our educational strength in the United States is inadequate in the field of Southeast Asian studies was the subject of comment by Professor John K. Fairbank of Harvard University, at the International Congress of Orientalists at the University of Michigan in August of 1967. It takes ten years, Professor Fairbank points out, with work in the Chinese and Vietnamese language, as well as the politics, history, anthropology, and economics of Vietnam to produce a full-bodied scholar in the Vietnam field, and we have only recently begun to organize the research and curricular programs through which candidates can acquire the necessary training.

On the other hand, the necessity of teaching and learning in America about Southeast Asia will not wait upon a ten-year period for the incubation of scholars. We know enough already about the way in which direct experience in the Asian culture, combined with language training, practice teaching, and community development projects can quicken the process of preparation to teach about Asia. If we cared to do so, we could, through Government and foundation-sponsored teacher education programs, mount a major program of teacher education right now which could serve as an international example of what can be done when a powerful democratic country uses its resources to the full in an effort to serve the true needs of the peoples of the world. Aside from the immediate training of teacher volunteers for Vietnam, we could develop one-, two-, or three-year M.A. and B.A. programs in Vietnamese studies, Peace Corps style, calling for volunteers through such organizations as the International Volunteer Service and the twenty-two other organizations already at work in South Vietnam with a handful of 350 teachers and workers.

We could finance hundreds of Vietnamese teachers and American student-teachers to work together, and would thus come to grips with the fact that for the years to come, no matter what the outcome of the war, we are going to need more and more teachers in the United States who are able to teach intelligently about the Vietnamese, the American, and the Asian people. The sooner we begin both to help the Vietnamese with a larger supply of teachers for their own country and a larger degree of understanding of their problems on our part at home, the sooner we can help to repair the damage they are now suffering. If the Defense Department can afford training in the Vietnamese language and culture for 9000 to 11,000 servicemen, we can certainly afford to train an equivalent number of civilian volunteers.

We should be planning at this moment for a Federal program of subsidy for selected veterans of the Vietnam war, both Vietnamese and American, to become teachers in Vietnam in the crucial period of reconstruction following the war's end. Although we will not be able to put highly qualified scholars of the kind described by Professor Fairbank into the field, that is not the major problem facing the Vietnamese. They need a new educational system, and we should make a national and international project out of helping them to get it.

THE CULTURAL OBLIGATIONS IMPLIED BY THE INTERNATIONAL EDUCATION ACT

In view of the situation of the United States in contemporary world society and the negative mood of Congress, the formal action of the Congress in passing the International Education Act of 1966 can be seen to be nothing less than a radical move in the direction of a world concept of education and a new cultural policy for the Government. If the implications of the Act were carried out in practice, education would become, for the first time in the history of the United States, a major element in foreign policy. Conversely, foreign policy would then be subject to analysis and decision based on long-range world-inclusive educational goals. The intention of the International Education Act, as construed by President Johnson in his public statements, is to advance the cause of education everywhere, in cooperation with "all nations, friend and foe alike," with a wish to "receive as much as we give, to learn as well as to teach."

While the Act directs attention to the necessity of building an international dimension directly into the American educational system and cites ways in which existing resources and programs of Government agencies can be used for education in an international dimension, Congress has moved in the opposite direction, granting funds for military programs, cutting back or canceling funds for international, cultural, and social needs of all kinds. International education has no constituency in this country except among those educators and citizens who believe in it strongly enough to make their views known publicly and to work directly with Congressional Committees and Government agencies to press for its advance. It is time that that constituency took appropriate action.[6]

At best the constituency is a small one, made up mainly of specialists in area studies, international relations, government and political science, and it has not much relation to the community of educators. I have remarked earlier the lack of direct connection between the academic departments and research centers in which the specialists work and the actual programs for the education of teachers. As a result, it is very hard to find scholars who have specialized in a given world area who know or care very much about its educational system, or ours, and very hard to find educators with a scholarly knowledge of the political science and sociology of the area handled by the scholar.

Because the task of preparing teachers in the subject-matter fields has been handed over to the departments, whose members are usually not thinking about how their students can best become teachers, there is no central thrust within the university community at any point toward intervention in foreign policy questions having to do with education and internationalism, no deep concern that the modern American teacher must act before his pupils and the community as an interpreter of the situation of America in world society. In other words, there is no basic attitude being developed within the educational system toward the foreign policy questions handled by Congress in the area of education itself.

While the colleges for teachers, the State Colleges, and the undergraduate colleges and universities remain starved for scholars who can teach and who possess depth in knowledge of foreign cultures and world affairs, the assumption continues to be made that if research and scholarly exchanges occur at the university level, the results of that research and those projects will find their way to the public school teachers and into the school and college curricula. This is not what happens. As a matter of fact, even in those institutions where there are large numbers of American faculty members who have worked abroad, on AID projects, on Fulbright grants, or in the

[6] A full discussion of these matters is to be found in the Proceedings of the Conference on World Education, 1966.

foreign service at large, little effect can be seen as a result of their experience and research on the undergraduate curricula of their own institutions.

Dr. Don Davies, Associate Commissioner, U. S. Office of Education, put the matter clearly when he asked, at the Conference on World Education, "How do we influence 25,000 school systems, 150,000 school administrators, and two million teachers, all of them already in the elementary and secondary schools of the country? This is a problem that will not be settled merely by changes on college and university campuses . . . If you are talking about such things as openness to differences in culture and ideas, you will have to remember that if the School Board and its staff does not accept that as a proper aim for the school, you are whistling in the dark. Whatever may be our strategy, it has to be one that includes a strategy for bringing about change in a very large and complicated system of public education."[7]

James Becker, speaking at the same Conference, referred to some of the practical projects now going on with teachers and communities. "The work of these people," said Becker, "makes a sharp contrast with the way the physicists went about forming the school curriculum with the Moses Method—a few physicists get up a mountain and come down with a curriculum. One of the main problems is that we have not yet found any effective ways of feeding the results of these special projects into the bloodstream of the elementary and secondary schools . . . It is not a lack of research or a lack of ideas, it is the fact that you can't get any kind of hearing for the ideas in the climate that now exists . . . The University may even have a special project with social scientists working with the schools, but the project consists of a few scholars who have a deep interest in it, and the rest of the institution pays little attention . . ."[8]

The emphasis in the work in international education which has already been done, and done well, by Education and World Affairs and other organizations, has been on the analysis of the undergraduate and graduate liberal arts curriculum and the need for its reform by the inclusion of materials in world affairs and non-Western cultures. But the unsolved problem of EWA and the organizations, associations, and Government agencies which are develop-

[7] Proceedings of the Conference on World Education, p. 35.
[8] Ibid., p. 36.

ing ideas and policies in international education is how to inject these ideas into the educational planning of the schools, colleges, and universities. The relation between that task and the work of the colleges of education is slight, even in cases where colleges of education have held AID contracts for the development of foreign educational systems.

The problem before us is one of stimulating interest and initiative within the colleges and universities to become active in considering a total shift in attitude toward the content of contemporary culture and to ask what, of all the things which can be taught to the contemporary student, is most worth their knowing. Coupled with that shift must be another one, toward a concentrated and continuous interest on the part of the colleges of education in the policies and decisions about education and international affairs made by Congress and the Administration. This means the inclusion of materials in education courses drawn directly from Government documents, reports of hearings, statements, and speeches of Government officials on cultural policy at home and abroad, ranging from the reports of the National Endowment for the Arts and Humanities to the International Cooperation Year and Government Conferences on Education, White House Conferences, and research publications of the U. S. Office of Education and the Department of State.

Those of us who believe that the entire content of the arts and sciences curriculum should be reshaped to bring it in touch with advances in the state of contemporary knowledge, including knowledge of contemporary world society, are at present in the minority. The curriculum-makers in the colleges and universities are concerned mainly with variations in the sets of requirements for general and special education to achieve a proper balance between them, rather than with an analysis of the content of the curriculum itself to determine whether or not it is drawing upon resources of knowledge now available and relevant to the needs of the student and the citizen in the 1960s. The universities and the colleges of education need, as much as does the Government, a reformulation of cultural policy. At present, few universities think of themselves as parts of a cultural system which has direct connections with the conduct of American foreign policy in its intellectual and cultural aspect. The Government governs, the schools and colleges educate, according to general assumptions laid down by national policies in whose formulation the educators of teachers seldom share.

THE ROLE OF THE INTELLECTUAL

One would assume that in the educational system of a democratic society in which there is no sharp division between the university and the society it serves, the colleges and universities would instinctively take part in efforts to formulate and to influence the conduct of foreign policy, particularly in its cultural dimension. But this is not the case. It is customary among intellectuals, when considering matters of power and the power structure of a given situation, to question the motives and intention of those who use the power. Among liberal intellectuals in particular it is usual to find a sharp distinction made between idealists without power and politicians or Government officials who exercise it, with suspicion of the latter and praise for the former.

If one considers the political process from the point of view of the intellectuals, their role is to act as critics of existing policies and to raise the question as to whether a given policy or act is consonant with professed ideals. Every society thus has trouble with its intellectuals, no matter how authoritarian the society may be, as one can see in contemporary conflicts within the Chinese political apparatus, in Spain under Franco, in Jugoslavia under Tito, in the Soviet Union from Stalin to Kosygin, and, in a different context, in the United States.

In the liberal democracies, the problem is handled by assuring to the intellectuals and the universities a freedom of expression, and taking the position before the world that such freedom is an ideal for all societies. It is for this reason that the United States is most often criticized for its failure to solve its own social and political problems, whereas the less open and more controlled societies, which do not make the same claim for individual freedom, receive milder criticisms in the court of world opinion, partly because political repression of intellectuals is considered normal in those societies. In fact, a good deal of the criticism from abroad, including much of that produced by writers in the Soviet Union, is based on prior criticism of American policy and action developed by American intellectuals writing for American readers.

What is seldom noticed is that a large portion of the world's intellectuals have a psychic investment in the cultural and political life of the United States, and often use it either consciously or unconsciously, as a testing point, not only for American intellectual and social behavior, but for the values and validity of their own political and social structures. I wish to persuade the reader that the very openness of American society to the intellectuals who denounce it and the continuous flow of criticism we receive from abroad, are not only signs of political strength but indications of a cultural power which is the envy of the propagandists who inveigh against it. I would also wish to persuade the reader that American citizens, teachers, intellectuals, and artists who travel abroad, with or without Government subsidy, not only have the same rights to express their opinions about American ideas and policies that they have at home, but that it is a favorable sign of the strength and value of a democratic society when these rights are freely granted and fully exercised.

Another part of our cultural power lies in the sheer amount of interest the world takes in us, with our daily lives and Government actions scrutinized by a stream of foreign experts, and the whole world seeming to feel free to take part in our politics, liking or disliking our Presidents, our habits, our films, our arts, and ourselves. My hope is that we can manage to go on being as interesting to the world as we now seem to be, and that the beginning we have made in developing new cultural policies designed to develop an international context for American ideas can be extended radically in the future.

CULTURAL POWER AND INTERNATIONALISM

The circumstances demand not only a shift in cultural policy in the direction of internationalism and away from the notion that we should urge the American case on everyone who will listen, but it must include a more precise definition of what the policy is intended to accomplish. It has been assumed for years that it would be good for American relations abroad if courses and institutes in American culture, American literature, American studies, could be organized on foreign campuses in order that American ideas and values should become known and understood, that students abroad would have direct access to the materials of American culture.

It has also been assumed, implicitly when not explicitly, that the main purpose of bringing foreign students and scholars to this country is to give them direct access to the reality of America, its culture and its educational system, in order that a better and more favorable understanding of our aims and values might exist abroad. There has always been an implicit political motive which, in broadest terms, could be described in the conventional phrase, "strengthening the forces of democracy by building friendship with foreign countries," or, in the language of the Bureau of Educational and Cultural Affairs in explaining its student programs with African countries, "improving the competence of friendly regimes and . . . increasing their understanding of American values, policies and actions."[9]

I am not suggesting that there is anything base in these purposes, or that there is any harm in being friendly and wanting others to be, except that the emphasis has been so heavily in this direction that it has obscured other important aims; the kind of intellectual and social experience available to the visiting scholars and students has been too limiting and, in a sense, too artificial.

I can recall, for example, speaking to classes in American studies in universities abroad, where the students either had no particular interest in the subject of American philosophy, culture, and education, or were taking for granted that the American professor in their midst was there to persuade them of the virtues of American life and letters as an apologist for its political and social system. The students were much more interested in the relations and comparisons between American ideas and those of other cultures, especially their own, much more interested in an opportunity for criticism and discussion than in academic exposition. My experience with intelligent foreign students in this country has been that the stereotypes of American ideas and cultural deficiencies which students bring with them from abroad are more often than not reinforced by their experience on the American campus and within the American community.

It is true of course that the operation of any government, abroad or at home, reflects the cultural habits and social preconceptions of the people whose government it is. Americans are accustomed to competing with each other in the normal course of their lives, and

[9] Hearings before a Subcommittee of the Committee on Appropriations, House of Representatives, 90th Congress, Part 2, Department of State, U. S. Government Printing Office, Washington, D.C., 1967, p. 575.

to judging people and institutions according to competitive ranking, in baseball, tennis, scholastic averages, television programs, or public opinion polls, with a national and personal desire to be first, to score the highest. American institutions of all kinds, including the educational and cultural, are rated according to their prestige, fame, productivity, wealth, size.

In their personal lives and social customs, Americans seek recognition for their virtues, and freely bestow such recognition on others as a normal part of their personal and social relationships. We want to be the first; first in space, as President Kennedy once said, without saying why we should be, first in whatever we do. We have built one of the most comprehensive systems of mass communication and image-making the world has ever seen, and we are the home of advertising and public relations. We tend to believe that virtues, talents, skills, and capacities go unrecognized if unpublicized.

It would be odd, therefore, if a large part of these elements in the national character were not expressed in the American conception of cultural policy and educational operation abroad, if we did not demand results from those policies which are measurable, in explicit admiration for our cultural artifacts, in the approval of our ideas, appreciation for our performers, support of our policies. In any number of ways we look for a return on our cultural investments in terms of political approval, "friendly relations," understanding. We want the question answered, Are you pro- or anti-American? without realizing that even to raise the question in part falsifies the answer.

On the other hand, the policies as they are administered suffer the defects of the culture, defects so endlessly described by American social critics. The policies suffer from the inability of most Americans to distinguish between holding an idea oneself because one believes it, and "selling" it and oneself to others. The purpose of cultural exchange, and the reason for developing a cultural policy in the first place, is to advance the cause of education and of the intellectual and cultural interests of all concerned. This is an end in itself, from which may or may not flow other advantages to the sponsors. The appearance of the American Ballet Theater Company before Soviet audiences is a gift from the dancers to the Soviet people which they accept gladly, as do Americans the art of the Bolshoi. The dancers happen to be American or Russian. When Andrei Voznesensky declaims his poems before Americans, or cries in protest in Russia, "I am . . . a human being made of flesh and blood, not a puppet to be pulled on a string . . ." he strikes a response in our country, because we recognize in him, and he in us, the common bonds which exist between one man and another, the common modes of experience through which we can share each other's bounty.

If, in consequence, certain political or other advantages accrue to either country, if Americans and Russians can learn to admire and understand each other through the arts, this is the natural and happy result of all experience in the arts. But it has little to do with the quality of wisdom in the ideologies or foreign policies of our respective Governments. The arts bring the world's people together on common ground, as do science, education, and the sharing of all mutual interests. The ideal cultural exchange is of the kind represented by the Montreal Exposition, where the arts, ideas, and architecture of the world can come together freely in an atmosphere which allows each object, performance, and idea to make its own statement before an international community.

I am arguing for a total foreign policy based on cultural values which inform and enlighten its decisions and acts, and against one which considers the arts, education, and cultural affairs to be merely instruments of support for a foreign policy and national posture already decided upon by the Government. The intellectual, cultural, and moral values are primary, the foreign policy must flow from them, not the other way around.

THE NEGLECT OF THE CULTURAL ELEMENT

In the continuing stream of analyses of how American foreign policy is made and administered, the whole question of cultural policy as a factor in foreign relations has been, in the title of Charles Frankel's book, *The Neglected Aspect of Foreign Affairs*.[10] One of the neglects lies in what the cultural policy fails to include. The policy concentrates on the formal educational and cultural institutions in our own and other countries and neglects to include, for example, American scientific and technological advisory services abroad, the Atomic Energy Commission, the Arms Control and Disarmament Agency, the Atoms for Peace program, and the

[10] *The Neglected Aspect of Foreign Affairs*, Charles Frankel, The Brookings Institution, Washington, D.C., 1965, pp. 156.

variety of programs run by Government agencies—Labor, Agriculture, Commerce, etc.—through representatives in the Embassies abroad. The intellectual community of foreign countries is organized much more tightly as an élite body than is the American and is much more in touch with itself. Scientific advisers working with foreign governments are directly involved with problems of disarmament, arms control, nuclear proliferation, the peaceful uses of atomic energy, education, and international research. They usually have direct and indirect connections with other scientists and scholars not in government service who are interested, or who could become interested, in this kind of problem.

The members of this part of the intellectual community in foreign countries seldom have any relation to American cultural activities abroad, partly because they lie outside the regular institutional arrangements for the activities, partly because science is not considered a part of culture or its affairs, and partly because the cultural affairs officers too seldom hold an interest in or knowledge of the larger questions raised by philosophers, scientists, and men of letters. Their interests are more likely to be administrative than intellectual, and their work, accurately described in Mr. Frankel's book, more related to the disposition of administrative matters than to the discussion of cultural or philosophical issues with local intellectuals and educators. There is, for example, an international peace research movement in which Americans have played a leading part, and which could become the basis for regional international conferences sponsored by the United States through its cultural agencies, or for visits by American specialists in the field.

In the field of education, some of the same difficulties are to be found, in the separation of cultural activities from education, with education defined as a body of practices, institutions and curricula in which experts are involved. There has not yet been an adequate clarification of the role in international education of the United States Information Agency with its obvious involvement with American cultural institutions, and the relation between its educational functions and those of the Cultural Affairs Officers, or the relation between the educational advisors and consultants in AID projects with the planning and programs in cultural activities organized by the State Department. The visiting scholar with educational interests and knowledge who travels to foreign countries for lectures and conferences with foreign colleagues seldom meets the American educators who are at work there, nor are there cultural events dealing with broader educational and social questions in which the AID educators take part.

The division of responsibility for "culture" between the USIA and its "fast" media—films, radio, magazines, public information—and the State Department's Cultural Exchange in the "slow" media—intellectuals, books, performers, exhibits, scholars, and teachers—is based on a fallacious distinction between the purveyors of information about American life and values and the exponents and practitioners of the arts, the sciences, and education. An information service is neither a propaganda instrument nor a cultural eunuch. A Voice of America speaks for America and its democratic culture, and the information it conveys is loaded with values derived from the culture, including the values of objectivity and of truth-telling.

In fact, the entire area of education has never been a central concern in foreign policy planning, especially as this has to do with the education of teachers and the kind of international cooperative research and teaching which could add a large and important dimension to the cultural element in foreign affairs. As is the case in the United States as a whole, the education of teachers has always been far down on the list of priorities, "education" has been separated from "culture," and the neglect at home is reflected in the neglect of a policy for teacher education abroad. The continuing and tragic manifestation of such neglect lies in the refusal of Congress to put any money into the very instrument it created in the International Education Act and the Center for Educational Cooperation. We are simply throwing away our chance to take the leadership the world system of education so badly needs.

THE STATE DEPARTMENT AND THE EDUCATORS

As of now, the relation between American education and American foreign policy has been one in which students and faculty members in the colleges and universities consider the State Department, as the operating agency for the administration and manufacture of foreign policy, to be a major counterforce toward true internationalism. The relationship between the State Department and the intellectual community, both inside and outside the universities and schools, is at best uneasy and, normally, unsatisfactory. Part of the unsatisfactoriness is unavoidable, since the State Department is an instrument for making policy according to Washington views of what constitutes the national interest, whereas the university is an instrument for the development of informed opinion and critical judgment about all policies, in world affairs or anything else. It exists to provide a continuing debate about what is in fact the national interest. Those invited by the State Department to serve on advisory panels for policy decisions are drawn from a strong group of university research scholars and others whose work in public policy matters is recognized, a good many of whom have interchangeable roles between the Department and the Universities, or are doing research in political and social issues as an extension of Departmental projects.

Again, an unavoidable problem arises in trying to maintain independent bodies of scholars in the universities whose research can produce fresh insight and thought *because* it is carried on outside and because its assumptions differ from those of the Government, while at the same time maintaining on the part of the outsiders a degree of influence on the policy-makers. I am thinking of issues like United States policy toward Communist China, or toward Southeast Asia, or toward the antiballistic missile system.

But the center of the problem as far as the entire educational system is concerned lies in the relation between U.S. foreign policy and all its dimensions and the bulk of the university faculty members who are not on advisory panels and whose main intellectual and academic responsibilities lie in teaching undergraduates and high school students. At the time of the teach-ins on the Vietnam question, the feeling in the universities was that dissident views on the campus were considered by the State Department, the President and his staff to be those of amateurs and bemused people without access to the cables and the inner circle of information and experts within the Government. On the one hand, membership in the inner circle, when extended into the academic community, tends to neutralize the member as far as public disagreement is concerned; on the other hand, nonmembership disqualifies the critic, and the State Department takes the role of explaining its policies as if these were the only ones which could be held by reasonable men who understood the problems.

The approach is publicly evident in the foreign policy conferences organized by the State Department for the benefit of educators. Responding to a serious interest on the part of the Department in making its policies and procedures known to educators, Department officials, from the Secretary of State to the heads of various bureaus, have appeared these past three years before an invited national audience of administrators, professors, and teachers from a range of institutions, many of them colleges for teachers. I am prepared to believe in the sincerity of the motives of the Government in providing the opportunity for educators to hear directly the rationale which the policy-makers hold for the decisions they have made and are making.

The State Department has little enough opportunity for such explanation, and there is something incongruous in the fact that the military budget allows for the expenditure of millions of dollars for information services connected with its work, by which large numbers of newspaper and television reporters, persons thought to be influential, including educators, are flown to military installations and military briefings, while the State Department has an infinitesimal budget for its information services. The educators who attend the foreign policy conferences consist of those whose institutions or whose private means can provide the funds to make the trip possible.

Once they arrive, however, the educators enter a situation in which the Department spokesmen seem not to consider themselves to be partners in an intellectual and political enterprise, but owners of a policy they must protect against harm. The result is that the educators are put in the role of potential purveyors of Government policy, not as teachers concerned to consider world affairs from a broad international point of view. The fact that the educators seem to accept their role eagerly is one of the depressing items which must be reported. One senses that the educators feel grateful that they have been allowed to pay their own way to the State Department and flattered that the State Department is willing to bring out its experts to expound on the validity of the policies it has adopted.

The Conference for educators does give to its participants a sense of the reality of the issues, since the issues are presented to the audience by persons responsible for dealing with them. This is an experience which few educators have the opportunity to undergo, and it results in a heightening of interest in the issues themselves on the part of those who attend. But if the purpose of American education is to provide the teachers and students in the schools and colleges with an international point of view, it is difficult to see how the State Department contributes to that purpose simply by reciting the reasons why its present policies are correct and indisputable. One would hope that in subsequent conferences of this kind, university scholars whose qualifications for foreign policy discussion are equal to the occasion could present alternate views for discussion by State Department officials and that the central problem of increasing the flow of ideas between the educators and the policymakers on a whole variety of issues, including that of improving the teaching of world affairs and raising the level of informed criticism of Government policy, could occupy the attention of the participants. Otherwise such conferences give the impression of being the State Department's answer to the teach-in.

One of the most interesting examples of what might be accomplished by a change in format came in a panel discussion at the 1967 Conference, in which a veteran reporter from the Washington *Post* challenged the entire information policy of the State Department in the presence of its principal information officer, and raised fundamental questions having to do with the relation of national security and the free flow of information to the public. In the subsequent discussion, substantive issues were raised about the Government's attitude to freedom of the press and the right of citizens, students, and teachers to know more than they are ordinarily told on issues of serious importance to educators and of consequence to the education of teachers.

The State Department has a genuine role to play in the education of American teachers, both in the dissemination of information about Government policies and the problems with which the Department deals, and in the opportunity it has for working with the university community on the development of cultural policies relevant to the new position of the United States in world society. What is needed as the basis for a new policy is the conception of the United States as an international culture, along with the idea that the American point of view is not "American" but international. Our purpose in America could then be seen, not as an effort to induct foreign scholars and students, or those we visit abroad, or ourselves, into an American culture and an American curriculum, so that we will all appreciate and support America and the West, but as an effort to enrich our curriculum and other cultures with the points of view, skills, and knowledge of scholars and students from everywhere. We should ask our visitors to join us in teaching Americans about the world, arranging our studies and theirs around sets of common interests and common problems.

The proposal is that the United States should become a meeting-ground for the people of the world, a place where we can pool the world's resources for the benefit of all. We should ask our visitors to bring their instruments and play their music, act their plays, read their poems, dance, sing, compose, paint, and write with us in our schools, colleges, and communities as resident artists and scholars, encouraging everyone to teach everyone else whatever it is he knows. Abroad, we can take the initiative in creating, not American outposts, but international centers where American students, teachers, artists, and scholars can work with their counterparts from elsewhere on common tasks for varying lengths of time.

THE IDEA OF REGIONAL WORLD CENTERS
FOR EDUCATION

The possibility would then exist of uniting the world's educational system into one which draws upon the intellectual and cultural resources of as wide a variety of countries as can be persuaded to join with us, and we would create a powerful counterforce to tendencies within the world community toward fragmentation and nationalist attitudes. We would also break down the conception of confrontation between East and West, by moving the center of gravity of Western initiatives into the African, Asian, and South American continents, and thus helping to remove the distinction between We and They, the distinction between a powerful industrialized West and an underdeveloped East and South.

We have already applied this point of view in certain parts of American foreign policy, in the Peace Corps, in the Atoms for Peace program, for example, and more recently in the proposal to create a world network of regional water resource centers to share scientific and technical knowledge and to develop cooperative research and study of present and future water shortages. At the first major international conference on the problem of the world's water resources, attended by 5000 persons from 90 countries, in Washington, May 1967, President Johnson opened the proceedings by announcing the establishment in the United States Government of a Water for Peace Office. Mr. Johnson told the Conference delegates that, "The United States is prepared to join others in establishing a network (of regional water resource centers). We will provide our fair share of the expert assistance, the supplies and equipment and the financing."[11]

This point of view about water is especially relevant to all those matters having to do with the educational shortages, present and future, which afflict the contemporary world. It is time we announced that we were "prepared to establish a network of regional *educational* resource centers" where the education of teachers and of students in the problems of the contemporary world could be conducted as an international enterprise. Mr. Johnson, at the water conference, raised the questions "How can we engineer our continents and direct our great river systems to make use of the water resources we now waste?" and "How can we curb the filth that pollutes our streams?"[12] A revised version of those questions is equally relevant. If we were to construct a version of these questions in cultural terms, it would read, "How can we develop our continents and direct our great educational systems to make use of the educational resources we now waste?" and, "How can we curb the misinformation and bias which pollutes our political and cultural relations?"

An example of what I have in mind can be drawn from an International Conference on Social Psychological Research in Developing Countries, held at the University of Ibadan, Nigeria, for a week in January of 1967.[13] The Conference was organized jointly by the University of Ibadan and the Center For Research on Conflict Resolution, along with the Doctoral Program in Social Psychology, of the University of Michigan in Ann Arbor. It was sponsored by the Nigerian Association of the Behavioral Sciences, the Society for the Psychological Study of Social Issues (U.S.), the Scientific Council of Africa, and the International Social Science Council.

Over one hundred persons attended, fifty of them official delegates, the rest observers from universities, government agencies, and research institutes in the African countries; the delegates included 21 social psychologists from Africa, 16 from the United States, 10 from Western and Eastern Europe, the rest from Latin America,

[11] Address to the International Conference on Water for Peace, by President Lyndon B. Johnson, May 23, 1967, Washington, D.C.
[12] Ibid., p. 5.
[13] Further information can be obtained from Dr. Charles Pidoux, c/o United Nations, BP 492, Niomey, Nigeria.

the Middle East, Asia, and Australia. The symposia were organized around problems in education and the diffusion of knowledge, issues in social psychological research, and problems in development and social change. Aside from the papers read and the topics debated, plans were discussed for international cross-cultural research, regional workshops in teaching and research, teaching in the African universities, research on international tensions, and ways in which the resources of social psychologists could be applied to education and development problems in the new countries.

If even a limited number of scholars in this and allied fields—those having a direct relation to teaching and education, anthropology, sociology, political science, philosophy—were to come together from around the world, taking time away from the home country on a planned international schedule for one month, three months, six months, or a year at a time, with graduate and undergraduate students as interns and research assistants, tutors, teachers, teachers' aides, etc., a whole new area of international cooperation could be opened up, through the efforts of Americans and other nationals, of the kind who put together the Conference in Ibadan. The Institute for Educational Research and Studies in Tehran,[14] on a very modest budget from the National Teacher's College in Iran, has already been one center of cooperation with the UNESCO Institute for Education in Hamburg, Germany, for a project in the International Evaluation of Educational Achievement. The use of American funds and American aid from the educational community in combination with Iranians and others could support some very interesting and useful teaching and research in international education by building upon the present efforts of Dr. Iraj Ayma and others in the Institute in Tehran, to make an International Center for Education in that country.

THE NEED FOR A CULTURAL POLICY

Admittedly, it is easier, although still very difficult, to deal with the technology of water than it is to handle the relations between cultures, since political issues immediately intrude in the latter enterprise. On the other hand, the formation of a cultural policy consistent with Mr. Johnson's point of view about water would give

[14] See *Progress*, newsletter (mimeographed) from The Institute for Educational Research and Studies, Box 3071, Tehran, Iran, 21 pp.

direction to a series of other international policies which are directly
related to the American educational system. There is a marked difference between the tone and content of the President's statements
at the Water Conference and at the International Conference on the
World Crisis in Education in October of 1967, although the emphasis on technology remained constant. The President, at the Education Conference, called for the use of the technologies of television,
satellite communication systems, microfilming, etc., to extend education to the largest possible number of the world's people. But the
President made no proposal about regional world centers for the
study and development of educational ideas and intercultural research, no declaration of policy of the kind which would have committed the United States to extending into reality the declarations
and provisions of the International Education Act, or of the President's speech at the Smithsonian Institution in 1965.

It may be true that the Conference on the World Crisis in Education was not the proper place for an international policy statement
by the United States. But without such a statement, or without
some practical manifestation of the international intention of the
United States in calling the World Education Conference in the first
place, the participants and those who took note of it in the educational community of the world could conclude that the Conference
was either a propaganda device to draw attention to the American
rhetoric of internationalism or was a way of bringing together client
countries for consultation about problems in mutual aid.

In any case, at some point and in some direct way, a statement of
American cultural policy must be made if there is to be clarity about
American intention in supporting the cause of international cultural
self-determination and world education. One of the first items in
need of clarification by a statement carrying the weight of the presi-
dency is the question of what kind of educational and social research is to be carried on by what agencies of the United States
Government, and what kind is the proper province of the universities
and for what purposes. Such a policy statement, one would hope,
would eliminate all the colleges and universities from classified or
secret Government research of any kind, and would eliminate the
colleges and universities from all military research on whatever
subject.

In positive terms, it would assign to the universities the area of
research and teaching in the field of world affairs, foreign policy,

and international education, inviting the scholars of the world to join the American universities and their counterparts on other continents in an effort to find solutions to problems in international conflict and in international cooperation to avoid mass violence. I am thinking of a policy statement by the United States of the same degree of significance which marked the statement in the United States Constitution about the separation of church and state, in this case separating all military and clandestine Government research from the free inquiry of scholars in the universities.

One good way of identifying the areas of proper university inquiry would be to ask whether or not, whatever the research might be, it could be used as material for teaching in the undergraduate colleges. If, for security reasons, it could not be so used, it has no place in the life of the American university. If the results of university research could not be made available to the world community of scholars, "friend and foe alike," to use the President's phrase in justifying the International Education Act, and if the research itself could not be conducted anywhere in the world by any serious international group of university scientists and scholars, then it should not be carried on in American institutions of higher education.

Such a declaration of policy would have immediate effects. One of the first would be to assert a serious degree of control over the kind of research in the social sciences now being carried on by the Defense Department and its allied agencies, both public and private. We would immediately shift a large proportion of the nine million dollars spent annually by the Defense Department on the study of social conditions abroad into the State Department, which at present has less than one million dollars for what can surely be called a major area of foreign policy. When only one percent of the total Government budget for the study of foreign societies is spent by the State Department, it is clear that the focus of effort in all these matters lies outside the scope of the very agency whose responsibility it is to understand the world before acting on it.

A NEGATIVE EXAMPLE

The Camelot Project, for example, sponsored by the Defense Department with a staff of university social scientists organized to study the ways of forestalling revolutions in selected Latin American countries, would never have been suggested or allowed had there been an overall policy based on a philosophy of democratic internationalism, and had this policy been properly administered by the State Department. Were a study of revolutions to be conducted it would not have been put forward as a military-political project whose results might possibly be used against the country in which it had been carried out. If it were to be done at all, it would not have been the work of American social scientists or of university scholars employed by the military, no matter how honest their motives or their scholarship.

It would have been carried out by a team of international scholars with the cooperation of the university community in the Latin American countries, and its results would have been published for the world community to read. In fact, a serious international study of the causes of revolution might produce some very useful recommendations for reorganizing the economic and social systems of the countries where revolutions are imminent. But it is unlikely that a unilateral study by the military of one country of the political conditions of another can be regarded as anything but disguised counterintelligence.

One would hope that a form of self-imposed discipline on the part of American educators and social scientists would prevent collaboration of the kind represented in the Camelot affair, or in the use of Michigan State University as a cover for intelligence operations in South Vietnam. In the absence of the self-discipline of scholars, and in the absence of restraint on the part of Government agencies, an official policy for university research and American scholarship in foreign affairs is an absolute essential, if cultural and educational affairs are to be considered a positive and honest element in American foreign policy.

One approach to such a policy can be found in the statement by the Fellows of the American Anthropological Association, in which the nature of international integrity in research and education is clearly described:

> The human condition, past and present, is the concern of anthropologists throughout the world. The study of mankind in varying social, cultural, and ecological situations is essential to our understanding of human nature, of culture, and of society.
>
> Our present knowledge of the range of human behavior is admittedly incomplete. Expansion and refinement of this knowledge depend heavily

on international understanding and cooperation in scientific and scholarly inquiry. To maintain the independence and integrity of anthropology as a science, it is necessary that scholars have full opportunity to study peoples and their culture, to publish, disseminate, and openly discuss the results of their research, and to continue the responsibility of protecting the personal privacy of those being studied and assisting in their research.

Constraint, deception, and secrecy have no place in science. Actions which compromise the intellectual integrity and autonomy of research scholars and institutions not only weaken those international understandings essential to our discipline, but in so doing they also threaten any contribution anthropology might make to our own society and to the general interests of human welfare.[15]

This is not the place to review at length the serious damage done to American cultural relations with other countries by the covert subsidies of the Central Intelligence Agency to educational and cultural organizations in the United States and abroad. It is enough to say that serious damage was done, and that the CIA actions put in jeopardy the integrity of American students, scholars, teachers, Peace Corps Volunteers, and every other representative of American culture who travels abroad for study, research, or public service. Many of the British and European intellectuals who had written for *Encounter*, for example, under the impression that it was an independent journal with American and British co-editors, were outraged to learn that they had been writing for a magazine supported by CIA money.

The British editor Stephen Spender, having heard rumors from other writers in the United States, Europe, and England of clandestine CIA support to his magazine, asked his American co-editor about it directly, and was told that the rumors were false when, in fact, the American knew that they were true. There is nothing I have seen in the magazine's publication record to indicate that the editorial policy was slanted in deference to American interests, and it is generally acknowledged that *Encounter* has been one of the most important intellectual journals in the West, one in which the serious philosophical, literary, and political issues in Eastern Europe and the Western world have had a full opportunity for treatment by some of the best of contemporary writers.

But the attitude of the Europeans and British toward the CIA

15 Statement on Problems of Anthropological Research and Ethics, by the Fellows of the American Anthropological Association, 1967; American Anthropological Association, 1530 P Street, N.W., Washington, D.C.

episode is either one of cynicism that the Americans with their rhetoric of freedom and democracy should have been caught in a hypocritical counter-intelligence act, a kind of intellectual U2 incident, or a sense of betrayal in being tricked into writing for a magazine subsidized by a foreign Government. At the very least, it is a naïve way for a country to run its cultural affairs, since any serious analysis of the idea of that kind of subsidy, aside from rejecting its hypocrisy, would have indicated that eventually, among writers and intellectuals, the most skeptical and perceptive breed of all human kind where politics is concerned, this sort of secret would inevitably be exposed. What is now to prevent the assumption on the part of any country that Fulbright scholars, or any other American received into foreign universities as colleagues, are not gathering intelligence data on the people and institutions giving them hospitality?

The point is that there has to be an American cultural policy, before the fact, not after, and that the policy has to be large-minded, consistent with the claims of a democratic society which says that it is concerned to be honest, open, and truly international in its relations with other cultures. We have to decide whether we want a policy designed to draw together the intellectual community of the world and to serve the world's interests, or one deliberately designed to work in the American self-interest as a combination propaganda and counter-intelligence arm of the U. S. Government. If it is neither one nor the other, it will be assumed to be the latter. Once we get a policy, we have to see that it is administered in keeping with its spirit.

THE ROLE OF STUDENTS

Again it is the lack of a clear understanding of the role of cultural and educational affairs in American foreign policy which makes it possible for decisions like that of the CIA in giving covert support to American students abroad to be sanctioned by four successive Presidents of the United States, or to be made at all. One of the deepest ironies in the relation of the CIA to the work of the National Student Association lies in the fact that at a time in the late 1940s and early 1950s when the United States Congress, the public, and the Government were suspicious of political action of any kind by students, were unwilling to grant them responsibility for social or educational policy in the universities, or to provide funds for inde-

pendent student action, at home or abroad, the one organization in
the entire country which did trust the students was the most sensitive of them all, the Agency in charge of counterintelligence.

Those of us who were working in international and national affairs
with students during those earlier years found that it was nearly impossible to raise funds in support of international student projects,
either from private sources, foundations, university budgets, or, least
of all, the Government. The Congress, in the grip of the McCarthy
disease of the 1950s, could not imaginably have been considered as
a source of funds, nor could the State Department, then infected
with the same ailment. But more than this, so little consideration
was given at that time to the idea that students, or even educators,
had anything to offer to the furtherance of American foreign policy,
or to the development of new patterns of thinking about foreign affairs at home, that with the exception of one or two of the smaller
non-CIA foundations, it was unthinkable to most of those who might
have furnished financial help to students and intellectuals that such
help would serve a useful purpose.

The students have by now proved over and over again the quality
of their ability, the degree of their responsibility, and the extent of
their readiness to carry out tasks in cultural and social affairs far
beyond the recognition they have received for the things they have
already done. Most of it has been done without adequate support
and against serious obstacles. The World University Service, with
its world-wide projects in international education and community
development, the Collegiate Council for the United Nations, the
volunteers in the Poverty programs, the Peace Corps, the International Volunteer Service, aside from the National Student Association and the projects sponsored by many religious organizations,
have all been part of an undefined cultural policy which the students have been carrying out by themselves. We can only imagine
the power of action which would be released were there funds now
available on a sufficient scale to finance properly the work of students in international education.

THE STUDENTS AND THE GOVERNMENT

At this stage in the development of the student movement there
are informed and serious persons in the United States Office of Education and in the Peace Corps who stay in touch with the student

leadership, have direct knowledge of the student movement, and understand the enormous potential which lies in independent action through student-organized projects. Government grants for international student projects in teacher education are needed and should be administered on a broad scale. But we have had enough experience with the niggardliness and contentiousness of Congress in supporting budgets for cultural and international projects, even those which are in no way political, to warn us that appropriations adequate to apply a wide and generous policy of support for students in the field of teacher education and international affairs are going to be very hard to come by.

The idea proposed in Government quarters for a public agency with a non-Governmental Board of Directors to make grants to student organizations and student-run projects in international affairs has merit, although it has the danger in it that its tie to the Government would tie it to Government policy. It is that danger which caused the National Student Association to cut back its international programs after canceling its CIA subsidies. Should an agency for the support of international projects in education by students and others be established, its administrators and policy-makers would have to be at least as perceptive as the CIA in supporting students whose ideas run counter to those of the Government. One model suggests itself in the National Endowment for the Arts, which has a panel of distinguished artists, writers, performers, and cultural leaders appointed by the President to a National Council to make policy decisions about grants and to approve the ones presented to them by the staff of the Endowment. Education and World Affairs, drawing its financial support from foundation sources, is able to remain independent by reason of the quality of its Board of Directors, the talents of its staff, its financial independence, and its colleague relationship with Government officers in the agencies and Congress.

Everything else being equal, the EWA model would be preferable to one which depended on Congressional appropriations. The danger is, in any case, that unless an enlightened attitude to cultural policy and international education is clearly established in the Congress and Administration, and unless there is strong national and Administration support for those policies, each time the appropriations come up for review the students and volunteers who have had fresh, interesting, provocative, or dissident views to express will be attacked by Congressmen and hostile witnesses; appropriations will be available only to conservative projects and compliant students and teachers.

It is literally true that as far as cultural freedom in international politics is concerned, we are still not very far from the McCarthy period, and the normal approach of Government agency officials both to their own work and to Congress is one of caution. The caution has become more pronounced during the past two years as the Government commitment to the military operations in Vietnam has grown in size and intensity. Since most of the country's student leadership is on record as opposing Government foreign policy, in Vietnam and elsewhere, it is doubtful that it would be possible to mount a serious student-run project in international education or cultural affairs without a staff composed of those students most likely to be attacked in Congress. As for private sources, the policies in Foundation grant-making are very conservative when it comes to supporting student projects, especially those which have to do with international affairs and teaching.

An example of what we can expect, and therefore guard against, is provided by the cancellation for 1968 of the Congressional college intern program, one of the most successful of all Government programs in bringing college students closely in touch with the actual working of government and national policy-making. The cost for 1300 students was $327,000, an amount struck from the budget by the House Appropriations Committee on grounds of economy, although it is generally conceded that the reason for ending the program was that a group of interns, during the summer of 1967, circulated and published with signatures a statement against the war in Vietnam, released, according to one of the interns, "to convince the policy-makers that some of the most respected elements of our young society are concerned with our actions in Vietnam." The House action was denounced by a handful of Congressmen as punitive and shortsighted, who interpreted the decision, in the words of Representative Hervey Machen of Maryland, as a way of "serving notice to the young people of this country that we cannot afford dissent and we want complete control over the people we bring in to see the government in operation."

The Office of Economic Opportunity is one of the few Government agencies which works directly with students without an intervening link to colleges and universities; an OEO grant supports the National Student Association's Tutorial Assistance Center through which more than 250,000 students across the country are helped, through an efficient, inexpensive, and well-run program, in the work of tutoring children in the inner cities and rural areas. The entire operation of the poverty program has given scope to student initiative, which is rare in the operations of Government—from Head Start teachers to VISTA volunteers, the students command the respect of their Government supervisors and have been given a large degree of autonomy and responsibility outside the conventional Government and university supervision, sometimes with consequent political rumblings in the communities where they serve. Such rumblings are heard whenever young people concern themselves to take social action which has political effects. It is time for this country and its Government to realize that if we mean what we say about creating a society for and of equals, we are going to have to support the right of young people to *be* equal, and to act on behalf of equality and liberal democracy.

In the wake of the CIA disaster, what is needed is a strong, positive, and convincing statement from the Administration, preferably from the President, that this country trusts its students, that it wants to give them full support in funds and assistance to carry out the educational and cultural tasks at home and abroad which they are fully equipped to do, that we do not believe in turning American students into hidden agents of counterintelligence, and that we urge them to express their honest views about their country and its policies wherever they go. Unless support to students and their education in world affairs is given in this spirit and with this kind of clarity of purpose, no Government-sponsored organization will have the mandate it needs in order to replace the CIA as the sponsor of student internationalism. Nor will the students believe that their Government either needs them or wants them to represent America abroad, or that it trusts them to come to their own conclusions about the issues in world affairs which disturb their consciences.

The national policy for grant-making, by all agencies, both public and private, should be one which treats students as the equals of any other applicants and judges their projects on the merits. Most of the best work by student organizations in teacher education and international affairs has been carried out without the supervision or control of university or government authorities; often its high quality is due to the fact that the work *is* unsupervised and not subject to the unnecessary inhibitions of academic convention.

An example of the kind of work in the international field which can best be done by students is to be found in a project during the fall of 1966, organized by the National Student Association with support from the State Department, for a travel and seminar program involving eleven visiting Bolivian student leaders. The itinerary, personnel, and content were arranged by the students in consultation with the U. S. Government and with the Bolivians. One Bolivian student came in advance of the others to act as co-director of the seminar, the content of which was planned to include discussion of mutual problems in educational and social change in Latin America and the United States; the visitors had a chance to visit a cross section of the activists in the American student body and to see what they were doing in community action, the Poverty Program, civil rights, and educational reform.

THE PHILOSOPHY OF INTELLECTUAL AUTONOMY

In a genuine sense, the students in this project and in others run by the National Student Association and comparable organizations were making cultural policy by the approach they took to their responsibilities toward the visitors and by the content of the program they planned. The particular character of the American student movement lies in its concern for social service and community action, as well as for the autonomy of students in running their own organizations. In contrast to student movements elsewhere, which are either controlled by government officials or are tied to national political parties, the American student movement is honestly and fervently independent, unwilling to follow the guidance of the national political parties, even in those cases where they have formal affiliations.

American students also have a point of view about their relation to the society they are trying to change. Unlike most student movements abroad, the American students seldom consider themselves to be part of an élite by reason of their University status, nor are they very interested in debating abstract political theory, except as a basis for social and political action. One of the main contributions they make in relation to American foreign policy is to demonstrate in action to those students with whom they work, here or abroad, a philosophy of social change in which the student becomes an ally of the members of his own community to achieve goals which they share. The concept of volunteer service in the public welfare is built into the student organizations, along with policies of student autonomy. As part of the university system, the students are now challenging their Government and their society on a broad range of issues in world affairs and social change, particularly where these policies, as in the case of the CIA subsidy, are to them a retreat from open democratic principles.

The university system has the major responsibility for preserving the integrity of American cultural policy, and university scholars and teachers have the duty of keeping themselves and their Government honest. Their major instrument for doing that lies in their professional associations and in the work of the universities themselves. But they also have the duty, through their example and initiative, of helping to establish in the world community of intellectuals the standards of intellectual impartiality and honesty which are best developed through international communication and joint scholarship. The mere fact that American intellectuals are relatively free from political control and that they have access to sources of funds for open research which, by comparison with what is available to foreign scholars, are incredibly large, lays a duty upon the Americans to work in the interests of international scholarship and education, since the others are so much more limited in the conditions for their own initiatives. The world needs a world code for scholarship on the order of the Universal Declaration of Human Rights, and in the absence of an Eleanor Roosevelt as the American spokesman for a world point of view, the joint efforts of American scholars must be put into service on behalf of the international ideal.

It is no longer possible to assume the right of an American social scientist or educator to enter the culture of another country, collect research data having to do with his private interests or the interest of his Government, and to return home with his booty, having done no more than to have taken the time of his foreign colleagues and informants and to have accepted their intellectual and political hospitality. A cultural policy based on a concern for increasing the world's knowledge of itself, and of using knowledge for the international benefit would demand that the university community act as the major counterforce to the use of the sciences and arts for nationalist political gain.

In the interim stage toward full internationalism in scholarship, the increase in the study of American society by foreign scholars on a bilateral exchange basis would decrease the unavoidable insularity of American sociological assumptions. I am thinking, for example, of the contribution Gunnar Myrdal has made to American and world understanding of the American race problem, because of his ability to conceive the American problem in non-American terms.

This means cooperation among international scientists and scholars to produce work of use to all, with American subsidies to support the kind of open international research which enlightens and benefits the society in which it is conducted and the others to which its results are distributed. It is another reason for establishing regional education centers rather than conducting unilateral research projects along with bilateral exchanges.

THE TEACHER IN INTERNATIONAL AFFAIRS

But above everything else, it suggests a new conception of international education which starts with the idea of bringing together the teachers and students of the world to make common cause. We need to begin developing a different conception of the world intellectual community to include not merely the élites of scientists, scholars, artists, and writers, but the teachers and students of the world's educational system. The teachers and the students constitute the network of persons in whose hands lies the rseponsibility for teaching and learning what the world community needs to know. Or, to change the metaphor, students and teachers are the agents of transmission of the ideas and values which exist in any given cultural period or in any region of the world.

A culture consists of the body of ideas, habits, customs, and belief which holds a society together and gives it its distinctive character. Not all of it can be conveyed to others, or even to itself, so much depends on what part of it is singled out. In the United States, for example, there are a youth culture, an Afro-American culture, a Puerto Rican, Spanish-American, Italian-American, and Indian culture, a culture of poverty, of the middle class, of the intellectuals. But when educators and others begin to do something about it, culture is always a matter of putting on art exhibits or adding courses in Western civilization or literature to the curriculum, or building cultural centers, or putting on performances of opera, music, ballet, plays. These are essential elements in the culture but do not begin to exhaust its content.

Similarly, the content of a culture does not become available either to its own members or to the members of other cultures until its words and ideas are transformed into meaning by persons who make the effort to learn what they mean. That is why so much is conveyed from one culture to another through the arts, particularly through plays, poems, novels, and films, where the reality of the lives of the characters in their own context is relatively easy to grasp. When the members of a national culture exchange words and ideas only with each other, or when only the élite understands what is being said either inside or outside a national culture, in science or in art, there is no serious means of communication across the world's cultures. The world's teachers supply that means.

For the teacher has a special privilege and a special role when he goes abroad to teach. To teach and to learn is to go to the heart of another culture, that is, to take one's place within the privileged situation of a company of friends who have something to give and something to learn from each other. To teach is to enter the lives of others at a level deep enough to make mutual understanding possible. To teach the children of another man is to enter his life as well as the life of his child and his family. To work with other teachers in their own school is to join a community, not simply to take an assignment. The schools and colleges are the places where the cultural values and the true images of a society are represented in what is done there, and it is the intermingling of cultural values from the full variety of the world's people which can furnish the texture of a new kind of knowledge within the American educational system.

Further, when a nation-state deliberately conceives its cultural policy as an instrument for injecting its own point of view into the culture of another nation-state, it creates strong resistance to itself within the intellectual community at large where the use of ideas as weapons or ideological instruments is quickly noted and automatically classified. Among the English-language newspapers and magazines sent abroad by the Soviet Union, for example, the consistent policy of presenting facts and ideas about the Soviet Union in a favorable light not only gives the language of the presentation an unhealthy glow like that of bad advertising copy, but it makes it almost impossible for a serious reader to take it seriously.

Similarly, when by political selection the books in USIA libraries abroad are chosen with a view to including only those which present the United States in a favorable light, the library becomes in large degree useless to serious people. Or when most of the educators sent abroad on AID or other Government missions are administrators and educational practitioners, their presence in other countries generates no intellectual excitement which could produce fresh thinking in new dimensions of educational, cultural, and social change. To the intellectual community abroad, the educational practitioner from America then seems more to be a U.S. civil servant with anti-intellectual tendencies than a lively mind representing a lively democratic culture.

On the other hand, when the question is put in different terms, as, for example, How can the citizens of one country have open access to the ideas and culture of another country? it is not simply a question of the cultural apparatus in each country turning out new and approved products for export. It is a matter of how the educational systems can combine their resources to write books, make films, make new courses, new recordings or television programs, which in the eyes of the teachers and educators of all countries can give a true insight into the character and quality of every culture. In the long run, this can only be done by the intermingling of teachers and students within a world educational system in which all national cultures are treated with a full degree of equality and a full degree of objectivity.

An example can be drawn from the work of the World Law Fund which, on the basis of research studies of the kind produced by Louis B. Sohn and Grenville Clark in the field of world law, has developed new materials which deal specifically with international problems as part of an ongoing search for institutional ways of creating a stable world order.[16] Having developed new curricula for teachers in universities and secondary schools in the United States, and having tried them out in more than 150 institutions, the Fund has conferred with Indian, German, Soviet, Latin American, African, and Asian educators with a view to using international materials of this kind on a world scale within the universities and schools. The Fund has also started a World Models project on five continents in which

---

[16] See, for example, *Legal and Political Problems of World Order*, compiled and edited by Saul H. Mendlovitz, a reading and discussion guide for seminars in international affairs. Published and distributed by The Fund for Education Concerning World Peace Through World Law, 11 West 42 Street, New York, N.Y., 856 pp.

scholars in the international field are preparing research statements on the kind of world order they see as possible and desirable from the point of view of their region of the world. No matter what the cultural or political differences may be from country to country, the common problems of international organization and the role of each culture in developing a world system can and should be studied, and should become part of the common body of knowledge with which the teacher deals within his own educational province.

It is for this reason that in the long run the goals of the internationalists throughout the world can only be realized by paying direct and consistent attention to the problem of the education of teachers. Teachers in the primary and secondary schools of the world are the neglected element in international affairs. They are poorly paid, are lacking in status within their societies, and in many instances poorly educated in comparison with their colleagues in the universities. In most countries the normal school or teacher training institute is still the established rule. When plans are made to increase the international dimension of education, either in this country or abroad, the teachers and their education have been the last things which the policy-makers take under consideration. The average number of teachers from the United States sent abroad annually for exchange of teaching posts, language and area studies instruction under the Fulbright-Hays Act is 700. The total number of teachers coming to the United States under the same program for instruction in American education is 400.

A NEW EMPHASIS ON TEACHING AND TEACHERS

What is needed is a large-scale increase in the attention paid to the work of teachers of all kinds through the existing apparatus of cultural exchange and foreign aid. It is gratifying to note that after the recommendations of President Johnson's Smithsonian Institution speech of September of 1965 and the recommendations of Secretary Rusk's special task force for "a broad and long range plan of worldwide educational endeavor," preceding the preparation and passage of the International Education Act, there was a marked increase in attention to education on the part of a number of Government agencies. The Inter-Agency Council for Educational and Cultural Affairs, whose Chairman was then Charles Frankel, started some good work in coordinating the operations of agencies of Gov-

ernment which not only have a part to play in the expansion of
international education, but have budgets with which to expand
them. The Inter-Agency Council includes the State Department,
members from HEW, the Department of Defense, AID, the Peace
Corps, the U. S. Information Agency, and observers from the Bureau
of the Budget and the Smithsonian Institution.

The major source of aid for international education, at least until
the Center for Education Cooperation receives its funds, lies in AID
and the U. S. Office of Education under the supervision of the Assistant Secretary for Education of the Department of Health, Education and Welfare. Putting international education into the Office of
Education means connecting it to the ongoing work of the American educational system, and the eventual protection of its budget
from the biennial cuts administered by Congress for foreign aid
projects of all kinds.

In the meantime, it is an international tragedy that this country,
through the shortsightedness of the Congress, has not set in motion
the work of the Center for Education Cooperation. The urgency of
the need for such a center was described accurately four years ago
by John Gardner in his report on "AID and the Universities," in
March 1964.[17] The Center, as designated in the International Education Act, is to serve as a channel for communication between U.S.
missions abroad and the U.S. educational community; it is to direct
the programs assigned to it by the Department of Health, Education and Welfare, and assist public and private agencies conducting
international education programs abroad.

The Center was designed to be a clearing house, a link between
the domestic programs of schools, colleges, and universities concerned with world affairs and the kind of educational activities
which can be initiated abroad. The idea of the Center if based on
the need for *continuous* interchange and cooperation between all
countries, in education, cultural affairs, science, and technology,
with the appointment of Education Officers in the United States
foreign service, and the development of new manpower within the
American colleges and universities for service in international education and development programs in foreign countries. There was
also to be an American Education Placement Service, to give rele-

[17] "AID and the Universities; a Report to the Administrator of the Agency
for International Development," by John W. Gardner, Education and World
Affairs, 522 Fifth Avenue, New York, N.Y., April 1964, 57 pp.

vant information to Americans who wish to serve abroad—school and college teachers, professors and administrators, either retired or on sabbatical leave, Peace Corps returnees who wish to continue their work abroad, and others. The Service could eventually develop into a world teacher exchange through which the flow of teaching talent could move internationally through collaboration with foreign governments and their educational systems.

In the meantime, until the Center is established, the educational programs of AID, aside from the Peace Corps, have been the major source of funds and opportunity for conducting international education. The particular virtue of the educational work of AID lies in the fact that it is directly linked to the problems of social and economic development of the countries where aid is provided, and is therefore involved in an immediate way with the problems of developing a viable social structure. Educational questions have to be answered in practical ways, including the basic question of how to educate teachers and how to get enough of them.

THE EDUCATIONAL PROGRAMS OF AID

The increase in educational work abroad by AID over the past three years has for the most part gone unnoticed by American educators and the public, and although the amounts of money allocated are still only 5 percent of the total foreign aid budget, they have made it possible to put more time and effort into programs which needed both. In 1965 the education funds in AID amounted to $131 million, moving from there to $137 million in 1966, $189 million in 1967, $198 million in the present year, with $251 million proposed for 1969.

The following are some of the areas in education in which AID is now working, after starting up some new and expanded projects in 1966:

(1) English language teaching and research for the Near East, South Asia, Africa, the Far East, with a budget increase from $2 million to approximately $3.5 million.

(2) The Summer Teaching Corps, for Summer Science Institutes and the National Education Association Overseas Teach Corps, through which American teachers go abroad—to Latin

America, Africa, and Asia (in 1967, 245 of them went) to carry on teacher education programs in intensive summer sessions.

(3) School to School partnerships, through which, in collaboration with the Peace Corps and the Partners of the Alliance Program, schools in the United States, 120 of them in 1966, 503 in 1967, each provide approximately $1000 in funds for building schools abroad, and usually follow up that contribution with a continuing relationship in the supply of books and equipment. As this part of the program develops, there will be a great many more opportunities for collaboration between foreign and American schools by exchange of students, ideas, faculty members, and curricula, with joint research projects included.

(4) Institutional Grant Program, through which AID will give support "to American research and educational institutions for increasing their capacity to deal with programs of economic and social development abroad," depending on the appropriations; the amount for this is calculated at $10 million.

(5) A program of research and planning has begun for the use of new educational technologies, mainly television, in the developing countries including Colombia and Jamaica where projects have already started, and El Salvador where a comprehensive educational system based on television is planned, to serve, with a five-year budget of $7.5 million, as a model for possibilities in other Central American countries and elsewhere in the world.

There are now teams from 71 American universities at work in 38 countries on AID educational missions, although as yet there is no comprehensive evaluation or even description of the overall policy and details of the educational programs themselves, especially as these apply to the education of teachers. One of the difficulties in the operation of AID educational programs lies in the fact that AID is a contracting agency for services, and, unlike the Peace Corps, which has a self-corrective mechanism for evaluation of the educational work it is doing, has no research component to turn in judgments as to whether the programs contracted for are accomplishing what is needed and what was bargained for.

THE LACK OF A RESEARCH ARM

In the two educational fields in which AID research is done, Education and Human Resources, and Institutional and Social Development, $6 million has been spent since 1962 for eight projects in the former and $2.75 million for 16 projects in the latter, on a range of topics from the feasibility of applying new educational media for use with large populations of illiterates, to comparative social change in the developing countries. The contracts for the research have been awarded to universities and to independent research agencies and institutes. Only one of the 24 projects has dealt with teacher education and in the one case the research had to do with techniques for training teachers of English.

A typical instance of the difficulty already referred to in doing American-sponsored social research without international participation can be seen in a Brandeis University project to study the political attitudes of youth as a factor affecting economic development. As the official summary in 1967 points out, "No suitable location has been found for field trials. Difficulties with the problem of 'sensitivity' remain unsolved."

But aside from basic research whose results could be expected to help in giving direction to policy-making for the use of American educational and economic aid, there is at present no systematic way in which AID can inform itself about the educational results of the teams from the universities at work in the 38 countries where they are located. When AID is faced with the question of assigning particular contracts to colleges of education and universities for work abroad, it must simply work through the going establishment, rather than, as is the case with the Peace Corps, take part in developing its own educational and training programs for those in its service. As a result, whatever weaknesses or strengths exist in the philosophy and practices of teacher education in the United States, or in a selected college of education or university and its staff, are exported by AID to the country we are trying to help.

After reviewing the programs of teacher education conducted on the American campuses, my concern is that we have no way of knowing, although any number of ways of suspecting, the kind of educational results being achieved by the help we are giving to foreign countries. If the philosophy and practices of the conventional

American college of education are used as a model for the formation of new programs of teacher education abroad, then we can assume that the same programs of general education, education courses, academic credits, grades, examinations, lectures, and textbooks are being reproduced, and that what is considered to be standard American practice is being presented to the developing countries as the best kind of modern education available.

Reports on the progress of AID educational projects abroad, prepared by those who are conducting them, do not give an indication of how the results would be judged by persons outside the field of professional education, and we are back with the problem of the closed system in which educators, most of whom accept a common set of assumptions about what constitutes good professional education, are the judges of what constitutes a good program in the education of teachers. Most of the answers to questions about the actual content of educational programs, the kind of teacher education being developed, the evaluation of them, the possibilities for educational research, international education, student teaching by American students under AID auspices, are simply not available, since no independent research has been carried on, even of the survey kind.

There is a great range of possibilities for the use of AID projects in general as instruments for the education of teachers, and as the means not only of giving help to foreign countries, but of learning as much as possible about the educational process in other cultures. Americans as well as non-Americans need to find the ways in which liberal and vocational education can be joined together in countries greatly in need of both, and the ways in which scholarship and research in the social and behavioral sciences can be joined with educational research and training abroad and at home. I have been able to find no particular point of view about the education of teachers in the plans being made by AID, nor have I found in the universities any point of view about the potential use of AID as a source of new curriculum development and teacher education. The policy suggested by a brief passage in John Gardner's "AID and the Universities,"[18] through which AID would take more responsibility for training people for the field, and would work with the universities in doing so, has not been put into effect, except in

[18] Op. cit., pp. 36, 37.

the case of the half dozen special programs similar to those at the Harvard Graduate School of Education, Teachers College, Columbia University, and Stanford University.

AID AS A TEACHERS COLLEGE

If the full degree of importance which the education of teachers should command in AID planning is to be realized, it will have to come through considering the AID mission overseas as a breeding ground for new talent among the foreign students and teachers and among the Americans who go there to help them, rather than as merely a service mission by experts from America. As I have already argued in connection with the collaboration of colleges and universities with the Peace Corps, specific B.A., M.A., and Ph.D. programs should be organized by joint programs of AID and colleges of education, with internships, which could well be arranged through existing funds already allocated to educational missions abroad, to give the opportunity for AID to have the help of young, enterprising, and educationally uninhibited student-teachers abroad. These students could work with their foreign counterparts on joint research and teaching projects as part of their preparation to teach from an international point of view at home, and to prepare themselves for service abroad in the future.

In this way, AID would be able to recruit some of the most enterprising and interesting of the young people interested in education for future service in AID, while at the same time would have the benefit of fresh thinking and educational help during the period of the internship. With a plan similar to the one already suggested for the colleges and the Peace Corps, student-teachers and teachers from the host country could return with the American students to their home campuses, there to continue the joint research and teaching in local American schools as well as in the college where the American is taking his graduate or undergraduate degree.

In the long run, as well as the short, this would mean the development of a new kind of professor of education, as has been suggested in relation to the Peace Corps—one who is at home in a foreign culture, is skilled in the art of preparing and supervising teachers, and in possession of a body of knowledge based on direct experience and foreign study. Such professors would be the source not only of ideas and administrative talent for AID, but of fresh thinking in curriculum and teacher education on the home campus. A few such persons already exist, but they are so few and the possibilities are so great for increasing their number, that it is crucial that a new concept of AID as an instrument of cultural and educational development for teachers of all kinds be substituted for the present concept of a contracting agency for educational services.

I also like John Gardner's idea of increasing the two-way flow of people and ideas between cultures, in a style like that of the United States Geological Survey, which has direct relations with several hundred American faculty members and graduate students who are on call for periods of varying duration.[19] If the colleges of education wished to start programs in which their faculty members and graduate students considered the experience abroad with AID as field work in education and as preparation for teaching, a new kind of base could be made within their own institutions for the spread of the whole concept of education as social development and for increasing the interest of the student body in foreign service within the social development agencies. This would immediately strengthen the quality of teacher education in world affairs, both in the kind of persons attracted into the field and in the content of educational experience available to them there.

I say this because in the literature of international education, both in Government statements and elsewhere, more people show an interest in training manpower for overseas service than for educating teachers. Over and over again, the teacher is omitted from mention, and it is assumed that to add an international dimension to education, it is only necessary to establish what are called "centers of excellence" for research, graduate work, and "international programs." One seldom sees recognition of the fact that it is the teacher who is at the center of the whole issue, and that unless the highest level of attention and effort is given to the education of teachers and the teachers of teachers, this kind of international center will have little effect on the educational system, either in providing intelligent and concerned young men and women for service abroad or for teaching at home. It will simply give us more research specialists.

[19] Ibid., p. 37.

Throughout this book I have said over and over again in various ways that these present years are of unprecedented importance and unrepeatable circumstance in the opportunities they provide to the United States for educational, cultural, and political leadership in the world, and that these kinds of leadership are so closely intertwined that it is impossible to deal with one without linking it to the others. I would like to say it once more, this time in the form of a final conclusion.

If we do not take advantage of these opportunities now, we will not have them again. The world is moving past us.

What it finally comes down to is a matter of injecting a new and radical philosophy of internationalism into the stream of history. Throughout the slow movement of the centuries toward the present age, the philosophers, visionaries, and poets have put before the world the ideal of a common humanity, joined together in mutual concern for the welfare of all, assuring to each the protection and nurture accorded to him in the language of the most recent of these documents, The Universal Declaration of Human Rights of the United Nations. In previous centuries, and until now in this century, it has never been possible to construct a practical world program through which the ideals of the Declaration could be realized, or even to communicate between one part of the world and another as to the necessary working arrangements through which such fulfillment might be possible. Now, at least, we have the advantages of communication. We are all in touch with each other.

But there is one other item which is new and of transcendent importance. Until now, there has never been a country which has had at its command so incredible an array of powers and instruments for achieving a peaceful world order, and which at the same time has put forward the stated intention of achieving national security by international agreement rather than by conquest.

This is not the place to argue the honesty of that intention on the part of the United States. It *is* the place to point out that the honesty of intent will be proven or disproven by the reality of American acts and by the character of the opportunities seized or neglected. We have by now heard enough about the American commitment to share our cultural and educational resources with the world, and in so doing to help bring about new forms of world education of benefit to all. There are now those among us, both here and abroad, who believe that without action in the very near future to put these intentions into effect, not only will the chance be lost but the stated commitments will be clearly identified as the product of speech-writers and not of the will of statesmen.

The American emphasis must now be completely practical. If there is to be world education rather than a series of bilateral cultural alliances calculated in the American interest, arrangements will have to be made for the use of American funds to support multinational educational projects. Aside from the United States, there is no other country willing and able to take the necessary international initiatives.

The United States called the International Conference on the World Crisis in Education in October of 1967, for the declared purpose of bringing the world's educators together to consider and to do something about a world crisis in education. There either is or is not a world crisis in education, and if a Conference is called on that subject by the United States, the natural assumption on the part of those invited is that the United States thinks that there is one, and therefore must have some notion of the nature of the crisis and the ways to its solution. Yet the stated American position was rhetorical rather than practical—"Can we train a young man's eyes to absorb learning as eagerly as we train his finger to pull the trigger?" asked President Johnson.

The answer is of course yes, provided we set about it properly. But nothing is decided or aided by calling for an International Education Year in 1970, as did that Conference, unless an explicit plan is produced for the use of American funds on an international scale for making it possible for the teachers and students across the world to work with one another on the central educational problem—how to develop teachers whose teaching is relevant to the present and future lives of the world's students.

Everyone knows that the countries and people most in need of education are those least able to afford it. Everyone knows that the United States has the money to spend and has been spending it at the rate of nearly $30 billion a year on the war in Vietnam, for what it claims is an international purpose. We have now succeeded in demonstrating, to ourselves and to the world, the ineffectiveness of unilateral military force in solving political and social problems. This would be a magnificent time to make a different kind of demonstration, to show what could be done to create a viable world society by the use of our science, our technology, our cultural and our educational resources. If, in order to do so, we are forced to seek a political solution to the present war in Asia, this is greatly to our advantage. Until we try another kind of demonstration, we will never know whether it would work, or whether world education in the full meaning of the term is indeed possible.

Appendix A

DESCRIPTION OF THE STUDY
ON WHICH THE PRESENT BOOK IS BASED

The study was conducted by the author at the invitation of the American Association of Colleges for Teacher Education, whose then Associate Executive Secretary, Dr. Kenneth Barker, now Dean of the College of Education at the University of Akron, had been active in the field of international education. In 1962 Dr. Barker with his colleagues in the Association had conceived the idea that a full-scale study of the preparation of teachers in the field of world affairs should be conducted, preferably by a person whose scholarly interests lay in philosophy and world affairs but who was not himself directly involved in the professional education of teachers.

The research began formally in February of 1966, with a staff consisting of the Director, Harold Taylor; a research associate, Crane Haussamen; and an administrative and research assistant, Miss Miriam Willey. Michael Rossman, Miss Martha Darling, and Miss Clara Grossman served as research assistants for shorter periods.

An Advisory Committee was invited to serve throughout the project, and consisted of:

H. Kenneth Barker, Dean of the College of Education and Dean of International Programs, University of Akron

Henry Steele Commager, Professor of American History, Amherst College

Peter Gillingham, Executive Associate of Education and World Affairs, Counsel to the House of Representatives Task Force on the International Education Act

Francis Hamblin, former Dean of the School of Education, George Washington University, and, 1966, Chairman, International Relations Committee of the American Association of Colleges for Teacher Education; presently vice-president for Academic Affairs, State University of Arizona, Flagstaff, Arizona

Frank Klassen, Associate Executive Secretary of the American Association of Colleges for Teacher Education

Brian Urquhart, Office of the Secretary General of the United Nations

Harris Wofford, formerly Associate Director of the Peace Corps in charge of the Office of Planning, Evaluation, and Research; presently President, State University of New York in Old Westbury

The method of research was to visit a cross section of fifty-two colleges and universities where teachers are prepared, chosen to include a variety of categories, small, large, rural, urban, private, public, in each region of the country; to review existing literature in the field; to confer with educators, Government officials, students, United Nations personnel, and others with direct experience in and knowledge of the field of world affairs, including officials and members of private organizations and public bodies. In addition to the campus visits by Harold Taylor and Crane Haussamen, two conferences were held, one on the role of students in educational reform, with a representative national group of forty students engaged in educational reform and teacher education, on October 22–23, 1966, in New York City, the other on world education, with representatives from Government, including some who were instrumental in developing the legislation for the International Education Act of 1966, educators, students, university scholars and administrators, at Airlie House in Warrenton, Virginia, December 9–11, 1966, financed by the Kettering Foundation. An edited version of the proceedings of the World Education Conference has been prepared and is available from the Association.

The colleges and universities visited during the study were:

Antioch College, Yellow Springs, Ohio
Ball State University, Muncie, Indiana
Berea College, Berea, Kentucky
Bloomsburg State College, Bloomsburg, Pennsylvania
Brooklyn College, New York, New York
University of California, Berkeley, California
University of Southern California, Los Angeles, California
University of North Carolina, Greensboro, North Carolina
Chicago Teachers College North, Chicago, Illinois
University of Colorado, Boulder, Colorado
Columbia University, Teachers College, New York, New York
University of South Florida, Tampa, Florida
Fisk University, Nashville, Tennessee
Flint Community College, Flint, Michigan
George Peabody College for Teachers, Nashville, Tennessee
Georgia Southern College, Statesboro, Georgia
College of Great Falls, Great Falls, Montana
Hamline University, St. Paul, Minnesota
Harvard University, Cambridge, Massachusetts
California State College at Hayward, Hayward, California
Hunter College, New York, New York
Southern Illinois University, Carbondale, Illinois
University of Illinois, Urbana, Illinois
Indiana University, Bloomington, Indiana
State College of Iowa, Cedar Falls, Iowa
Kent State University, Kent, Ohio
University of Kentucky, Lexington, Kentucky
West Liberty State College, West Liberty, West Virginia
Lady of the Lake College, San Antonio, Texas
Lincoln University, Lincoln, Pennsylvania
Los Angeles City College, Los Angeles, California
Michigan State University, East Lansing, Michigan

Western Michigan University, Kalamazoo, Michigan
New York University, New York, New York
Northwestern University, Evanston, Illinois
Ohio University, Athens, Ohio
New York State University, International Studies and World Affairs, Plant-
    ing Fields, New York
State University of New York College at Plattsburgh, New York
Queens College, New York, New York
San Francisco State College, San Francisco, California
Stanford University, Stanford, California
Temple University, Philadelphia, Pennsylvania
Texas Christian University, Fort Worth, Texas
North Texas State University, Denton, Texas
Southwest Texas State College, San Marco, Texas
Utah State University, Logan, Utah
West Virginia State College, Institute, West Virginia
Eastern Washington State College, Cheney, Washington
Wayne State University, Detroit, Michigan
Wilmington College, Wilmington, Ohio

At most of the institutions a general pattern of a two-day visit was followed, consisting of (1) Conferences with faculty members of the College of Educa-tion or the Department of Education and the administrative officers connected with the education of teachers; (2) Conferences with members of the arts and science faculty involved in international programs or courses dealing with world affairs and non-Western cultures; (3) Visits to education classes and others where possible; (4) Conferences with students in teacher education programs and other students interested in education and world affairs; (5) Conferences with appropriate administrative officers of the institution, including Deans of Arts and Science, Provosts, Presidents, Directors of International Programs and Centers, depending on availability and areas of responsibility for educational policy.

On occasion addresses were made to convocations of students and faculty members, at faculty meetings, before groups of students; on other occasions classes were taught in education and philosophy, to evoke discussion of educa-tional issues and to gain a sense of student concerns and interests. Nine con-ferences attended in connection with the study had a range from the United States National Student Association Congress in Urbana, Illinois, in August 1966 to a Conference on International Education and Teacher Education at the University of Kentucky, and an NDEA Institute on teaching about peace and war at Wayne State University.

Other information was solicited from appropriate organizations and individuals through correspondence and conferences; file materials and memoranda were prepared on the basis of this information for the use of the staff, the Director, and the Advisory Committee.

Over the past ten years, the International Relations Committee of AACTE, which has 775 member institutions in which 90 percent of the country's teachers are prepared, has been the central planning body of the Association for inter-national programs and activities in increasing the involvement of educators of teachers in the field of world affairs. Through the Committee, international edu-cation has been an integral part of the agenda of the Association's annual meetings, to which some fifty foreign educators are invited. Regional conferences have been held each year at universities throughout the country at which proposals, projects, suggestions for international education have been discussed, with consequent practical results on the home campuses.

Among these projects are:

1. Overseas study tours for American educational administrators, through a contract with the Bureau of Educational and Cultural Affairs in the Department of State, for thirty-day visits to examine educational systems and conditions in foreign countries. Approximately 100 administrators have visited six European and Asian countries.

2. Inter-institutional affiliation projects have been carried out with arrangements made by the Association with 30 American colleges and universities for direct links to foreign teacher education institutions for exchange of faculty, texts, curriculum material, college publications, faculty and students, depending on the resources of the American institution.

3. Through arrangements made with AID, educational administrators from abroad have been brought to this country for administrative internships in American colleges and universities, where the foreign visitor spends six to nine months at the American institution for study and practical experience in educational administration. Nineteen administrators from Asia, Africa, and Latin America have participated.

4. Four annual seminars for teachers in social studies have been arranged under a contract with the Bureau of Educational and Cultural Affairs attended by Central American teachers, with staff provided by American teacher education institutions. Two hundred teachers have participated.

5. In collaboration with the Office of Overseas Schools of the Department of State, the Association has provided educational aid to seven overseas schools in Europe, Asia, Africa, and Latin America, for improvement of the quality of teaching, staffing, and curriculum.

6. A series of pilot projects in education for international understanding has been organized in eleven American colleges and universities in collaboration with the National Council for the Social Studies, and has ranged, according to the interests and financial ability of the institutions involved, from introducing international curricula into the present programs, participation in travel-study programs abroad, to the development of exchange programs with foreign students and faculty members.

7. Liaison has been established with the major foundations, private organizations, and Government agencies with an interest in international education, including the United States Commission for UNESCO, the United States Committee for UNICEF, the Peace Corps, Education and World Affairs, the Ford Foundation, the Carnegie Corporation, and the Asia Society, which has developed valuable guidelines and materials for the use of Asian studies in the education of teachers.

Among the future research activities planned by the Association are:

(a) A major review and assessment of American technical assistance overseas in the field of teacher education, beginning with a report on the character and content of the involvement of the Agency for International Development in education, to be carried out under a contract with AID.

(b) A review of the administrative internship program (Number 3 above) with a view to considering the extension of the program in the future.

(c) An analysis of the present state of staff resources, curricular practices, innovations, financial commitments, and possible involvement of colleges and universities in the education of teachers in world affairs, to be conducted under a grant from the U. S. Office of Education.

There are, of course, other projects in international education for teachers which have been set in motion by other organizations and institutions, but the extent of AACTE efforts, with stringent financial limitations both in the local institutions and in the Association itself, is an indication of the present scale of effort in national initiatives within the teacher education movement.

The Conference on World Education

Another part of the author's study had to do with the implications of the International Education Act of 1966, and the present and future possibilities for collaborative effort in international programs of teacher education between private organizations, colleges and universities, schools, colleges of education, and the United States Government. The Conference on World Education, mentioned above, brought together many of those in this country most directly concerned with the International Education Act, including some who were instrumental in developing both the legislation and the ideas on which the legislation was based. The Conference resulted in a document which not only contains the substance of the papers and the discussion, but serves as a report of one phase of the study findings.

Documents

The reader may be interested in two other sets of documents. The first is the U. S. Government publication of the Hearings before the Task Force on International Education of the House Committee on Education and Labor of the 89th Congress in March and April of 1966,[1] and the accompanying Government publication of selected readings to supplement the International Education Act, prepared by the Task Force on International Education of which Congressman John Brademas of Indiana was Chairman.[2] The former document is a set of statements about the problems and possibilities in international education, presented by a cross section of the country's best informed representatives of higher education, private organization, and Government. In the latter is to be found one of the best compilations of research findings and writing on the subject of international education that is available anywhere, with individual sections on a full range of topics from the problems of internationalizing the

[1] Hearings before the Task Force on International Education of the Committee on Education and Labor, House of Representatives, 89th Congress, Second Session on H.R. 12451 and H.R. 12452, Washington, D.C., March 30, 31; April 1, 4, 5, 6, and 7, 1966. 453 pp. Washington, D.C. Printing Office.

[2] *International Education; Past, Present, Problems and Prospects*. Selected Readings to Supplement H.R. 14643 prepared by the Task Force on International Education, John Brademas, chairman, Committee on Education and Labor, House of Representatives, U.S., 564 pp., U. S. Government Printing Office, Washington, D.C.

curriculum, to those of strengthening the faculty and teaching resources in higher education and the schools.

The second set of materials is the series of pamphlets recently published by Education and World Affairs on international education and the professional schools, in Agriculture, Engineering, Law, Business Administration, Public Administration, Medicine, Public Health, and Education.[3] The research was conducted under the overall supervision of a Study Committee of twenty educators, headed by Dr. T. Keith Glennan, President of Associated Universities, Inc., and involved the work of four task forces in the areas under consideration. The introductory section of these documents presents the problems of adapting the work of the professional schools to accommodate new international responsibilities, and provides a basic rationale for the proposition that all institutions of higher education, in whatever field, have both opportunities and duties in connection with international education. The reports on the professional schools themselves provide valuable analysis of the present state of professional education in its international aspect, and equally valuable suggestions and recommendations for further activity.

Other reference books, handbooks, and publications with relevance to the education of teachers in world affairs are included among the standard publications of UNESCO, the United Nations, and other international organizations, as listed in the Foreign Policy Association regular bulletin, INTERCOM.[4] The September–October 1967 issue of INTERCOM contains a valuable survey by James M. Becker of the present state of teaching and curriculum in the field of world affairs in American schools and an account of research and projects designed to improve the situation in the schools and colleges. Mr. Becker's article, the bibliographical and other references, along with the description of an eighteen-month research study of education in international affairs being conducted by the Foreign Policy Association, make this document a concise and basic reference work for those concerned with the education of teachers in internationalism.

[3] Hearings before the Task Force . . . , ibid.

[4] INTERCOM, issued six times annually by the Foreign Policy Association, 345 East 46 Street, New York, New York. September–October 1967. 88 pp.

Appendix B

SOME EXISTING ORGANIZATIONS
WHOSE WORK CAN BE EXTENDED INTO
THE INTERNATIONAL EDUCATION OF TEACHERS

The World Confederation of Organizations of the Teaching Profession

The most wide-ranging international network of organizations of teachers is the World Confederation of Organizations of the Teaching Profession (WCOTP)[1] with 151 national teacher groups from 95 countries, representing a total membership of five million teachers. An Assembly of Delegates is held once a year, attended by approximately 500 leaders of teachers' organizations, with an agenda which gives the delegates a chance to exchange ideas and to develop programs for their own countries. Among these are regional meetings and seminars on topics ranging from teaching science in the Asian elementary schools (Manila, December 1964) to the status of the teaching profession (Niamey, Nigeria, September 1963) and a seminar in the role of teachers in nation-building (Tunis, March 1967). Two publications, *Echo* and a quarterly, *Education Panorama*, serve as a means of reporting the work of the national organizations to each other and of exchanging ideas and information about educational programs on an international scale; a very interesting series of books on "Man Through His Arts," sponsored by the Confederation and supported by UNESCO, gives substance to the UNESCO project on the "Mutual Appreciation of Eastern and Western Cultural Values."[2]

A council on the Education of Teachers operates within the Confederation, with obvious possibilities for carrying out programs in international teacher education which, if funds were forthcoming, could do many of the things recommended in the present Report. The difficulty lies, as is so often the case in international education, on the stringency of the budget-making for other than national education systems at a time when nearly every country in the world is in trouble with its own expanding needs for education, and the education budget has to fight its way against other national priorities. There is not yet a powerful constituency in the international field to support the idea that international education is a matter of high priority for all national systems.

The range of existing budgets, both personal and public, within the colleges of education, the universities, the State Departments of Education (as in the example of New York State), the foundations, and the Federal programs is

[1] World Confederation of Organizations of the Teaching Profession; 1330 Massachusetts Avenue, N.W., Washington, D.C. 20005.

[2] Obtainable from the New York Graphic Society, Greenwich, Connecticut.

broad enough to make it possible that American initiatives for organizing study-travel projects, visits by foreign students and educators, research and practice teaching projects here and abroad could stimulate new activity through the Confederation and its existing set of world connections. Here is a structure ready for international use on a much larger scale than any other in the field of teacher education. It remains to see what more can be done.

The Smithsonian Institution

The Smithsonian Institution is one of our major national resources for the development of teachers with an international point of view, since the nature of the Institution's work in the past fits it admirably for an extension of this dimension in the future. Already there are teams of researchers affiliated with the Smithsonian at work in anthropology in Brazil, Mexico, Greece, Turkey, Burma, and Iran, as well as in the United States, on archaeological problems, making clearer "the processes by which human groups respond to, adjust to, or break down under the impact of sudden overwhelming changes imposed from outside sources, by providing information on such processes in primitive tribes subjected to such changes. This work permits analysis of languages, ideas, concepts and attitudes that lie behind the more visible and material segments of rapidly disappearing cultures."[3]

Under the heading of "Urgent Anthropology," the Smithsonian Office of Education and Training intends to collaborate in an international effort to recover ethnological data while it still remains available, by training ethnographers both here and abroad, cooperating internationally with anthropologists, preparing guides and manuals, etc. The opportunities for building a system of international teacher education into this kind of research await only the extension of present efforts by the award of fellowships, travel funds, and other aids to teachers in the social sciences and humanities.

The same set of extensions can be made throughout the other fields with which the Smithsonian Institution is concerned, in fine arts, history and science, particularly in the field of ecology and the study of ecosystems through the Institution's Office of Ecology, where problems in population biology and population dynamics can furnish the setting for educational studies related to the evolution of societies.

Oceanography provides another field in which the Smithsonian has already taken initiatives which could be turned in the direction of teacher education on an international scale; a full variety of American research resources and agencies, from the National Aeronautics and Space Administration to the Lamont Geological Observatory, are cooperating through the Smithsonian in a program of wide implication for the future of education in those sciences connected with the study of oceans and the ocean floor. Enterprising educators with an interest in teacher education could give the same kind of reading to the Smithsonian Institution reports already recommended in the case of the National Science Foundation. Out of such review and consideration of available resources could come new plans of benefit to all concerned.

[3] *1967–68 Smithsonian Research Opportunities: Fine Arts, History, Science,* Office of Education and Training, Smithsonian Institute, Washington, D.C., 1966, 153 pp.

The Educational Development Center

The progress of Educational Services Incorporated (now the Education Development Center) from a primary interest in the reform of the American science curriculum into the field of the social sciences and humanities demonstrates not only the close relationship between the natural and social sciences which can be established when they are considered in the light of problems in curriculum-making and teaching, but the way in which such problems can be intelligently attacked when university scholars and school teachers put their heads together in the solution of common problems.

A United Nations Teacher Corps

During the course of the work with members of the United Nations Secretariat and delegations and of the Society of Friends in planning the World College pilot project of 1963, I discovered a serious interest on the part of many in the possibility of an International Teacher Corps, which might be supported by the United Nations, with direct connections to the U. N. Institute for Training and Research and the Economic and Social Council. Since that time, an interest similar to that developed by the International Secretariat for Volunteer Service has continued among members of the United Nations and other internationalists. One way of furthering that interest would be to expand the work of UNICEF into the field of teacher education.

Since 1961, UNICEF, in collaboration with UNESCO, has been supplying equipment for teacher education institutions and elementary schools connected with them in nearly fifty developing countries—typewriters, scientific apparatus, library books, mimeographing machines, and other items—in addition to carrying on some in-service training for teachers. The assignments of professional educators from around the world for the latter have been made by UNESCO and, since the work of UNICEF is supported in part by the host countries where UNICEF projects are in operation, there is already present in that body a truly international apparatus for education with interconnections between ministries of education, international educational organizations, and foreign educators on a world-wide rather than a unilateral or bilateral basis.

It is thus possible that through UNICEF a United Nations Volunteer Teacher Corps could be established, with volunteers recruited on a world-wide basis among students who are near the completion of their preparation as teachers, among graduate students interested in educational service abroad, and young teachers at the beginning of their careers in teaching. The purpose of the Corps would be fourfold: to expand the kind of technical help now given by UNICEF to countries needing it, to extend that help into the education of teachers in internationalism, to provide opportunities, on the one hand for student-teachers to immerse themselves in the educational system of a culture other than their own, and on the other to provide such assistance as the student-teachers are capable of giving to the children and educational system of the country to which they were assigned. The assignment could be for two years, after which the Corps member would return to his own country to complete his education and to begin, or resume, his teaching career.

Nominations of candidates for the Corps could be made to UNICEF by the participating countries, assignments to teacher education institutions and allied schools could be made by the host countries, and, in certain cases, programs of research and curriculum-building might be worked out jointly between teacher education institutions in various countries. Costs for the Corps could be shared by UNICEF, the host country, and the cooperating teacher education institutions. Because UNICEF is already working with UNESCO and is in touch with the major world organizations of teachers and with a variety of educational institutions around the world, the task of communication and organization could be shared by a sizable number of persons and groups interested in internationalism in the education of teachers.

There is no doubt that the contribution which the members of an international Corps of this kind could make to world education would be direct and invaluable. Teacher education institutions everywhere would benefit from the opportunity to work with highly qualified student nationals of other countries on educational problems common to them all. Assistance in teaching in areas of the school curriculum where talent is not fully available—in science, mathematics, foreign languages, comparative education, history and the social sciences, agricultures, public health, and other fields—could be supplied by the presence of the Corps members. In cooperating with UNICEF, educational institutions would find new means of making connections with each other through a strong and widely admired international organization whose central purpose is to help the world's children through whatever means are possible.

World Education Centers

An example of new thinking for American international programs is provided by the work of Stewart E. Fraser at George Peabody College for Teachers in Nashville, Tennessee. Dr. Fraser is Director of the International Center and professor of International and Comparative Education at the College, the Center being his own creation, established three years ago with practically no money and no staff. To a certain extent, both these conditions can be put down as educational advantages since, without funds, grants, or other emoluments, there are likely to be no restrictions on the ideas around which the program forms, no elaborate conditions, committees, and all-university bodies to clear, approve, and otherwise modify programs which should be given a chance to be tested in action. Without staff, one is then forced to look into present resources, which in Dr. Fraser's case were the doctoral students in international and comparative education at Peabody, approximately one third of the twenty of them from foreign countries, the rest American.

Dr. Fraser's ideas for extending the concept of international education into residential international centers have grown from the raw experience of establishing the Center which he heads, and in many respects parallel the main recommendations of this section of the report. It also contains parts of the World Urban Teaching Center idea proposed for San Francisco State College. Having taken note of the fact that international residential centers for foreign students seldom make use of the resources of the students or of residence in developing international education programs, Dr. Fraser proposes that American campuses consider the establishment of what he calls Residential Academic Centers for International Education, where the training of teachers, educators, specialists, and research scholars to work in overseas development tasks would be part of the program, along with the study of international, comparative, and developmental education for use in teaching in the United States.[4] Dr. Fraser points out that:

"International Houses in America, with multi-universities in their neighborhood, cater to all faculties and all disciplines. Their cohesiveness is nurtured primarily through social and residential, rather than through professional affiliations or contacts. The concept of a residential center devoted *solely* to exploring the common problems of education throughout the world and developing both specialists and strategists to overcome them is different when contrasted to the goals of traditional international houses. The involvement of social scientists jointly viewing the theme of developmental education in a residential community setting cuts across many of the traditional boundaries that have risen between academics, educators, and those concerned with the training of teachers. A residential center devoted to the study of the 'accelerating and inhibiting factors' in international education offers a framework for cohesive study that the customary international houses cannot and do not necessarily wish to offer."

There are elements in Dr. Fraser's proposal similar to those in operation at the Center for Educational Development in the Harvard School of Graduate Education and the Center at Stanford, except that in his case Dr. Fraser proposes a direct relationship between (a) the tasks and personnel involved in international teacher education and research, (b) the International Center, and (c) the other intellectual resources of the university or universities, in the region where the Center is established. In addition to regular degree programs, the residential center for international training would offer cultural and orientation services for Americans going abroad, to teach, to advise, to do research. One third to one half of the residents would be Americans, the rest from a cross section of countries, mainly graduate students, who would be available not only in seminars within their own ranks for cooperative research and study, but for teaching in the local school and community programs.

The emphasis would be on intellectual and cultural exchange between various cultural groups already committed to working in international and developmental education, and on acting as a focal point for research in the extension and improvement of the international curriculum in American public schools. Visiting educators from other American institutions could come for limited periods of work in a congenial international setting, using the documentary and resource materials of the Center. Dr. Fraser, whose thinking also parallels that of the New York State University Center in Planting Fields, and of the proposed Institute of International Education in the College of Education at Ohio University, has in mind the use of all the disciplines of the social sciences in furnishing the manpower and materials for a continuing interchange of international ideas between faculty members and students of this and other countries. Collaboration with the Peace Corps and other Government programs, particularly those of the Center for Educational Cooperation, would follow naturally as an operational principle from the basic idea.

Through consultation and cooperation with the Peace Corps and other agen-

---

[4] Dr. Fraser's ideas for the centers are developed in two papers, "Residential Academic Centers for International Education: a Proposal for Their Establishment in the United States," *Peabody Journal of Education*, March 1966, and "Some Aspects of University Cooperation in International Education," *School and Society*, April 16–30, 1966, pp. 234–38, 240, 242, 244. Additional ideas in the area of international educational exchange are contained in *Governmental Policy and International Education*, edited by Dr. Stewart E. Fraser, John Wiley and Sons, New York, 1965.

cies, colleges of education could establish educational centers for summer programs, work camps, hostels, etc., in foreign countries to which their students would be sent, and where Peace Corps personnel, both Volunteers and supervising staff, could help in study and work programs designed for teachers.

Colleges of education, in collaboration with other parts of the university, could organize student research projects on problems in food production, birth control, technology, medicine, which could be carried out with the help of Peace Corps Volunteers while they were abroad, other Volunteers when they returned, and the faculty and student body of the sponsoring institution. Coincident with this might be a program of volunteer professors who would agree to go with a group of a dozen students for a half year to a year to work in countries where arrangements might be made by the Peace Corps in connection with the Centers suggested in Dr. Fraser's proposal.

Aside from the establishment of formal programs, one of the most effective ways of giving the teacher education candidate the kind of foreign experience he needs, would be to arrange on an individual basis for a promising student-teacher to go abroad for a semester or a year to one of the regional centers conducted by various American universities, or simply to make an arrangement with the East-West Center and the University of Hawaii for an integrated program of Asian studies carried on over a three- to six-month period for a selected group of juniors or seniors in a teacher education plan. Or, if there were World Affairs Centers of the kind described above, a student could be sent for one semester to study at another college where there is a World Affairs Center, preferably one staffed by returned Peace Corps Volunteers, foreign students, and others who are directly interested in education and teachers.

One simple device which could be used within the United States or by any college abroad is to send a qualified faculty member with fifteen students with him to a community in the United States or in a foreign country selected in collaboration with the Peace Corps, or other appropriate organizations, and supervise individual study, teaching, and community development projects for one semester or two, resulting in research papers, curricular materials, etc., from each of the students, and possibly a monograph or a research report on the project by the faculty member. The work abroad would be coordinated with the course requirements and previous studies and experiences of the students in the program.

Some Examples

The International Institute for Educational Planning in Paris has identified ninety-nine international, regional, and national organizations in the field of research and training in educational planning. Undergraduate and graduate students of education from the United States and elsewhere could travel to other countries for joint research and comparative studies with other students and teachers, using the facilities of appropriate organizations in making the arrangements.

The Association of Overseas Educators, with headquarters in Wiesbaden and Washington, D.C., has a potential membership of 30,000 persons who have had overseas teaching experience, with a present membership of 300; the Association has local chapters throughout the United States, runs a lecture program, cultural relations seminars, foreign student and teacher welcoming and orientation projects, supplies a newsletter, and has a Foundation for Educational Exchange for research, publication, and education on questions having to do with teaching in world affairs.

There is a body of experience within the membership of the Association which should be fully used in the education of teachers, both for those in preparation and those already in service. In collaboration with other organizations, for example, the National Education Association's Teach Corps, the Association could conduct a wide range of research and action programs in teaching through (a) autobiographical accounts and research findings of experience overseas for use in education courses, (b) the spread of information about overseas opportunities for American teachers, (c) special seminars and training programs for students interested in foreign service, (d) organization of year-long seminars in foreign cultures with six- to eight-week study-travel trips during the summer, (e) research in curricular materials based on the members' foreign experience and relationships abroad, (f) exchange programs with schools where members have taught, (g) development of one- and two-year projects for service abroad, in which the school system grants special leave and special inducements for recruiting foreign service teachers, and the school planned the project specifically to enlarge and deepen its curriculum in world affairs, (h) full use of the experience of the returned teacher in school and community education, with national planning to include selected returnees in work in a variety of schools other than their own, along with projects in curricular development conducted jointly by colleges of education and nearby school systems.

Appendix C

TWO ORGANIZATIONS WITH PROJECTS INVOLVING FOREIGN STUDENTS AS TEACHERS IN THE AMERICAN PUBLIC SCHOOLS

The Ogontz Plan

An example of what can be done by private initiative is shown in the work of a group of citizens in Philadelphia who started the Ogontz Plan for Mutual International Education, by which qualified foreign students at the University of Pennsylvania and other universities in Philadelphia have been recruited to teach in the Philadelphia public schools. The purpose of the Plan stated by its sponsors, International House in Philadelphia, and Mr. Carl Stenzler, Chairman of the Ogontz Plan Committee, is "to add to existing school curricula a greater emphasis on the international humanities; the objective study of other peoples and cultures, by bringing into the schools . . . foreign students who identify with world peoples about whom we know too little . . . and to broaden the perspective of foreign students so that they will be better able to understand the United States."[1]

Five students representing five different parts of the world come to a given school for one half day a week for three weeks, to present classes in foreign cultures carefully prepared in advance in consultation with the local teacher, with payment made to the student-teacher from the regular school budget for substitute teachers. Beginning in 1962 with one school and five student-teachers from Liberia, India, Turkey, Sweden, and Japan, the program has grown until in 1966–67, 142 foreign visitors from 51 countries (110 graduate students, 13 undergraduates, 9 professionals, 10 wives of foreign students) from 19 universities and colleges in the Philadelphia area have worked with 14,000 pupils in 50 elementary and secondary schools, in 19 school districts in 7 counties and 3 states.

The program has been successful not only in bringing a direct awareness of the reality of foreign cultures to the children in the participating schools, but it has been effective in helping the foreign student to become involved directly with educational problems and American values of which he would have otherwise been ignorant. In addition, through the relation to the other teachers in the schools and to the parents of the children, the foreign students have become enmeshed in the community life of the area, and their ideas and points

[1] Ogontz Plan for Mutual International Education, sponsored by the International House of Philadelphia, 140 N. Fifteenth Street, Philadelphia, Pa., 19102. Carl Stenzler, Chairman, International House.

of view have been a source of mutual education in the adult society of which they could otherwise not have been a part. A variety of extensions of the idea are immediately possible, including trips by teams of foreign and American students to outlying areas for symposia and teaching, community forums, college seminars, adult extension classes, television programs, discussion of films about foreign countries, and many more.

There is no reason why the Ogontz Plan could not be used nationally as a model for communities everywhere in the United States, nor why programs comparable to it could not be sponsored by colleges of education who might import selected foreign students to join in practice teaching programs already under way, nor why the Plan could not become the basis for new policies in the recruitment of foreign students through Government funds to establish direct relationships with teacher-education institutions abroad. The question of how to inject the element of a world perspective into the American educational system could then receive a direct answer, without our having to wait to influence the curricula of colleges and universities, educate a generation of new teachers, while leaving the present teachers, nearly two million of them, untouched by the ideas available to them in the resources of our foreign student population.

Nations Incorporated

Another model for cooperative effort among community organizations, the universities, the schools, and foreign students, is to be found in a project organized by a group of internationally minded citizens in the Bay Area of San Francisco, under the title Nations Incorporated, with financial support from local foundations, businesses, and individual donors.[2] The work is concentrated in a Summer Workshop of Nations, now completing its sixth year, to which are invited high school juniors and seniors for three-week sessions of intensive study, lectures, seminars, and conversations, led by selected foreign students who are doing graduate work in universities in California and elsewhere, and aided by visiting scholars who have special knowledge to add to the work in African, Asian, Latin-American, and Middle East areas. Dr. Robert Scalapino, then Chairman of the Department of Political Science at the University of California in Berkeley, was responsible for bringing university resources to bear on the organization of the first workshops.

The summer Workshop of 1967 was held at a conference center in La Honda, near San Francisco, with 100 high school students divided into study groups of approximately 25 in size according to the country and area of their particular interest, each with a staff of two foreign instructors and one American classroom teacher who served as moderator. The design of the Workshop is one which aims to involve the students in a serious consideration of the cultural, political, religious, economic, and educational problems of the countries chosen for study, and to give them a sense of immediacy of the foreign cultures and their people by bringing them closely in touch with young graduate students from abroad whose knowledge of their own society and its problems is personal and direct as well as scholarly. During the evenings, special lecturers in related topics are introduced to speak on the arts, foreign policy, education, along with films and special sessions having to do with careers in world affairs, the Peace Corps, and the problems of world society.

One of the most important of the attributes of the Workshop of Nations

2 Nations Incorporated, Franklyn M. Barnett, Executive Director, 2428 Hillside, Berkeley, California.

and of Nations Incorporated itself, lies in the outreach it has acquired into the existing educational and community life of California, and the possibilities of its extension into a series of similar projects across the country. Largely through the enthusiasm of a sixteen-year-old student who attended the 1965 Workshop, a similar project was organized in Ithaca, New York, by Dr. William Lowe, Assistant Dean of the College of Education at Cornell University, for the summer of 1966, in collaboration with the Assistant Superintendent of Schools and a committee of citizens in the Ithaca community.

The first International Workshop in Ithaca was attended by sixteen high school students and, with a design similar to the California program, the second was held in 1967 with a focus on Latin America at both of the two-week sessions. The instructors are graduate students from Central and South America studying in a wide range of disciplines at Cornell. North American public school teachers are also involved, including the director, a history teacher from a local high school. Additional lectures, seminars, and demonstrations are provided by the faculties of Ithaca College and Cornell University. All the educative agencies in the area have cooperated, with financial help from individuals, businesses, service clubs, children's groups, units of Cornell and the Center for International Programs and Services of the New York State Education Department.

The implications of this kind of project for the education of teachers in world affairs are clear, and have already begun to work themselves out in California, with initiatives taken by the Director, Mr. Franklyn Barnett, and Dean T. Reller of the School of Education at the University of California, for proposed cooperation with local school systems for Teachers Workshops, awarding inservice credit for weekend conferences and continuing seminars. Here, the presence of the foreign participants in full status with their American colleagues and teachers not only makes use of a neglected resource for the development of a serious and informed interest in world affairs on the part of teachers and students, but provides the opportunity for the foreign participants to engage in a much more direct relationship with American educators and each other in dealing with common interests and problems than is possible under any other circumstances. Some of the same effects obtained in the pilot project for a World College[3] have occurred in the Workshop of Nations—the intermingling of ideas and points of view from a variety of foreign participants who have usually not had an opportunity to work closely with each other, either at home or in the United States.

But above all, it is again the sense of immediacy of access to the foreign culture as seen through the eyes of its representatives that makes this approach to the education of teachers so important an experiment both in educating the educators and their students, and in making an impact on the community at large. Films of the Workshop in session, as well as television tapes of selected speakers and sessions, have been made for use in local schools and on local television stations; plans are under way for the student participants in the summer programs to serve as teachers' aides when they return to their schools in order to bring the materials developed during the summer into regular school classes. A combination of this approach with the Ogontz Plan for the use of foreign students as teachers in the schools themselves, in collaboration with the student aides and the teachers who have served in the special summer workshops, suggests itself as an extension of the work already going on.

Mr. Barnett has already investigated possibilities for this kind of extension through conferences with educators at nearby universities, and through sugges-

[3] Described on pp. 167–70.

tions that the universities, through their departments and colleges of education, develop their own programs in collaboration with Foreign Area Studies centers and allied departments where foreign students could be most helpful. "I believe," says Mr. Barnett, "that the problem is essentially one of finding a mechanism to work within existing structures." Some of these structures include not only the State system of education in California, but the Center for Educational Cooperation in Washington, the U. S. Office of Education, the regional center of Projects to Advance Creativity in Education of the San Mateo County Department of Education, and the American Association of Colleges for Teacher Education. The operating center could be in the department or college of education, where one person could be appointed to act as director of international programs and could call upon foreign students and scholars as well as members of area studies centers in university faculties.

Appendix D

THE UNESCO PROJECT IN EDUCATION FOR
INTERNATIONAL UNDERSTANDING

The UNESCO project in Education for International Understanding and Co-operation, initiated in 1953, furnished its first report of findings in 1965.[1] The Report indicates a growing number of institutions around the world with a commitment to work in curricular reform and experimental work in extending the range of student involvement in world affairs. The project began with thirty-three schools in fifteen countries, each of which was to devise its own programs and to carry them out in whatever ways seemed best to the teachers, who were asked to select one of three themes or areas of study, the rights of women, other countries, peoples, and cultures, or the principles of human rights. By the time the Report of the project was issued in 1965, the number of schools involved had risen to more than three hundred, of which fifty-five were institutions for teacher education in forty-three countries of Africa, Asia, the Middle East, Europe, Latin America, and North America, with a wide range of cultural traditions, stages of development and economic and political systems.

In addition to the work of supplying materials—booklets, posters, filmstrips, bibliographies, etc.—the UNESCO Secretariat arranged, in cooperation with the members of the Project, a series of regional conferences, meetings, and seminars in Europe, Latin America, Asia, and the Middle East; a full international meeting to sum up results after ten years of work was held in Paris in 1963. Aside from the general stir in the schools involved in the project and the specific programs which developed from the initial stages into what, in some cases, were important reforms in school and teacher education curricula, in several countries national organizations took up the idea and extended it throughout their own educational systems. For example, in India, which began with nine schools and thirteen teacher-training institutions, the Indian National Commission for UNESCO started a nation-wide project on the same lines as the parent experiment; by 1964, 350 secondary schools and teacher institutions were involved in workshops for teachers in world affairs to prepare new materials and syllabi, and to circulate available information which the Secretariat in Paris had been collecting over the years.

This has made it possible for the comparatively small size of the project in its beginning to expand in ways which promise additional expansion in the future, and indicate that if the Center for Educational Cooperation under the International Education Act begins its operations in Washington, D.C., there

[1] "International Understanding at School: an Account of Progress in UNESCO's Associated School Project," UNESCO, Paris, 1965, p. 22.

are a good many precedents and existing intercountry connections which can link the American schools to a large number of educators and institutions around the world. In the modest terms of the UNESCO report, the results so far have "led to the development of a great variety of examples of activities which can be carried out by the ordinary school or teacher-training institution and which are therefore of general education significance" and have demonstrated that "not only is it possible to teach for international understanding without overloading or disrupting the school programme but that such teaching enriches the content and increases the impact of school subjects."

The impact on teacher education has not yet reached a similar level of significance, although some progress has been made. At a regional seminar held in Hamburg in 1958, where teacher education was a key point in the agenda, it was agreed that the study of the "techniques of education for international understanding should find a place in the professional training of all teaching students and that the methods and programmes developed from this work should be used by the students in their periods of practice teaching in demonstration schools."[2]

In Belgium, Ceylon, and Spain, where this idea has been taken seriously, students have in fact carried out such work in their practice-teaching periods. Graduate students in Ceylon have started projects of this kind in different parts of the country, maintaining contact with their colleges of education by reporting to them about progress and receiving guidance and sample materials in exchange. What remains for Americans, both through the American UNESCO Commission and through AACTE and other organizations, is to circulate the ideas and materials to the colleges of education, and to organize similar projects in the spirit and approach of the original undertaking.

Internationalism and Access to Higher Education

The close connection between examinations and curricula in the schools and colleges, and the even closer connection between examination systems and the development and maintenance of social classes within each society, make the concept of educational testing one of the most important ideas in the entire field of international education. As may be apparent, my own views of the conventional examination system, with its ties to sterile methods of instruction and obsolete curricula, are that it is a naïve and coarse-grained way of dealing with human talent. When one considers that almost the entire world's educational system uses the examination as a screening device in the selection of those who will receive the benefits of further education, further that is, than the first five to eight grades of school, it is possible to argue that a thorough analysis of the relation of social inequality to educational methods, including the use of conventional examinations as a device for the selection of educable talent, is the most important place that anyone could start in a review of the problems of world education.

A pioneer study in this field, carried out by Dr. Frank Bowles, now adviser on international education to the Ford Foundation, was organized in 1959 by the Joint UNESCO-International Association of Universities research program, through an international commission of educational experts representing a variety of world regions and educational systems. It was the first time that a systematic effort had ever been made to join together a cross section of educational systems throughout the world in mutual efforts by educators and scholars to

[2] Ibid., p. 40.

focus attention on one major problem of concern to all. The results of the research,[3] published in 1963 after two years of field work, conferences, and study by Dr. Bowles and his staff, from 1960 to 1962, furnish the basis for the consideration of nearly every major problem in international education and in planning for education on a world scale in the future. If taken seriously by educators in the United States and elsewhere, the conclusions reached and the educational issues raised could be used as the materials for a continuing effort in educational reform in institutions of higher education everywhere in the world.

The core of Dr. Bowles' findings is contained in his statement of five hypotheses about world-wide admissions programs. "The problem of admission to higher education," says Dr. Bowles, "is only superficially administrative. At base it is educational, rooted in the purposes and goals of the educational community. If the result of the study is stated as a finding that the present admissions process is educationally inadequate, an entire set of new approaches to the problem is uncovered. These may be presented as five hypotheses to be tested against the established facts of the workings of the process:

1. "The annual entry into higher education represents not more than one-third—and in some countries as few as one-tenth—of the students of superior ability who start the admissions process with the intention of preparing for higher education. The other two-thirds of the group are eliminated by present methods of examination, selection.

2. Much of the elimination, even in countries with well-developed educational systems, is the result of social inequalities which take the form of financial barriers to continue the education, particularly in the secondary schools.

3. The present programmes of preparation for higher education are educationally inadequate as evidenced by high rates of failure to complete higher education programmes after entry.

4. Current methods of selection make insufficient use of secondary school information about the intellectual capacities and interests of individual students.

5. The facilities and programme offerings of higher education are incapable of satisfying the existing demands for entrance to higher education by properly qualified students. At their present rates of development the inadequacy ten years hence may well be frightening.[4]

The implications of these hypotheses for the education of teachers add to the sense of urgency felt by educators who have looked at the problem of aid to developing countries through the improvement of their educational systems. The Bowles study raises new questions about world education at some of its most important points, including the problem of part-time professors in institutions of higher education in the developing countries, the limitation of entry into the teaching profession at universities controlled by those who have a professional interest in limiting access to teaching, the inadequacy and low status

[3] *Access to Higher Education*, Volume 1, the International Study of University Admissions, by Frank Bowles, UNESCO and the International Association of Universities, International Document Service, Columbia University Press, New York, 1963, p. 212.

[4] Ibid., pp. 30–31.

of teacher training institutions in nearly every country in the world, the intricate interconnection between higher education and the secondary and elementary schools, between education and the political, social and economic forces in each society.

In his discussion of the expansion of the world's educational opportunities, Dr. Bowles sets the problem in its American and world dimension when he says, "In operation, higher education has before it two choices for discharging (its) responsibilities. One method widely employed but now being modified is to control student-entrance by examinations, a type of control ordinarily operated through a series of eliminations. Another method is to control student entrance through advice based on the student's performance, judgments of student abilities, and expressions of student preference—in short, control through orientation or guidance."[5] Dr. Bowles proposes an emphasis on the second alternative—revision both of admissions and curricular policy to bring to all young people in elementary, secondary school and after it, education which combines the two crucial elements—the ability to perform useful tasks, and the ability to understand oneself in the context of cultural, intellectual, political, and historical traditions of world society. Future studies of international education will have to take into account the findings of the Bowles research, both as a method of collaboration among teachers within the world-wide educational community, and as a means of focusing attention on the key issues in social, political, economic, and educational development.

[5] Ibid., p. 168.

Appendix E

GENERAL AND SPECIFIC RECOMMENDATIONS

General Recommendations

1. That educators stop thinking of the education of teachers primarily in terms of formal academic requirements and professional courses and consider instead the ways in which their intellectual interests and experiences in the affairs of the world can be increased in range and quality.

2. That the study of world affairs not be considered a special area in international relations and world history for those being trained to teach in the field, but that the content of the entire undergraduate curriculum—particularly in the social and behavioral sciences and in the humanities—be revised to reflect a world point of view of man and society and to involve all students in ideas, materials, literature, and comparative studies from the cultures of the world.

3. That the emphasis in teacher education be shifted from the continual discussion of certification problems and procedures and that responsibility and support for new programs be placed where it belongs: in the hands of students and teachers, working together with the academic and professional departments of the universities, with the schools, the communities, and the community agencies now cooperating with colleges of education, educational laboratories, and centers for the study of urban, rural, and international problems.

4. That the colleges and universities be reorganized to give students a high degree of responsibility for conducting their own education, for developing their own study projects, for teaching themselves through research projects, field work at home and abroad, student-led seminars, tutoring children and fellow students, and inclusion in policy-making bodies within the colleges and universities.

5. That a nation-wide volunteer Student Corps of approximately 25,000 students be organized with government subsidy as an extension of the ideas and programs of VISTA, Head Start, the National Teacher Corps, and exchange Peace Corps. Service and study in foreign and American communities should be considered a regular part of teacher education programs.

6. That the American campus be considered a central place where students assemble to learn what they need to know in order to become educated and useful. The rest of the world, both inside and outside the United States, should be considered a general world-wide campus where students from the United States and other countries come together to educate each other with the help of scholars and teachers.

7. That we take as models for new programs in the education of teachers projects developed within the Peace Corps, Exchange Peace Corps, National Teacher Corps, VISTA, Head Start, International Secretariat for Volunteer Service, International Volunteer Service, the Experiment in International Living, and other government and voluntary agencies concerned with social change and world affairs.

8. That the standard pattern of two years of general education requirements, an academic major, and a specified number of professional courses and practice teaching in the junior and senior year be radically modified (a) to allow the student at the beginning of his preparation to become directly involved in teaching, in the schools, in the community, and in his undergraduate college and (b) to allow for a high degree of flexibility in meeting the academic degree requirements. The new program would accept as meeting these requirements field work abroad and at home, Peace Corps and other kinds of voluntary service, independent study, student-run seminars, practical experience in research, and projects in the community.

9. That state departments of education take as their primary role—rather than the regulating of certification of teachers—the planning and initiating of new programs in international study (abroad and at home), international curricula, and international relationships with schools, teachers colleges, universities, and ministries of education in other countries.

10. That the education of teachers—for all levels of education, from nursery school to graduate study—be made a primary concern of the government and of the colleges and universities.

11. That wherever there are programs and organizations with international connections—government bureaus, AID, Overseas Schools, the National Science Foundation, Institute of Mental Health, UNICEF, the Atomic Energy Commission, Experiment in International Living, university centers abroad, the Smithsonian Institution, the Council on International Educational Exchange—a component of teacher education be included in the existing structure. The intellectual and financial resources available to these organizations can be used to develop teachers with international experience.

12. That foreign students—both graduate and undergraduate—be considered a primary source when recruiting student-teachers and teaching assistants for service in American schools and colleges, and that student-teachers be recruited from foreign countries specifically for teaching duties.

13. That international teaching centers be established on American campuses, with connections and exchange arrangements with institutions abroad for educational research, international curriculum making, practice teaching, and teacher education.

14. That educators of teachers turn their attention to the primary importance of the creative arts both in national and international education; and that the painting, sculpture, theater, music, dance, and literature of other countries be presented to American students and teachers through visiting students, artists, performers, and scholars; and that international festivals of the arts—ranging from dance to films—be sponsored and arranged by colleges of education.

15. That the content of professional education courses be revised to include the study of foreign cultures and educational systems as a central component, co-

ordinated with study and practice teaching abroad and the expansion of connections between American and foreign schools, teacher education institutions, and universities.

16. That serious and concerted political action be taken at the earliest possible moment to secure funds for putting into effect the legislation of the International Education Act.

17. That in connection with the administration of the International Education Act and other government programs, approximately 10,000 federal fellowships and/or scholarships be provided for student teachers—undergraduate and graduate—and young teachers already in service in the public schools and colleges, to make possible a year of study and practice teaching in foreign countries as a component of their preparation for teaching in the United States.

Specific Recommendations

In what follows, the more specific recommendations in relation to internationalism and world affairs are listed in summary form, according to the categories in which they fall.

1. New forms of collaboration with the Peace Corps should be worked out through state departments of education, colleges of education, and universities to include Peace Corps service as a regular component in five- and six-year curriculums leading to the B.A. and M.A. degree and the teaching certificate.

2. Taking the concept of Peace Corps service abroad as an organizing principle, existing curricula and requirements for the teaching certificate should be modified to allow development of individual study programs during the undergraduate years for those intending to serve in the Peace Corps after graduation and for others interested in foreign affairs, international education, and international service of all kinds. This would include not only special junior-year-abroad programs for student-teachers, but summer travel-study projects, international education workshops, and institutes in foreign countries and on American campuses, staffed by foreign students and teachers as well as their American counterparts. The courses and individual study plans in history, sociology, anthropology, foreign languages, literature, comparative education, and the arts would be chosen by the student and his faculty adviser to make up a comprehensive individually planned curriculum for that student.

3. Special graduate programs leading to the M.A. and Ph.D. degrees should be organized for returning Peace Corps volunteers. They would include practice teaching, flexible study programs, and curriculum development projects based on the previous experience of the volunteers in study and teaching abroad.

4. The Exchange Peace Corps idea should be extended, both through the expansion of government programs of the kind now being conducted by the State Department and by initiatives from the colleges and universities, to permit foreign students already in this country and others to be recruited from abroad to teach in the American schools and to participate in community development projects.

5. Individual faculty members in colleges of education should be assigned to liaison work with the Peace Corps for the development of study-teaching proj-

ects abroad for American student-teachers, with connections to foreign ministries of education and the American embassies abroad.

6. Returning Peace Corps volunteers should be recruited for teaching and research assignments in colleges of education which would collaborate with local school teachers, student-teachers, and high school students interested in foreign affairs. The returned volunteers, selected on the basis of their ability and readiness for the work, would be asked to develop and test experimental curriculums—using materials and experience from abroad—in cooperation with elementary and high school teachers and a supervising faculty member from the college of education. Other volunteers should be recruited to serve in the college in developing new study programs and to advise students interested in entering the Peace Corps or similar foreign service projects.

7. The master of arts in teaching should be expanded in concept and program to include a three-year M.A. for the B.A. graduate. Six months of the senior year would be spent in preparing for Peace Corps service under special curricular arrangements; two years would be spent in service abroad, during which time the graduate student would submit research reports to and exchange correspondence with a supervising faculty member at home and possibly a member of the Peace Corps staff in the resident country. The program would end with six months of study on the home campus and practice teaching nearby. Similar extension of the master of arts in teaching idea could be made with help from, although not necessarily service in, the Peace Corps in a two-year curriculum. One year would be spent in volunteer service abroad, with six months of preparation beforehand and six months of further study and teaching after the year abroad.

8. Four-year Peace Corps doctorate programs should be established. The two years of foreign service would be linked to a doctoral thesis based on field work, in a style similar to doctoral programs in anthropology.

9. The idea of the Stanford undergraduate regional centers abroad should be extended to include specific projects in teacher education for juniors and seniors taking the teaching certificate with the B.A. degree. This idea would emphasize the collaboration of foreign nationals who are student teachers and teachers with American counterparts.

International Programs Possible Through Existing Organizations with International Connections

1. Wherever there are AID programs in educational development, the sponsoring universities should include graduate and undergraduate students of education in the country teams. They would perform research, studies, and community development work as assistants to a university faculty member.

2. Faculty members serving abroad on educational missions for AID or other U. S. Government agencies should, if possible, arrange for graduate students of education to accompany them in one or another capacity (on university fellowships or government and foundation grants) for the development of curriculum materials and direct experience with foreign educational systems.

3. Organizations like the International Secretariat for Volunteer Service or UNICEF should arrange for B.A. graduates from a number of countries, includ-

ing the United States, to form volunteer international teams for work in education, teaching, and research. Academic supervision and credit would be given by the institutions to which the students are attached.

4. The Office of Overseas Schools, administered by the U.S. Department of State, should collaborate with colleges of education and U.S. school systems in establishing practice teaching and curriculum and research projects in U.S.-supported schools abroad in which student teachers could serve for periods from one semester to two years while remaining connected with their institutions at home.

5. Through consortia like those involved in the American Association of Colleges for Teacher Education, Great Lakes College Association, and the Regional Council for International Education, colleges and universities can combine their resources abroad and at home in developing educational programs for undergraduates and graduates who intend to enter the teaching profession.

6. Projects similar to that undertaken by UNESCO in its Education for International Understanding and Cooperation should be duplicated by other international organizations to create new links between teachers in a variety of countries for exchange of students, teachers, materials, curriculums, tapes, films, and other educational instruments.

7. International study projects similar to that sponsored by UNESCO-International Universities Association on admission to universities should be organized on a broad scale through existing organizations with international connections; for example, the World Academy of Arts and Sciences, Universities and the Quest for Peace, the World Law Fund, the World Confederation of Organizations of the Teaching Profession.

State Departments of Education;
Certification and Professional Education Requirements

1. That special arrangements be made in cooperation with the universities and schools to evaluate foreign teaching experience by Peace Corps volunteers and others who have had teaching and educational experience abroad in order that (a) credit toward certification be awarded for bona fide work in education and teaching abroad, (b) students with foreign experience and interests be recruited into the teaching profession, and (c) regulatory programs of the departments exhibit a wider latitude in requirements for educational subject matter and practical teaching and field experience.

2. That the departments call upon colleges of education and universities for the development of new programs in international education for teachers and, as is the case in New York State, establish projects of their own for cooperation with educators and institutions abroad in the exchange of teachers and curricular materials.

3. That the courses in education accepted for the certification of teachers be thoroughly revised to include (a) comparative studies of foreign educational systems, (b) field work at home and abroad in study and experience with a variety of forms of education, (c) material drawn from the social and behavioral sciences—particularly cultural anthropology—which can introduce the student to foreign cultures within the context of national educational systems.

4. That faculty members in colleges of education organize two- to three-year projects in the development of new education courses with content drawn from foreign educational and social systems, through summer travel and study and through cooperation with foreign educators, returned Peace Corps volunteers and staff, and faculty colleagues who are experts in foreign cultures.

5. That colleges of education be encouraged to appoint scholars in the social sciences and the humanities who have an interest in education and world cultures, rather than relying on other subject matter departments and research centers in the university to teach students of education to become aware of social issues and world problems.

6. That the process of regional and national accreditation of programs of teacher education be revised to emphasize and encourage variations in the standard pattern of curriculum to ensure the inclusion of a maximum of foreign experience and study on the part of the student body.

7. That staff members be appointed to state departments of education with specific responsibilities for international education throughout the state and that through connections established between institutions abroad, state school districts, colleges of education, and universities arrange for exchange of faculty, international summer workshops, international curriculums, and joint study projects with foreign scholars and students.

8. That summer travel-study projects abroad be arranged for groups to include members of department staffs, state school board members, graduate students of education, teachers, principals, superintendents, and college and university president and deans.

9. That the work of staff members of state departments of education be arranged to include (a) travel abroad to establish liaison with foreign institutions, Peace Corps staff and volunteers, ministries of education, and American cultural affairs officers; (b) the appointment of foreign students and scholars as interns in the department; (c) joint research projects in international curriculums with foreign educators serving as interns and staff members; (d) conferences with experts in foreign affairs and area studies for consideration of curricular changes and content in teacher education programs.

10. That official as well as informal relations be arranged between state departments of education, the colleges of education, teachers of undergraduates, and community groups interested in international affairs—local World Affairs Councils, United Nations Associations, the Foreign Policy Association, the League of Women Voters, and similar organizations—so that the resources of these organizations can be put to use in the educational system and can work directly with teachers. This could include use of library and information centers, combined regional and state activities, conferences, panel discussions, television and radio forums with foreign students and scholars, visiting speakers, joint travel-study trips, etc.

11. That specially qualified professors from the state or from other states, returned foreign service officers, members of the United Nations Secretariat and delegations, staff members of nongovernmental international organizations be invited for one to two days of discussion with state departments of education staff members to review issues in education and world society related to the curriculum in international affairs.

Cultural Policy and Foreign Affairs

1. That a major policy decision be made at the highest level of government on the purpose and character of the work in international education and cultural exchange, to emphasize that:

(a) The use of American funds and educational manpower in international affairs should be to advance the cause of internationalism in the world community—not simply to cultivate friendly attitudes toward America, American culture, or American foreign policy.

(b) American education is part of a world system of education, and American resources should be used to the fullest extent possible to contribute to the welfare of all other educational systems.

(c) The education of teachers, in the United States and in all other countries, should receive maximum attention in practical programs designed to create a higher level of international understanding and cooperation.

(d) All government subsidies for American students, scholars, and intellectuals for service, research, and study abroad should be in no case covert, and that wherever possible teaching, research, and study on the part of Americans abroad be conducted in partnership with the nationals of the host countries, or with international teams in cooperative projects.

(e) The function of the university is to increase the store of knowledge and to teach and disseminate that knowledge for the benefit of mankind. Therefore, universities should not be used by their governments for research on military matters, either in secret or in open projects. The criterion for the selection of appropriate university projects should be whether they aid the spread of international enlightenment in the arts, sciences, and technologies and whether the results of the research could be taught to students in American or foreign universities and schools.

(f) Since the American universities are in a favored position in world society, with financial resources and a degree of intellectual freedom unknown in most other countries, they have a special obligation to set standards for intellectual behavior in relation to political and other controls which can give leadership to the world's intellectual community.

2. That university scholars take a more active and formal role through their professional organizations in following the issues and decisions in cultural policy as these relate to national and international affairs and that they take an active part in the formation of those policies by exercising their right of criticism, review, and political action where foreign policy is concerned.

3. That the AID program of educational assistance abroad shift its emphasis toward the education of teachers, and that this shift be reflected in the allocation of funds.

4. That the AID program in Vietnam be sharply increased in size and in budget to deal with the extreme educational problems now afflicting the Vietnamese

people as a result of the war, and that a major part of the effort go into the recruitment and education of teachers.

5. That a government program be developed through which qualified Americans who have served in the armed forces in Vietnam and in other developing countries and are familiar with the language and problems of those countries be recruited as volunteers to carry out teaching, community development, and other duties as civilians following their military service.

6. That other programs for the development of teachers and scholars with a knowledge of Southeast Asia be established, with a view to preparing large numbers of potential aides in the rehabilitation of Vietnamese education once the war ends, and in creating a larger body of scholarship and public understanding in the United States of the problems of Southeast Asia.

7. That the Educational and Cultural Exchange program of the State Department concentrate more heavily on the international education of teachers.

8. That plans be made by the State Department to be held in the United States and elsewhere, in which actors, composers, dancers, poets, painters, critics, and educators in the arts are brought together to share their performances, to translate each other's works, and to find ways of introducing their art forms into each other's educational systems.

9. That conferences of American and foreign educators be sponsored by the State Department to discuss issues in foreign policy, particularly in relation to cultural and social affairs.

10. That regional centers, initiated with American funds and administered by international committees, be established in various parts of the world for research and study of educational problems—curriculum making, teaching, translation, etc.—where an international student body could attend for periods from six months to two years, and the staff would be recruited on a world-wide basis.

11. That government subsidies be arranged for student-initiated projects in teacher education and international affairs through which American students could join forces with students from other countries in increasing their areas of common interest and common understanding, and that the former CIA subsidies to student groups be replaced by larger grants from open government and foundation sources—in each case administered through the authority of recognized educators, as in the case of the Fulbright awards.

12. That AID organize a research component in connection with its educational missions, in order that some objective evaluation may be made of the results of its educational work, and that the literature of educational research be expanded in an international direction. The research component could be built around projects carried out by qualified university and college of education faculty members, with graduate and undergraduate students of education recruited for the research staff as part of their work toward a degree in education.

13. That the American Overseas Schools be developed into centers for teacher education and international research, for practice teaching by Americans and host nationals, and for international curriculum experiments.

The Role of Students

1. The opportunity for teaching should be extended into the elementary and secondary schools by organizing the teaching system to allow time for children to teach each other in tutorials with appropriate assignments made by the teacher, in team projects, in assignments of junior high school students to groups of elementary school children, and volunteer service by high school students in the community, especially in poor rural areas and urban slums.

2. Education students and others should be invited to act as tutors to foreign students and to work with them in educational and study projects connected with the country of their origin.

3. Selected sophomores, juniors, and seniors should be invited by university faculty members to serve as tutors and teaching assistants for freshmen, with three-year plans made in which foreign experience by the students during summer terms or nonresident semesters can then be put to use in adding additional materials to existing courses in the humanities and social sciences.

4. Study and, if possible, practice teaching experience should be arranged abroad or in a "foreign" culture in the United States for all students who expect to be teaching a foreign language or a foreign culture.

5. Special language and study projects for student teachers should be arranged from the freshman year on in geographical areas where direct collaboration between teachers and students in bilingual communities is possible, as in the Spanish-American region of the Southwest.

6. During one semester of nonresident education, junior and senior education students should be asked to develop teaching and community service projects in communities other than their own—for example among the Navajos, in Appalachia, in urban communities—and to carry them out under faculty supervision and with the cooperation of local educational authorities and teachers.

8. Through arrangements made with foreign students already in this country, international projects should be developed by American students between the foreign students and their American counterparts for joint or parallel studies and practice in education in this country and in the country of the foreign student's origin.

9. Curriculum projects should be developed by student teachers studying abroad through which student film-making can become part of their contribution to the curriculum in the schools and colleges back home.

10. Students should be asked—where the talent and the equipment are available—to prepare video-taped discussions with foreign students and scholars for use in the classroom and in the community, over local television stations, and closed-circuit television on the campus.

11. More projects should be initiated such as those developed by Nations Incorporated in San Francisco, in which high school students work in intensive summer sessions with foreign students and teachers already in this country on issues in world affairs.

12. International curriculum-building projects should be initiated by American

colleges of education by establishing connections between students in their institutions and students abroad, with exchange of tape recordings, short stories, plays, poems, and other written materials, films, and comparative studies of family and social life. These could be similar to those conducted by the American Association of Colleges for Teacher Education in its interinstitutional affiliation project.

Index